AF804384

Toolbook for Health Care Redesign

Ruth I. Hansten, MBA, BSN
Principal
Hansten & Washburn
Bainbridge Island, Washington

Marilynn J. Washburn, MA, BSN
Principal
Hansten & Washburn
Bainbridge Island, Washington

AN ASPEN PUBLICATION®
Aspen Publishers, Inc.
Gaithersburg, Maryland
1997

Library of Congress Cataloging-in-Publication Data

Hansten, Ruth I.
Toolbook for health care redesign / Ruth I. Hansten, Marilynn J. Washburn.
p. cm.
Includes bibliographical references and index.
ISBN 0-8342-0907-1 (alk. paper)
1. Nursing services—Administration. 2. Organizational change. I. Washburn, Marilynn. II. Title.
[DNLM: 1. Delivery of Health Care—organization & administration—nurses' instruction. 2. Organizational Innovation. W 84.1 H251t 1997]
RT89.H373 1997
362.1'068—dc21
DNLM/DLC
for Library of Congress
97-21698
CIP

Editorial Resources: Lenda P. Hill

Library of Congress Catalog Card Number: 97-21698
ISBN: 0-8342-0907-1
ISBN-13: 978-0-8342-0907-7

Printed in the United States of America

1 2 3 4 5

Dedication

This toolbook is dedicated to all those who have (or will in the future) experience the pain, challenge, exhaustion, joy, and hope of care delivery system redesign, restructuring, or reengineering. We applaud your resolution and true grit, and know that your ability to continue to creatively refine and improve the health care systems in your community, sometimes seemingly against tough odds, proceeds from your trust in yourselves and your commitment to those you serve. We hope that sharing the tools in this book will inspire you onward, and help you overcome some of the inevitable obstacles to a better, user-friendly health care system.

Ruth and Marilynn
Hansten & Washburn
10042 NE Knight Road
Bainbridge Island, WA 98110
Telephone: (206) 842-1189 or (206) 842-0912

Contributors

Children's Hospital and Medical Center
Seattle, Washington:
Jaleh Shafii, RN, MSN Project Analyst
Mary Chmelik, RN, Project Analyst

Columbia Northwest Medical Center
Tucson, Arizona:
Dorothy Sawyer, RN, MN, Chief Nursing Officer

Legacy Health System
Portland, Oregon:
Judy McGee, Vice President Patient Care
Cynthia Evans, RN, MSN, Senior Consultant for Patient Care
Scott M. Mason, RN, Patient Focused Care Specialist
Lisa Shipley, RN, BSN, CCRN, Patient Focused Care Specialist and System Analyst
Renee Gillenwater, RN, BSN

MultiCare Medical Center
Tacoma, Washington:
Diane Cecchettini, Vice President Patient Care Services
Jolie Knudtson, RN, MBA, Clinical Director Adult Critical Care
Mary Ellen Swatta, Operations Improvement Director

Allina Health Systems
Minneapolis, Minnesota:
Jack Dobier, Labor-Management Coordinator

Griffin Hospital
Derby, Connecticut:
Lynn Werdal, RN, MS, Vice President Patient Care Services

Group Health Cooperative of Puget Sound
Washington:
Barbara Trehearne, RN, C, MS
Director of Nursing Resources

Holy Family Hospital
Spokane, Washington:
Cathy Simchuk, CNA, BSN, Assistant Administrator of Patient Care Services

Huntington Memorial Hospital
Pasadena, California:
Elaine Goehner, PhD, RNC
Joyce Johnson, PhD, RNC

Lebanon Community Hospital
Lebanon, Oregon:
Marvin Heskett, Director of Patient Care

Marin General Hospital
Marin, California:
Sandie McCreary, Director of Quality Management

Noyes and Associates, Ltd.
Bainbridge Island, Washington:
Betty Noyes, RN, MA, President

Norman Regional Medical Center
Norman, Oklahoma:
Kay Mitchell, Manager 5N
Suzanne Wyatt, Educator

Valley Medical Center
Renton, Washington:
Sheila Ball, RN, MBA, Quality Improvement Coordinator

Table of Contents

Foreword

There are an increasing number of interesting books and articles on reengineering, restructuring, learning organizations, total quality management, process improvement, and new theories of organizational improvement. Yet few actually tell you what to do on Monday morning. How do you implement these ideas? What are other people doing? What works well and what doesn't work well? What are the pitfalls in going down the path to improvement? How do you take all the information and turn it into some sort of knowledge that can be applied?

This book, *Toolbook* for *Health Care Redesign,* is a hands-on, practical application for implementing change programs and restructuring organizations. It is written from the perspective of the health care industry but it is in no way limited to issues in health care organizations. It applies equally well to all organizations and it is the best manual that I have seen for practical implementation of restructuring and reengineering. It helps YOU facilitate the change. It gives YOU the tools to make it happen. And it describes success stories and exercises that can be applied to YOUR organization.

Ruth Hansten and Marilynn Washburn write from hands-on experience and share with you what has worked for them and what hasn't. The book deals with four major areas: assessing the situation, planning for change, the intervention process, and evaluating for success. Within each of these areas are several tools and models, success stories, and case study examples.

This is without question the best book of making changes in organizations and specifically telling you how to do it.

James R. Legler, PhD
Professor
Wartburg Institute for Leadership
Wartburg College
Waverly, Iowa

Introduction

One or 2 million years ago, humankind learned how to modify the sticks and stones they had picked up off the ground. These tools, used in dwelling construction to cooking to games, made life more productive, more facile, and more fun. Complexity has increased to the point that some of our present tools, such as computers, require additional instruments and manuals to potentiate their use.

During the last 200 years in health care, we have developed astonishing and intricate technology and systems from the humble origins of a few herbs and a cloth to a feverish brow. During that topsy-turvy growth, we have rarely been afforded the opportunity we presently experience—the challenge to re-create a health care system that will provide rational health promotion and illness care to the population of our shrinking world. So, we are all "out there," working diligently in our own areas of expertise, attempting to find answers that make sense for our communities. And just as our forebears shared delight when such monumental tools as the wheel or the telephone were created, we hope you will experience at least relief, if not joy, by discovering and adapting the implements developed by another health care facility.

All of us in health care are attempting to make the health care system work for our patients and clients and ourselves, given the constraints of our current social and political situation. Sharing what works and what doesn't will help you refrain from re-creating the proverbial wheel. You may adapt the tools presented in this toolbook to your own situation and your own facility. Just as you have read in our newsletters and previous books, our work is based on operational, practical experience gained from our own clinical and consulting experience. Please share with us what worked for you, what didn't, and what new ideas and tools you've developed.

We have followed the scientific problem-solving process (quickly recognized by you astute readers as the nursing process) to consider tools and advice that can be used throughout the restructuring or care delivery redesign processes. Each area includes conceptual frameworks, to-do (or don't) lists, and advice, as well as tools that can be used during that phase.

We thank all of the contributors who were willing to share their work and the tools they created together through stressful and challenging times. They bravely have shared their mistakes and their victories in written format (often a difficult task!) in hopes of saving others time and effort. We have also included our own experiences in "damage control" during reengineering without naming facilities (thanks to you for the learning opportunities as well!). We salute you for your commitment to your patients and the health of our communities!

This book goes beyond a manual on reengineering health care facilities (there are already multiple good texts on reengineering theory) and focuses on the discrete tools that will facilitate the process. We, the authors, the contributors, and all of the health care organizations with whom we've worked would agree with Freeman Dyson, the physicist, in his 1979 book, *Disturbing the Universe,* when he asserts, "There is a great satisfaction in building good tools for other people to use." We hope you enjoy using them!

Ruth and Marilynn

SECTION ONE

Taking Time To Assess

Worst Case Scenario
"Making Assumptions"

Admittedly, we were new to the role of consulting, but that doesn't excuse the mess we found ourselves in when we contracted to assist a hospital during a difficult restructuring project. The hospital's situation was as follows:

"We've laid off many of the senior nursing staff, and are replacing them with nursing assistants. The remaining staff are angry, and have threatened to go to the media with their concerns. The union is upset, but we've done everything by the book. What we need you to do is to come in and present some team building sessions so that the new staff can work with the RNs."

No problem. We knew what to do. And despite warnings from the management team that ***"these people can be very rude,"*** we believed we knew just what was needed to make team work happen. The sessions were scheduled (with more emphasis on what dates we were available than on content) and staff members were assigned times to attend.

The first sessions were what could be described as that proverbial "baptism by fire." Yes, the staff members were unbelievably rude, demanding to know what we were being paid, walking out of the sessions, blatantly reading newspapers, and generally exhibiting unprofessional and obnoxious behavior. The newly hired assistants were more than concerned about their new jobs in such a hostile environment. Many refused to play our time-honored experiential game (guaranteed to build better teams), and sat victim-like while issuing a list of complaints about how management had "done them wrong."

It was more than obvious to us that we had failed to assess the situation, and had made assumptions regarding behavior and attitudes. Near the end of one very vocal session, one of the participants shared her observation: ***"You know we aren't stupid. We know we have to change the way we work and we are ready for it. But we resent the PROCESS in which the change has occurred."***

❶ TAKING TIME TO ASSESS

"What does not get counted does not count. Money is easily counted. Therefore, all too soon, money becomes the measure of all things. A just society needs a new score card."

Charles Handy

Although our opening scenario is truly a horror story, and we played a real part in it, there are several points to be made. Failing to assess any situation, whether it's a patient condition or the boss's mood, often leads to action based on assumption, or worse yet, action based on someone else's assessment.

Of course, having said that, it seems elementary. However, we are good at rationalizing why this essential first step is often skipped. Resistance is typically encountered by those who are in a hurry or are convinced that they know what is needed, based on their observations. Selling the idea of taking time to make an additional assessment is often not easy. In the previous story, the managers were correct. Their staff could be rude and were unhappy. But staff members were *not* unhappy about the need to change and, in fact, recognized the necessity for it. What made them angry was how the change was made. Having assessed that initially, we would have taken different steps to facilitate team building.

▼

Make your own assessment before determining if you can take actions that will be effective in achieving the outcome desired by both parties. Determine what information was used to formulate the initial assessment, and seek to validate it.

▲

There are countless methods for determining what's really going on in any given situation; some work and others serve only to cloud the real issue. This opening section of our book begins with the important analysis of which assessment tools work the best (in our experience) and also discusses some that have made our lives much more difficult than necessary.

THE INFAMOUS SURVEY PROCESS

Believe it or not, assessment is not synonymous with survey. Yet, it is incredible how many people, when faced with the need to determine what's going on, will recommend, "Let's do a survey!" What a novel idea! And the result is that staff and patients are surveyed endlessly. One organization we worked with had seven different patient surveys for the poor patient and family to complete before, during, and after the hospital stay! We question the value of the data received with this much questioning. People have limits and rights regarding the information they are willing to share. Careful attention must be paid to these issues for a survey tool to be effective.

When To Survey

This is an important strategic question to consider. If you have never involved the staff in a survey process, the field is wide open. If you have inundated them with written questions on a weekly or monthly basis before reading this, you have overdone it. Take a break and move on to the next section—you need a different tool!

There is no hard and fast rule regarding the number of times you may survey a given population. Knowing your staff (or the target group), and knowing the history regarding what previous assessment methods have been used, will be helpful in deciding which survey would be appropriate. To determine when to conduct the survey, the following criteria should be considered:

- What other methods have been used to assess the situation?
- Was a written survey done previously, and if so, when?
- What has been done with information previously obtained?
- What kind of information are you seeking?
- What degree of participation will be meaningful?

WHAT OTHER METHODS HAVE BEEN USED?

We will discuss other options in addition to the survey tool, as we continue this chapter. You may find that others before you have tried interviewing random or selected people, found answers in quality improvement data, tracked complaints or incidents, or drawn conclusions from their own observations (a limited and risky practice!).

WAS A WRITTEN SURVEY DONE?

This is important information to have. Many times we have asked managers or staff developers if they have done any type of assessment, and they will ignore a past survey attempt. "Yeah, we tried to survey the staff, but we only got a handful of responses." Or, "Sure, we did a survey a few months ago. Marge, what did you do with those results?" Persist in your quest. If the staff have been asked the same questions before, and perceive that nothing was done about their responses, they will be understandably resistant to your new attempt.

WHAT HAS BEEN DONE WITH THE INFORMATION?

Equally important to determine is the action taken on the data received. Were results shared in numerous ways so that the participants know that their input was received and valued? Or has the carefully collated stack of responses been filed away for later use? Better still, have actions been taken based on the results, and were those actions successful in achieving the desired results?

WHAT KIND OF INFORMATION ARE YOU SEEKING?

Subjective, intuitive information regarding an identified problem may be best obtained in a one-on-one approach. If you want some quick numbers and want to save time, a multiple-choice survey tool will be effective. People generally prefer to answer questions when enough information has been given to make the completion of the survey fast and easy; therefore, multiple-choice and fill-in-the-blank formats are often preferred. The problem with this approach is the limitation of individualized responses, which can alter the true assessment of the issue.

WHAT DEGREE OF INFORMATION WILL BE MEANINGFUL?

If you need to have a response from as many of the affected members of the group as possible, a written survey will be more efficient than an individualized approach. If a representative sampling is all that is necessary, select up to 10% of the group and interview them, or invite them to a focus group to respond to a select number of specific questions.

▼

If you are going to use surveys, design them to retrieve actionable data, communicate the results, and then take action!

▲

What Survey To Use

So, you're convinced that a survey is the correct choice. Now, what to ask? It's tempting to ask general questions that yield "nice to know" information. But keep in mind the rights of your participants, and do not alienate them by asking questions that are not clearly linked to the issue you need to assess.

▼

Specific, action-oriented questions will not only help to set standards and expectations, but will also create momentum for change.

▲

In the following pages, we have included survey tools that have worked well for us. Our intent is to provide you with a working platform from which to make your own survey, recognizing that it's much easier to improve someone else's work than to have to start from scratch!

ONE-ON-ONE: ASKING THE RIGHT QUESTIONS

There are times when a survey just won't yield the information you need to determine what action needs to be taken to improve the system or the department, or to correct the problem. Subjective, personal perspectives often call for the individual touch. However, there are a few cautions to this method to consider as well. Selecting a few people to interview will give you a limited (and slanted) view of the issue. Our experience shows that people tend to select participants based on personalities. For example, the following quotes depict this: "I always talk to the trouble makers—they're the most vocal about what's wrong" or "I only talk to those who volunteer or show interest in a positive way—I don't need the hassle of the ones who are not supportive!"

▼
If you randomly select representatives to interview, make sure you let everyone know the selection process.
▲

Random selection should be just that. If your target group involves staff who cover three shifts, make certain there is equal representation from each shift. Putting everyone's name in a hat is probably the fairest method of selection. This attention to detail may seem trivial, but participants will increase their resistance to the data collected if they perceive the data were not gathered in the most objective manner. We worked with one staff developer who scheduled "random" interviews, only to discover that staff members on the night shift were not included in the selection process. Of course, this validated the night shift contention that "no one ever includes us on anything" and generated a wall of resistance that sabotaged what could have been a beneficial reengineering project for everyone on the unit.

▼
Give serious consideration to the benefits of interviewing everyone.
▲

A well-conducted interview process, in which specific questions regarding one issue are asked, will not only provide well-rounded information about the current state of things, but will be therapeutic as well. You might want to limit your time spent with each person, but with so many potential benefits, who would not want to make the effort to meet with everyone?

Tool #1: Sample Surveys

ASSESSING THE ORGANIZATION

(This is a good tool for using in a focus group as well as in an individual survey.)

Where's the Team Spirit?

Assess your organizational environment for support of team development.
SA = Strongly Agree A = Agree N = Neutral D = Disagree SD = Strongly Disagree

____ 1. Vision (the direction the organization is going) and values (how to accomplish the mission) of our organization are clearly understood by all employees.

____ 2. The nature of our work lends itself to a team effort.

____ 3. Our organization has a history of "following through" on changes.

____ 4. Our managers exhibit good listening and interpersonal skills and can be supportive.

____ 5. Employees here believe they can share risky ideas and feel supported by management rather than criticized.

____ 6. Employees know their roles in getting tasks done and know when to let someone else do a certain task.

____ 7. Management believes that employees can and should make most of the decisions that affect how they do their work.

____ 8. Opportunities for feedback regarding job performance are available and timely.

____ 9. Personal growth through education and training is supported.

____ 10. Management empowers employees at all levels to make decisions that affect the quality of service to their clients.

Courtesy of Herrick, K., Northwest Organization of Nurse Executives, Hansten, R., & Washburn, M., 1993. [Portable Workshop].

AN ASSESSMENT OF A HEALTH CARE ORGANIZATION FOR SUPPORT OF CARE DELIVERY REDESIGN

Organizational Structure

Yes No

___ ___ 1. Is there an organizational chart?

___ ___ 2. Are there clearly defined reporting systems for staff supervising team members?

___ ___ 3. Is there sufficient communication among the various units?

___ ___ 4. Is the mission visible to everyone, and is it followed?

___ ___ 5. Are there interdisciplinary committees in which staff participate?

Quality

___ ___ 1. Is there a quality program that is currently in place?

___ ___ 2. Does the model focus on outcomes?

___ ___ 3. Is it supported by management *and* staff?

___ ___ 4. Are staff actively involved in the process?

___ ___ 5. Do staff participate in determining the criteria for measuring quality?

Safety in Practice

___ ___ 1. Are there policies addressing standards for safe staffing?

___ ___ 2. Is there a practice advisory committee that is involved in addressing problems related to staffing?

___ ___ 3. Are the policies directly affecting patient care evaluated for their consistency with state regulations?

___ ___ 4. Do staff have responsibility and autonomy for continually appraising the care delivery system and implementing changes as needed?

___ ___ 5. Are assistive personnel roles created or enlarged without the input and evaluation of the rest of the team?

___ ___ 6. Are there job descriptions and competency checklists for each member of the team?

___ ___ 7. Have new staff roles been developed with attention to state laws and rules?

Educational Resources

___ ___ 1. Are new personnel adequately trained and oriented (using validated competencies and measurable outcomes)?

___ ___ 2. Is there a system for providing additional skill development when the need is identified by an RN supervising an employee?

___ ___ 3. Is there a documentation process for establishing competency in all skills required by the job description?

___ ___ 4. Is there a mentorship or preceptorship program for all new personnel?

___ ___ 5. Is information regarding new changes in health care and health care regulations, including all practice acts, readily available?

Source: Reprinted from R. Hansten and M. Washburn, *Clinical Delegation Skills: A Handbook for Nurses,* p. 85, © 1994, Aspen Publishers, Inc.

continues

ASSESSING THE DEPARTMENT (OR UNIT)

(to prepare for strategic action planning)

Thank you for including us in your planning session! To facilitate the best process possible, we need input from you regarding your assessment of the "state of the department" at this time. Please complete the following questions, and return to the department manager by (date). This will give us an opportunity to review your comments and to prepare a summary for you before our meeting on (date 2 weeks later).

1. Identify two major strengths of your department.
   1.
   2.
2. List two areas that need improvement for this department to thrive.
   1.
   2.
3. What do you believe are two opportunities your department could take advantage of for further growth or effectiveness?
   1.
   2.
4. What are two issues that could have a potentially negative impact on the success of this department in the next two years?
   1.
   2.
5. If you could change one thing about this department, what would it be?

   How would you implement this change?

   What benefit(s) would this change bring to the department or the medical center?

   List two comments you have heard about this department from others within the facility.
   1.
   2.

continues

SHORTER VERSION OF "ASSESSING THE DEPARTMENT" TOOL

1. What is the most fulfilling part of your work with this organization?

2. If you could change two things about your work or work environment, what would they be? How would you propose to change these two barriers?

3. What spells success for you? (How would you know that the problems you've identified are solved?)

continues

ASSESSING MANAGERS

Transitions Assessment

1. Describe the most difficult challenge for you personally in dealing with the changes at your facility.

2. Give an example of a situation that you've dealt with recently relating to the changes.

3. What do you perceive to be the most difficult element of change and transition for the rest of your team?

4. What one aspect of managing the change process would be most important for you to learn?

Assessment Survey for Managers

Part A

1. List three positive results your unit has demonstrated related to the change in care delivery.

2. Describe any problems on your unit that continue to interfere with delivering quality care.

3. Identify any continuing educational needs.

Part B

1. List the three best qualities of your management team.

2. List three problem areas you would like to see improved, in order of priority.

3. As a manager, what do you see as your greatest need?

continues

AFTER CARE DELIVERY REDESIGN

(Once you've begun to make the changes this is an effective tool for assessing how it's going.)

1. What do you enjoy most about your present position?

2. What do you find the most challenging?

3. If you could change one thing about your new role, what would it be?

4. The benefits of working in the new system are...

5. The most difficult aspect of the new system is...

6. I still need...

continues

SURVEY FOR MANAGERS

(This tool assists consultants in preparing appropriate content for a planned workshop.)

Hansten and Washburn will be conducting a workshop for nurses to assist them in making sense of the changes and challenges in their role as registered nurses (RNs). We will be focusing on their survival during transition and how they interact with patients and coworkers, using outcomes planning, supervising and delegating effectively, and resolving conflicts and problems. The following survey will help us in making the skill-building exercises the most practical and effective for your staff.

1. Rate the following interpersonal communications or relationships in terms of difficulty and/or problems (1 is the most difficult, 3 is neutral, 5 is the best relationship possible).

    ____ Staff-Staff ____ Staff-Manager ____ Staff-Patient

    ____ Staff-Physician ____ Other (describe) ____________________

2. "If only all the RNs on my unit or in my department would ____________

    ____,

    then my life as a manager would be so much easier!"

3. When I tell the RNs that I expect them to be accountable, I expect them to

    ____.

4. The last 3 to 6 months, I have spent most of my managerial time on the following activities:

5. Describe a situation or scenario that has happened recently that frustrates you (for example, "If the RNs delegated, supervised, or communicated more effectively...the following situation would NOT have been a problem"). Use the other side for detail.

continues

SURVEY FOR HOSPITAL RNs

(to be used with the survey for managers)

Hansten and Washburn will be conducting a workshop for nurses to assist you in making sense of the changes and challenges in your role as an RN. We will be focusing on your transition and how you interact with patents and coworkers, using outcomes planning, supervising and delegating effectively, and resolving conflicts and problems. The following survey will help us in making the skill-building exercises the most practical and effective for you.

Years in nursing: ____ Degree in nursing: ____ Years at this facility: ____

1. My primary concerns about the change in the patient care delivery system are...

2. What is professional accountability? Please give examples.

3. Working in an RN leadership role in patient centered care (check all that apply)...

   a. is something I've done before.

   b. concerns me because of my legal accountability.

   c. I don't know yet.

   d. sounds exciting.

   e. I'll wait and see.

continues

(to prepare for a workshop or workout session)

Dear Hospital Leader:

We will be meeting with you once again on December 5 or 6. To prepare for these sessions, we'd like you to complete the following and bring the answers with you to these sessions.

- ❒ Positive outcomes and otherwise good things you noted this week are the following:

- ❒ Describe a meeting you attended this week. Were the planned outcomes of the meeting achieved? Was everyone on track? Did you feel satisfied with the process and the results?

- ❒ Describe a situation in which you gave positive feedback (formal or informal) to someone this week.

- ❒ In what way(s) have you maintained a 24-hour focus? How have you promoted interdisciplinary teamwork?

- ❒ Describe a complaint you had this week. How did you handle it? Were you satisfied with the staff's involvement in the resolution?

"Remember: some days you're the bug and some days you're the windshield."

(from an old Country/Western song)

Overcoming the Resistance

When we were at a large metropolitan hospital on the West Coast, preparing to assist in the facilitation of a major change in skill mix on a specialty unit, representatives of the hospital said, *"To tell you the truth, we're not sure anything will work. These people are not happy. They see management as the enemy and are tired of even the mention of the word change."* Typically, management wants a quick fix and seeks to achieve this by "throwing some education at 'em," but we held our ground. Before participating in any training, we wanted to assess the staff, get their perspective, and determine what kind of training would be needed. This called for a little one-on-one with every member of the team.

Armed with the following set of questions, (see Tool #2) we proceeded to meet with everyone on all shifts, asking for no more than 15 minutes of time. There was some initial suspicion and a polite refusal by one staff member, but everyone else willingly shared some honest perceptions of the current state of the unit. The result was not only an "eye-opener" for the manager, but when we did offer a workshop to this group, they were not only receptive, but actively participative.

Meeting one-on-one sends a strong message. It says you value others' opinions, demonstrates respect, and offers privacy for people to voice their concerns. Ownership is apparent, and we suggest that responses are more thoughtful and honest than those given on an anonymous survey form. The staff in the organization described previously were consistently amazed that "management must really think this is important, to spend so much time with us" and thought this action was a demonstration of the values of the organization.

Tool #2: Overcoming the Resistance

The Questions

Do people throughout the organization share values and vision?

Do cooperation and trust seem high throughout the organization?

Can people handle more change?

Will this change be seen as beneficial?

Will people be able to maintain dignity and self-respect?

Will this change be seen as mild?

What does this change mean to you now?

Do you know where and from whom to get answers regarding the change?

Have you read the information available?

Have you been to any meeting and shared your thoughts?

Source: Adapted with permission from *Beyond the Wall of Resistance: Unconventional Strategies That Build Support for Change,* by Rick Maurer, Bard Press. © 1996 by Rick Maurer.

WALK A MILE IN MY SHOES

There is no denying the effectiveness of this particular strategy for seeing first-hand what is really going on from another person's perspective. You have no doubt read of the stories of nurses "shadowing" doctors, doctors shadowing nurses, managers working on the unit for a day, and so on. Even our youth have had the opportunity to follow a member of the city government to experience politics from the front row.

We have often worked with leaders who have shaken their heads in dismay, noting *"I can't understand what they're complaining about. When I had that position, I always finished my work on time and certainly didn't have the problems they're complaining about now."* Well, if it's been more than 2 years since you had that position, a lot has changed. It may be time to get a new perspective about what the real situation is like. It should be no surprise then that we highly recommend this technique of assessment. Yes, it takes time, but the results, as demonstrated in the following success stories, are well worth the investment.

Success Story: Teamwalk

Sacred Heart Medical Center in Spokane, Washington, has been sponsoring a process called Teamwalk for the past five years. This project links an employee of one department for a 2-hour visit to another department of his or her choice. Enthusiasm runs high, as every year approximately 250 employees take advantage of the opportunity to walk a mile in a teammate's "shoes." *"It really made me stop and think of the big picture,"* says Roni Clark, a health unit coordinator who spent 2 hours in the admissions department. *"The day I observed, they had 125 admits! That really helped me remember that it's not just our surgical floor that Admitting is working with."*

Dee Jameson, RN, a member of the excellence-in-service committee that organized Teamwalk, says a primary goal is to reinforce teamwork, one of Sacred Heart's four key values. *"When you spend 2 hours with someone, you begin to understand their job,"* Jameson notes.

Success Story: The Dream Team

We all know that participation makes the change process easier and more successful in the long run. But, how do we facilitate participation as part of a restructuring project? The staff at Columbia Northwest Medical Center in Tucson, Arizona, have an interesting and effective answer: the Dream Team.

Getting Started

The administrative leaders at Columbia Northwest Medical Center knew that a change was needed to meet the increasing demands of the industry and to continue to improve the services offered by this acute care facility. Because this facility is a forward-thinking organization, with a culture that has been long used to encourage grass-roots involvement for making changes at the unit level, it is no surprise that leaders recognized a need to continue this level of participation as they considered an overall organizational redesign.

Administratively chosen, based on multidisciplinary representation and the need to involve employees who "question authority and challenge the status quo," seven members of the staff at Northwest became the "Dream Team."

These members were armed with a notebook containing 25 recent articles covering the good and the bad of recent restructuring projects, as well as their own copy of *A Whack on the Side of the Head,* by Roger von Oeck. Their mission was to answer the question, ***D**oes **R**estructuring **E**nhance **A**pproaches to **M**anaging patient care delivery?*

Data Gathering

Initially meeting once a week, the team gathered data in a variety of ways. Each member spent 1 or 2 days being a "patient shadow," following the patient throughout the day, noting how long waiting periods were, how many people interacted with the patient, and what was going right and what wasn't. Many "eye-openers" occurred, supporting the feeling that there was room for improvement in the way care was being delivered. One patient observer noted that when taken to radiology, "The patient was just parked in the hall, with no one to talk to, and told they would get to him when they could." Talking over patients, as if they weren't there, was also observed in elevators and hallways. The Dream Team also noted the positive side of things, learning there were many things they were doing correctly. Site visits and continual literature review were also part of the process because members used data from these to assess the big picture.

For more on how the Dream Team members put their data to work in an effective implementation plan, we refer you to Section Two for the rest of their story.

(Courtesy of Columbia Northwest Medical Center, Tucson, Arizona.)

Tool #3: Patient-Focused Caring Unit Assessment

Legacy Portland Hospital took a different approach to gathering data regarding what's really happening on the patient care units. Using a more formal process, they armed each of the charge personnel with the following form, asking them to target specific issues and to invite comments from the staff regarding each item.

PATIENT-FOCUSED CARING UNIT ASSESSMENT

Unit ______________________________

Date ______________________________

Manager ______________________________

Patient-Focused Care (PFC) Support __________

Area	*Comments*	*Recommendations*
EFFECTIVE USE OF RESOURCES		
Handling of chart		
Use of clinical associates		
Supplies, equipment, phones, computers, chart, and medication location		
Staff understanding charges, costs, labor-productivity measures (LPMs)		
Assignments		
Continuity of caregivers		
INITIATIVE		
Call lights		
Helping others		
Use of clinical paths		
Outcome planning		
Staff understand unit quality plan & monitoring (QP&M)		
Self-directed		
TEAMWORK		
Reports and rounds		
Delegation		
Unit communication		
Feedback and conflict resolution		
Unit decision-making		
Skill mix		
Satisfaction—doctors, patients, staff		
Degree of patient and family involvement		
RESPECT AND CARING		
Open and welcoming environment		
Patient knows caregivers' names		
Show value to other team members		

Courtesy of Legacy Health Systems, Portland, Oregon.

MANAGERIAL ROUNDS

People ask the difference between a leader and a boss. . . . The leader works in the open, and the boss in the covert. The leader leads and the boss drives.

Theodore Roosevelt

An excellent source for assessment data, often overlooked unfortunately, is the manager. We believe, with some organized direction, this role can be invaluable in determining what reengineering might be beneficial for improving the overall functioning of the department.

However, for many managers, managerial rounds have not been a part of their routine practice, having been replaced by the myriad of meetings and supported by the philosophies of shared governance, participative management, and self-directed work teams. Further emphasis should be placed on the process of managerial rounds. As a source of diverse information regarding the day-to-day progress of units' functioning, the development of staff members through coaching and role modeling, and the identification of systems problems. Realizing the demands of many other priorities, it becomes essential to maximize the time managers spend on the units. How do you make the most of this lost art of managerial rounds? Are there similarities to the clinical rounds of yesterday?

▼

"I discontinued the monthly meeting and instituted twice-a-week nursing rounds the following year. These nursing rounds provided occasion for me to meet patients formally, to discuss their nursing care, and to teach them. They also provided opportunities to role model, to teach staff, and to collaborate with the staff on issues identified in the group discussions which followed the rounds. Through collective problem solving, nurses improved their capacity to identify their own roles and to distinguish them from other team members' roles."

(Roberta Prim, Head Nurse at the University of Michigan Medical Center)

▲

Differentiation: Clinical Rounds versus Managerial Rounds

Clinical Rounds	Managerial Rounds
short term/this shift	use a 24-hour perspective, taking data from all shifts
focus on patient clinical picture	multifocused (staff/patient/family/other departments)
clinical outcomes of patient emphasized	outcomes (purpose of rounds) are planned before making rounds
observations limited to patients and families and duration of stay	observations are sequential with follow-through based on identified trends and emerging patterns
short-term problem resolution with a "fix-it-now" approach	emphasize accountability of all team members in resolving problems
identify opportunities for clinical improvement	maximize opportunities for role modeling of desired behaviors

As we continue to emphasize cost-cutting measures and the streamlining of care delivery, the cost of "rework" becomes a luxury no one can afford. Recent studies have discovered adverse events in 3.7% of 30,121 hospital stays and concluded that 80% were preventable (Lumsdon, 1995). Realizing that data do not change behavior, an additional advantage of routine managerial rounds places the manager in a position to obtain first-hand information through on-site observation, identifying adverse events before they become a written incident report on the manager's desk. Being there also affords the opportunity to develop personal accountability through coached problem resolution, thereby having a positive influence on the behavior that will help to reduce adverse events, which is much more meaningful than collating data in the sanctity of an office.

There are a number of challenges to the process of being routinely visible on the units you manage. It is apparent from the long list of advantages to be gained through this process that one cannot simply "show up" on the unit and expect success.

▼

Planning must occur prior to the event, and outcomes, or the purpose of the rounds, must first be determined. This is the primary requirement for success; otherwise, you can expect to experience the time-worn adage of "fail to plan, plan to fail."

▲

In addition to planning the outcome, there is an obvious need for excellent communication skills in the form of sharing observations and providing feedback. It is also necessary for the manager to be able to identify potential problems and assist or coach the team member in finding resolution. This is foreign to many of the "fix-it" approaches we have commonly observed in the past.

Tool #4: Guidelines for Making Managerial Rounds

Phase One: Planning

WHY: Determine your outcome for this assessment.

- patient/customer satisfaction
- staff performance
- effectiveness of unit operations

WHEN: Schedule to complement other manager's rounds and outcomes.

- at start of shift
- after meetings that take you away from the department
- end of shift

WHERE: Base location of rounds on planned outcome.

- patient rooms
- unit stations
- report room

WHO: Base who you interview or observe on the planned outcome.

- staff members
- patients, families, and visitors
- physicians
- other professionals

Phase Two: Ask the Right Questions

WHAT: Determine focus of questions based on planned outcome.

1. Patient and customer satisfaction
   - "How are things going for you during your stay on unit B?"
   - "What are your expectations during this hospital stay, and are they being met?"
   - "How are you doing?"
2. Staff performance
   - "How are you doing with planning assignments based on outcomes?"
   - "What made you mad today?"
   - "What took too long?"
   - "What went right today?"
   - "What caused complaints?"
3. Effectiveness of unit operations
   - "What job involved too many people?"
   - "What job involved too many actions?"
   - "What was too complicated?"
   - "What was wasted?"
4. Effectiveness of leadership
   - "What do you need from me that you are not getting?"
   - "How is my communication style working for you?"
   - "In what areas could I be more consistent, honest, and/or direct?"
   - "What am I doing right?"

IDENTIFYING WHAT'S ENDING

As William Bridges (1980, 1991) reminds us in his landmark book on transitions, change is not cumulative. There must clearly be some things that no longer occur or are no longer part of the picture because of the change. Often this ending is seen as a loss and has prompted the use of the grief process as a means of coping with change. We have found this idea of endings to be an effective part of assessment, helping the team member to get in touch with his or her feelings regarding the proposed change.

Tool #5: Assessing the Emotion of Change

IDENTIFYING THE ENDINGS

Create a metaphor to describe your feelings about the proposed changes:

To make this change, I have had to give up:

What stays the same for me?

Circle the feeling that most describes where you are today:

- Denial
- Anger
- Bargaining
- Anxiety
- Sadness
- Confusion
- Depression
- Acceptance
- Excitement
- or ____________________

What do I need to let go of to make this transition successful for me?

As part of the preparation, or warm-up, for our 2-day workshop (see "No Land in Sight" in Section Three) preparing staff for the proposed change, we have them complete Tool #5. There is typically some resistance to this degree of emotional discussion, but once the ice is broken, an excellent discussion generally follows during which the group has the opportunity to identify some of their fears and concerns regarding the impending reengineering project.

Although we have not done so, you may consider using this worksheet, or part of it, on an individual basis, distributing it to each member of the team and asking them to return it for your review.

The completion of the worksheet is self-explanatory, but there are some important aspects to each section and we'd like to take you through them one at a time.

Metaphorically Speaking

This is an excellent method for safely getting to the heart of the matter without putting someone on the defensive. Generally, people have fun with this question, often getting creative in their responses. Despite the potential light nature to this exercise, there are significant assessments regarding the individual response to the proposed change. Consider some of the metaphors in the following box, which were offered by nursing personnel before an organization-wide downsizing. Note the common, yet varied themes.

Create a metaphor to describe your feelings about the proposed changes.

A lack of understanding of purpose:

"I'm running a marathon or working out without water to drink, wondering if there is a reward for all this."

"I'm making a dress without a pattern."

"I'm on a train going toward a destination, the train goes back and changes course, and we never get anywhere."

A concern about the personal role:

"I'm part of a wildflower garden, not sure if I'll be mistaken for a weed before I bloom."

"I'm a windblown tree, wondering if I'll break or be flexible enough to withstand the storm."

"I'm in a car with multiple providers, we go over the bridge into a lake, and I'm wondering who will roll down the window as the water rises. The patient is on shore."

A sense of victimization:

"I'm at a four-way stop, and the other three streets are closed for construction."

"I have the recipe and the picture of the dessert, and it looks good, but I have to make it with one hand tied behind my back."

"I'm in a swimming pool with the water rising (management), and the lifeguard is not paying attention to me as I drown."

A sense of optimism:

"I'm at a concert, listening to the cacophony of the orchestra tuning up and anticipating the music ahead."

"I'm a circus performer with several plates in the air—I'm working hard to keep them moving, but the applause is worth it."

"I'm a child who has lost her family, but I have been adopted by a new family, and we are happy."

These responses quickly indicate the participant's readiness to move on, or resistance to the process based on fear, lack of information, or lack of support from leadership. We caution against the temptation to make any psychological interpretations, but to use the metaphors as a basis of trending the emotional responses of staff to assess their needs for reengineering to be successful.

To make this change, I have had to give up . . .

my parking place

working with my friends

my preferred shift or unit

my sense of routine and organization

It is important to make the distinction between the question on giving up and the last box on the worksheet relating to letting go. Giving up is generally perceived as an issue that is not negotiable—that as a result of the change, the person will no longer be doing or having this. Typically, respondents consider giving up as something over which they had no control; they consider it as a direct result of the project. Letting go, however, does involve personal assessment and choice; participants need to identify what aspect they are willing to change on the personal level to ensure success of the project.

We find it helpful to make this distinction through the use of the following story:

▼

Once upon a time, there were two monks who belonged to a religious order that strictly forbade any contact with women. Monks were not allowed to talk to a woman or touch her. One day, Brothers Peter and John were making their way through the country, and a tremendous rain came down, changing the roadway into a small and muddy stream that was very difficult to cross. They noted a damsel in distress, unable to cross the road, and calling for help. Brother Paul went to her rescue, picking the woman up and carrying her to safety on the other side of the stream. The monks then continued on their journey, but Brother John was quiet and appeared angry. Reaching their destination for the night, Brother Paul asked John what was wrong.

"Wrong? I can't believe you, Brother Paul! You picked up a woman today and carried her across the stream! You know that is against the order! I can't believe you!"

Brother Paul sighed and noted, "I may have carried her across the stream, but you are carrying her still."

Reps, P., ed. (1961). *Zen flesh, Zen bones: A collection of Zen & Pre-Zen writings.* New York: Bantam Doubleday Dell.

▲

This story helps to make the point that each of us is carrying some baggage we may need to get rid of for one reason or another, and that we do indeed have control over what we "let go" of.

What I need to let go of to make this transition successful for me:

my need to be in control all the time

my feeling that only I can do it right and no one else can do it as well as me

my need to be the only one

my distrust of management

Circle the Feeling

The emotions listed include those five that are part of the grieving process. Usually, there is a variety of responses, with some participants identifying more than one emotion. This is an emotional and turbulent time, and a discussion of the team's feelings can be beneficial in clearing the air and restoring a sense of connection and meaning to the project.

▼

Failing to assess feelings of the group will only result in the necessity to deal with emotional overtones repeatedly and stall the progress you had hoped to make.

▲

What Stays the Same

The responses here generally indicate the personal commitment to the mission of the organization or the work unit (if the mission is real and visible as part of the culture!). We emphasize the importance in identifying these constants; in a sea of continual whitewater, it is essential for people to know what represents solid ground. Be wary if your responses are limited to a personal perspective, such as the following:

- my paycheck;
- my job; and
- my seniority.

These self-absorbed responses often come from an insecure group, one in which trust of the "system" and management may not be strong. Work will need to be done to clarify the purpose of the project as well as the overall mission of the organization or team. If the connection of the team member to the overall sense of the purpose of the group is not made, there will be continued lack of participation, and effective change will not be possible.

Responses you hope to get include the following from a unit within a small hospital where the mission and vision of the organization were known to everyone.

What Stays the Same for Me:
the caring of the patients
the mission of the organization
my commitment to the patient and the profession
our commitment to quality
the team
my desire to do the best I can

Whatever responses you get, you will be better able to assess where everyone is at regarding understanding the scope of the proposed change, and have an idea of the degree of support or resistance present in the staff. From here you can begin to identify a plan for what the next steps will be.

PROFESSIONAL STEREOTYPING

Often, the completion of the "endings" worksheet will also reveal some interesting cultural biases. Staff members may honestly communicate that they need to let go of the idea that an assistant is "uneducated and does not care like I do" or that "the pharmacist only cares about the right dosage at the right time, and is not capable of understanding the patient's needs." With so much attention placed on cultural diversity, it is surprising to us that the culture of a particular profession can create these equally strong biases and behaviors, which, if left unaddressed, will only serve to get in the way of the most carefully built team. Consider the following situations:

Memorial Hospital's staff was enthusiastic when they began to implement a patient-centered care delivery model, but lately there's been trouble. It seems that the pharmacists on the units are in conflict with the nursing staff, wanting a more systematic approach, and stating the nurses are "too sympathetic" to the patients and tend to make mistakes in medicating too soon, without careful analysis of the patient's drug profile.

The new short-stay ambulatory center at St. John's was a dream come true (to both the board and administration). But, there is continual frustration within the multidisciplinary team, and the unit is now on its third manager. Physicians are saying administration is "too controlling" and focused only on the "bottom line," while patient techs are calling the patients "demanding" and "unreasonable."

Defining the Terms

professional patriotism: loyal and devoted support and defense of one's own profession, often made visible when challenged by an outside force; the feeling of ownership and pride in the unique contributions of one's own group

professional stereotyping: a fixed and superficial judgment about another profession, diminishing or eliminating the opportunity to appreciate the qualities of each individual within the profession (Herrick, 1993)

The devoted support of fellow professionals often surfaces in times of change, and the desired connection can be taken beyond pride and loyalty into an adversarial relationship between two disciplines. Closed minds and an exclusionary bias result when a group "circles around the campfire" of their colleagues, who are much more similar and less frightening than new multiskilled workers with less training and preparation or of different backgrounds. Territories are created and boundaries are reinforced as departments, and now agencies, have difficulty relating to each other.

Generalizations become the norm as various groups identify a behavior and the attribute becomes part of the stereotype of the role; for example, the RN from Memorial Hospital stated, "That's what you'd expect of a pharmacist, they are all compulsive." We are reminded of the situation when a nurse observed a new patient-care tech on a nursing unit. Standing by the ringing phone, he was busy with a chart and clearly not answering the phone. The nurse identified this as "lazy" behavior and used this example to reinforce her opinion of this level of care provider as a type with no initiative. Freely sharing this stereotype by stating, "This is just what I expected from techs, they're all lazy," to other members of her nursing team had a negative impact on the development of a well-functioning team.

▼

"Increasing importance will be placed on management's ability to manage a diverse work force. And diversity doesn't only mean race and gender. It also means functional diversity, now that cross-functional teams have become the new trend. Different departments with radically different cultures—such as research and development, marketing, engineering, public relations, purchasing—have to learn to work together in teams or work groups."

(Pelled, 1996)

▲

Assessing the Priorities

The process we have used to identify the barriers of professional stereotyping is similar to those processes you've used to overcome the negative attitudes toward cultural diversity. We would suggest the following tool from one of our workshops ["From Barriers to Bridges: Success Strategies for High Performing Teams" (Herrick, 1993)] for multidisciplinary work groups.

By using this tool, employees begin to understand their values and the main objectives and strengths of their own group. Common values often emerge as similar priorities are identified in the first part of the tool. Matching stereotypical characteristics in the second part allows for open discussion about where and when these ideas originated and whether they are valid judgments. Be prepared for some eye-opening exchanges as staff share their ideas. Some "hot buttons" may need to be insulated, and you will need to rely on the ability of a neutral facilitator to keep the discussion on an even ground. But the benefits are well worth the time, as we emphasize once again the importance of dealing with the "soft side" of change.

▼

"To see brotherhood in action, just watch a bunch of high school kids taking a final exam. There's no question of race, creed, or color. There is only one question: "Who's got the answer?"

Sam Levenson

▲

Tool #6: Assessing the Priorities

Ask each member of the team, department, or unit to complete the following, and then share the results in a facilitated discussion.

List three characteristics or behaviors that are particular to your job.

1. ______________________________
2. ______________________________
3. ______________________________

Describe the three main priorities of your job.

1. ______________________________
2. ______________________________
3. ______________________________

Match the role with the characteristic that you would most commonly associate with that role. You may use descriptors more than once.

Pharmacist:_____	a. athletic
Patient-care assistant:_____	b. detail-oriented
Lab technician:_____	c. friendly
Physical therapist:_____	d. caring
Registered nurse:_____	e. technical
Radiology technician:_____	f. busy
Financial accountant:_____	g. trustworthy
Secretary:_____	h. intelligent
Social worker:_____	i. professional
Manager:_____	j. problem-solver
Admitting clerk:_____	k. stressed
Volunteer:_____	l. supportive
Respiratory therapist:_____	m. strong
Physician:_____	n. methodical
Environmental services worker:_____	o. theoretical
Maintenance engineer:_____	p. authoritative
Security guard:_____	q. flexible
Administrator:_____	r. business-like
Dietitian:_____	s. retired
Medical records clerk:_____	t. tactful
	u. determined
	v. task-oriented
	w. careful
	x. mechanical
	y. fast
	z. analytical

FROM NOVICE TO EXPERT: WHERE ARE YOUR PEOPLE?

"The foundation of any work redesign or restructuring involves the assessment of basic clinical competencies," recommends Adonna Lowe, vice president of patient care and nursing with the St. Joseph Healthcare System in Albuquerque, New Mexico (Lowe, 1996). We would wholeheartedly agree, taking it one step further in recommending the assessment of the degree of proficiency staff members have attained in their practice. Clinical competency is indeed an essential cornerstone to successful redesign, but failing to fully appreciate the perspective and the educational development of the staff only sets the stage for unmet expectations regarding professional performance.

Consider the following situation in which we were asked to assist in the development of teamwork at a small community hospital:

> The edict had been decreed and indeed carried out. As an immediate cost saving measure, staff levels were reduced by 20%. To accomplish this degree of reduction, senior nurses were retired or laid off. Additional nursing personnel saw the writing on the wall and resigned, accepting employment elsewhere or leaving the field entirely. The remaining personnel were very young. The most senior person had only three years of experience, and the majority of the nursing personnel had been with this organization for less than a year because of continual turnover. The staff developer attended orientation one day, looking at a group of newly hired nurses, all of whom had associate degrees from the local community college and no previous experience. Choosing from her limited staff, the criteria for being a preceptor was reduced to those who had been with the organization for more than 6 months! These new recruits, joining those who had not been laid off, would be in charge of a newly restructured work force that relied on team leadership of various levels of assistive personnel.

The problems are probably obvious to you. Teamwork will be only a small part of the issue. One lesson to be learned here is that random layoffs to accomplish immediate cost savings will seriously impair the ability of the remaining staff to realize the expectations of the new team. Clinical competency is an issue, but beyond that, the degree of experience and perception of the staff remaining in the previous situation has not been assessed nor considered in terms of the feasibility of the proposed team project. Eliminating or losing personnel who have acquired expertise, leaving only staff who are in the "advanced beginner" or "competent" levels will leave you with a task-based, detail-focused group that is simply not able to see the "big picture" and respond in the way that you had hoped.

▼

Whether you have cut your staff or not, or you have high turnover or continual retention of a staff with longevity over ten years, you need to assess staff levels of clinical proficiency as well as competency.

▲

Because the majority of restructuring projects involve the advanced development of the nursing role, the integration of additional roles in a team approach, and the coordination of the whole process, leaders who can assume these new roles must be available. How do you know if the existing staff members have these abilities? You may be asking the impossible of staff members who are not "there yet," and will need continued support and additional training to be able to realize the dream.

From Novice to Expert

One model that is familiar to the nursing world is that of Patricia Benner's, *From Novice to Expert.* Her adaptation comes from the groundbreaking work done by Dreyfus and Dreyfus (Garland, 1996) in their studies of skill acquisition of chess players and Air Force pilots. As more experience and education are attained, an individual can progress through these stages of development with marked differences in approach to decision-making, problem-solving, organization, and work efficiency. However, as Benner and Benner remind us, "Some persons will tend to settle in a competent or proficient level because of personal learning styles, personal concerns, or organizational constraints that cause them to plateau at a level of practice" (Benner and Benner, 1991).

Although Benner and Benner have adapted the Dreyfus model to nursing, we suggest that the general implications are applicable in all fields of care providers. An understanding of this development will assist in planning what the next steps of a restructuring project are, and more importantly, in determining if the staff available are ready to lead the way.

Level I: Novice. Beginners who have no experience with the situations in which they are expected to perform must depend on rules to guide their actions. Following rules, however, has limits. No rule can tell novices which tasks are most relevant in real situations nor when to make exceptions.

Implications: work is organized by task; becomes disorganized easily

Level II: Advanced Beginner. One who has coped with enough real situations (or has them pointed out by a mentor) begins to identify the recurrent meaningful aspects of situations. An advanced beginner needs help setting priorities because she or he operates following general guidelines and is only beginning to perceive recurrent meaningful patterns. The advanced beginner cannot reliably sort out what is most important in complex situations.

Implications: in stable situations, follows orders and procedures; gets disorganized in unstable situations, and has a naive trust in standard protocols

Level III: Competent. Typically, the competent nurse (individual) has been in practice two to three years. This person can rely on long-range goals and plans to determine which aspects of a situation are important and which can be ignored. The competent individual lacks the speed and flexibility of the person who has reached the proficient level, but competence is characterized by a feeling of mastery and the ability to cope with and manage many contingencies of clinical care.

Implications: works with preset plans and goals personally identified; less naive about protocols and coworkers; develops own way of doing some things

Level IV: Proficient. One who perceives situations as wholes, rather than in terms of aspects. With holistic understanding, decision-making is less labored because the individual has a perspective on which of the many attributes and aspects present are the important ones. The proficient performer considers fewer options and concentrates on an accurate region of the problem.

Implications: reads situations better and sets priorities according to the situation as it unfolds

Level V: Expert. The person who no longer relies on an analytical principle (rule, guideline, maxim) to connect understanding of the situation to an appropriate action. The expert individual with an enormous background of experience has an intuitive grasp of the situation and concentrates on the accurate region of the problem without wasteful consideration of a large range of unfruitful possibilities.

Implications: fluid and skillful in managing; attends to both the most salient aspects as well as those that go unnoticed by less experienced staff

Source: Reprinted with permission from P. Benner, Stories from the Front Lines, *Healthcare Forum Journal,* pp 69–74, July-August, © 1991.

Nursing Expertise Self-Report Scale

Gayle Garland, a nurse educator in California, has developed a survey tool for the beginning assessment of professional development. Although still in the trial stages, it makes an effective first step in analysis of clinical performance. We are delighted to have the opportunity to include this tool and encourage you to share your data with Gayle by contacting her at the address provided.

Tool #7: Nursing Expertise Self-Report Scale

Please circle the answer that best describes you.

1. I am an: RN Other
2. My job is: Staff nurse Assistant Nurse Manager Other
3. Length of time since graduating as an RN:
   Under 6 months 6 months to 3 years More than 3 years
4. Length of time working on your unit:
   Under 6 months 6 months to 3 years More than 3 years
5. Previous experience in nursing prior to graduating as an RN:
   Under 6 months 6 months to 3 years More than 3 years

The following is a list of statements about nursing care. Please circle the number which best represents your agreement with the statement.

	Strongly agree	*Agree*	*Unsure*	*Disagree*	*Strongly disagree*
1. I often know ahead of time that my patient will take a turn for the worse.	1	2	3	4	5
2. I frequently draw on past experiences when making patient care decisions.	1	2	3	4	5
3. Quality nursing care results from strictly adhering to policy and procedure.	1	2	3	4	5
4. When I do patient care, only a few pieces of information stand out as critically important.	1	2	3	4	5
5. I am consciously aware of the process of decision making in patient care.	1	2	3	4	5
6. Emotional attachments get in the way of good nursing care.	1	2	3	4	5
7. When something goes wrong with my patient, I seem to know automatically what to do.	1	2	3	4	5

continues

		Strongly agree	*Agree*	*Unsure*	*Disagree*	*Strongly disagree*
8.	Sometimes I find it difficult to identify objective reasons for certain patient care decisions.	1	2	3	4	5
9.	The best way to give good nursing care is to get close to the patient.	1	2	3	4	5
10.	I find it time consuming to set priorities in patient care.	1	2	3	4	5
11.	I make my best decisions about patient care when I remain objective.	1	2	3	4	5
12.	In an emergency, things happen so quickly that I don't know what to do.	1	2	3	4	5
13.	I base my patient care decisions more often on the rules I learned in nursing school than on my experience in patient care.	1	2	3	4	5
14.	It seems obvious to me what things need to be done first for my patients.	1	2	3	4	5
15.	I use facts such as lab values and vital signs as my main source of information for making patient care decisions.	1	2	3	4	5
16.	I usually require a lot of information about a patient care situation before I am comfortable with making a decision.	1	2	3	4	5
17.	I do my best nursing care when I become truly involved with the patient.	1	2	3	4	5
18.	I am comfortable with altering standard patient care procedures when I see the need.	1	2	3	4	5
19.	Sudden patient care emergencies usually come as a complete surprise to me.	1	2	3	4	5
20.	Most often I find myself relying on gut feelings when it comes to patient care.	1	2	3	4	5

Source: Reprinted with permission from G. Garland, Self-Report of Competence, *Journal of Nursing Staff Development,* Vol. 12, No. 4, p 197, © 1996, Lippincott-Raven.

continues

continued

Instructions for Completing the Nursing Expertise Self Report Scale

Overview

The Nursing Expertise Self Report Scale was developed from Patricia Benner's model of clinical competence described in Benner, P. (1984). Benner described three changes in performance as the nurse progresses from novice to expert practice. One change is the reliance on rules and principles to the reliance on past experience to guide performance. The second change is a transition from viewing the clinical situation as a collection of equally important features to viewing the clinical situation as a whole, in which only a few features are important. The third change is the passage from detached observer to involved performer. Unique to the expert level of performance is the element of intuition. This scale is designed to measure self perception of these three transitions and intuitive decision making.

Self report methodology is widely used in psychological and human subject research. Self report methodology has the advantage of being versatile and direct in measuring feelings, values, opinions, and perceptions. However, the most limiting disadvantage is the concern for validity and accuracy of self report. **Therefore, the self reported level of competence derived from the use of this scale may not correspond to the observed level of practice for an individual nurse. This scale is not intended as a substitute for observation and testing of competence in the clinical setting.**

Potential uses for this scale include:

Designing educational offerings,
Discussion and planning for transitions in care assignments,
Individual professional development planning.

Validity and Reliability

Reliability testing was done using a test-retest method. Content validity was conducted by review of nurses in the practice of Nursing Staff Development.

Scale Scoring and Interpretation

The Nursing Expertise Self Report may be used with or without the demographic tool. Benner's model discusses a potential relationship between experience and expertise, therefore the design of the demographic tool.

Scoring—The Nursing Expertise Self Report Scale has twenty items scored using a Likert scale from Strongly Agree to Strongly Disagree. For items 3, 5, 6, 10, 11, 12, 13, 15, 16, and 19, the **Strongly Disagree** response is identified as the **Expert** response. For the remaining items, the **Strongly Agree** response represents the **Expert** response. **A value of 1 is given to the response that reflects novice practice. The expert response receives a score of five.** The potential minimum score assuming a response on each item is 20. The potential maximum score assuming a response on each item is 100.

There are no identified point values that demark any specific level of competence. Lower aggregate totals reflect self perception reflective of novice practice. Higher overall scores reflect self perception reflective of expert practice.

Results

The author requests that those who use the Nursing Expertise Self-Report Scale forward a copy of their findings and any comments to the address below. The author may be contacted for assistance also at the address below.

Copies of the original study may be obtained by contacting the author.

Gayle A. Garland, RN, C, MSN, CNA
9390 Carmel Road
Atascadero, CA 93422
(805) 461-3010

AND WHAT ARE THEY DOING?

Equally important to assessing feelings, biases, and barriers is a determination of who is doing what and how long it is taking. Although "walking in someone's shoes" will give the "flavor" of the job and identify some rights and wrongs, there are also tools for gathering more specific data related to productivity and efficiency. Although we do not claim to be efficiency experts and do not suggest you hire one, we do cite some benefit in doing a quantitative study of time and motion.

Baseline Work Sampling

MultiCare Medical Center in Tacoma, Washington wanted to identify the percentage of time workers were spending with patients. This would be important baseline data to determine quantifiable improvement or to evaluate if a change in the care delivery system would actually mean less time spent with patients. To complete their study, seven patient units were identified and volunteers were recruited to be observers. Staff activities were observed in the following manners:

- every 5 minutes;
- in 4-hour blocks;
- for all shifts; and
- over a number of various days.

It was important to factor in the night shift, as well as the weekend shifts, to form a composite of time spent with the patients. Their baseline data are shown in the Analytical Tool Set. (Refer to Section Four, "Evaluation" for a report on the success of their project.)

Tool #8: Baseline Work Sampling

Analytical Tool Set

- Establish baselines, internal and external
- Identify tools to teach: flow charts, Pareto, skill matrix, etc.
- Collect baseline work sampling

Percent of Time Spent with Patient Data Set

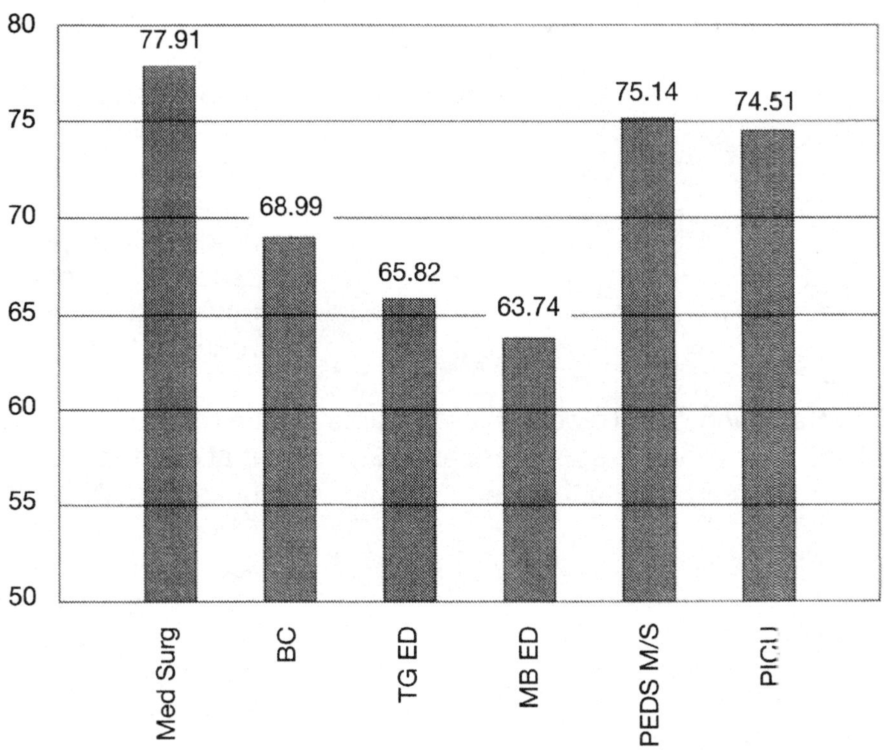

Courtesy of MultiCare Medical Center, Tacoma, Washington.

Tool #9: Components of CHMC Diagnostic Assessment

Component	*Purpose*	*Result*
Literature Review	To provide an overview of the current national trends in nursing practice redesign	The most commonly reported approach was to pair the RN with assistive personnel in a skill mix model.
Staff Forums	To solicit input from the CHMC's own health care team on opportunities to improve the delivery of patient care	RNs identified that they were spending a significant amount of time in non-nursing or non-licensed activities. Suggestions were made to incorporate assistive personal to perform these non-licensed tasks.
Work Sampling Study	To determine RN time spent in licensed activities	The results indicated that on the acute care units, the RNs spent 58% of their time in licensed activities. In the critical care units, RNs spent 64% of their time in licensed activities.

Source: Copyright © 1996, Children's Hospital and Medical Center, Seattle, Washington.

Diagnostic Assessment

Although time and motion are important, the Children's Hospital and Medical Center (CHMC) completed their assessment, collecting data in addition to completing a work sampling similar to that of MultiCare.

Survey the Literature

The first component listed in the CHMC diagnostic assessment is that of literature review. Many of us remember that any research project begins with an extensive search of the literature to see what has already been written and who has done what. The power of this information when shared with the staff is often forgotten, or not realized. The CHMC made copies of their review and made them available on all of the patient care units. Staff were referred to this bound compilation of information when questions arose such as, "Has anybody else done this before?" and "Has it worked?"

In a similar fashion, you may recall that the Dream Team of Northwest Hospital of Tucson was armed with 25 of the latest articles specific to their proposed restructuring.

▼

Assessment of what others have done is important to success, but sharing that assessed information is fundamental to facilitating the participation of the team.

▲

Ask the Staff

We have asked the staff a variety of questions, using a number of tools to guide the process. The CHMC offered a series of open forums in which small groups of staff were encouraged to come and to share their concerns and questions regarding the current state of practice of patient care. This open discussion approach offered the opportunity for staff to relate their own priorities and not simply respond to a predetermined list.

Observe the Staff

The time motion process used by the CHMC was similar in format to that of MultiCare Medical Center, but with an emphasis not only on time spent with the patient but on identifying the types of tasks being done and the level of preparation required to perform those tasks.

These data were supported by a comparable nationwide study done by the Hay Group in 1993, which determined that 52% of nurse time in hospitals was devoted to tasks that did not require professional knowledge (Hospitals and Health Networks, 1994). (See work-sampling graph from CHMC.)

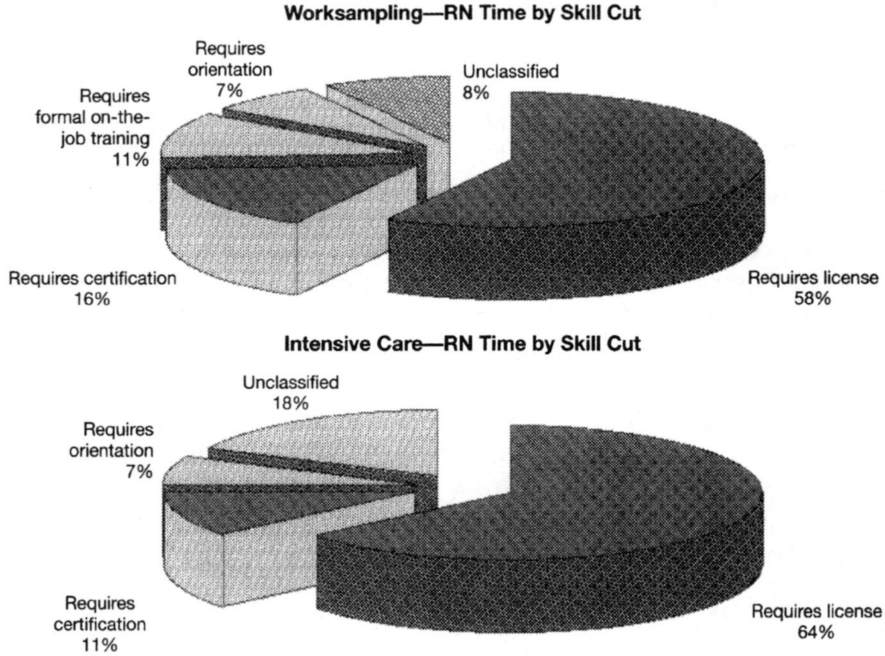

Source: Copyright © 1996, Children's Hospital and Medical Center, Seattle, Washington.

IDENTIFYING PARADOXES

Sometimes it's difficult to figure out what the real problems are. Insurer contracts are paying less and less on the dollar; reimbursement is at an all-time low; and the search is on to find more efficient and effective methods for providing service to preserve what little profit margin is left. But what needs to be changed? Where are the problems?

The answers often lie in asking the right questions, in directing thinking in a way that will yield useful information. What is needed is a catalyst—a stimulant, if you will—that will help people to focus their thinking on what's really at stake. We have adapted Gareth Morgan's (1993) work in the following tool about dilemmas and contradictions.

Tool #10: Dilemmas and Contradictions

Distribute this form during a small staff forum, or to a group of managers for them to complete. Have them complete it individually and then report to the group, generating a flip chart list of the issues that are shared. You will be surprised at the honesty and the work ahead of you!

What are the main contradictions encountered by people working here?

quality care	versus	__________
cost saving	versus	__________
patient safety	versus	__________
staff development	versus	__________
__________	versus	__________
__________	versus	__________
__________	versus	__________

Another approach to this directed discussion is the use of specific issues concerning one department. Realize that you are putting issues that you have assessed, either through direct observation or communication with staff members who have shared their perspective previously, on the form. In this example, we were working with an educator committee of a large hospital undergoing a merger with another hospital in the city. The educator group was at a loss regarding their direction, and unclear regarding what would be deemed "broken" and in need of fixing. We used this tool to help focus their thinking and to further assess what the real problems might be.

Educator chart

The educator group takes an overall view of the issues.	BUT	
The educator group coordinates activities related to education at ABC.	BUT	
The educator group meets regularly.	BUT	
The educator group has defined short-term and long-term goals.	BUT	
The members of the educator group willingly participate in regular meetings.	BUT	
The members of the group are clear on their roles.	BUT	

Their completed form revealed the following problems:

Completed chart

The educator group takes an overall view of the issues.	BUT	lack time and resources to fix issues; duplication of effort; no clear view of effectiveness
The educator group coordinates activities related to education at ABC.	BUT	no control over resources; pulled too many projects; hindered by other groups' demands
The educator group meets regularly.	BUT	have difficulty staying with agenda; don't have time to cover all the issues
The educator group has defined short-term and long-term goals.	BUT	everyday tasks not reflected in goals; no control over resources to achieve
The members of the educator group willingly participate in regular meetings.	BUT	hesitate to volunteer for action plans; time restraints limit productivity
The members of the group are clear on their roles.	BUT	others are not clear on our roles; changing hats too often

Tool #11: Visual Images

Sometimes a visual image will inspire conversation in an open and honest fashion. As described in the endings exercise, the use of metaphors is an excellent method for facilitating discussion that will help to energize the group for future action. We suggest you break your group into small groups of three to four people and have them complete the following:

Visual images

Think of an animal or other image to describe your department (hospital, work group, etc.). (You may draw it or describe it—be creative!)

as it was 2 years ago...

as it is now...

as it will be 5 years in the future...

Source: Adapted from G. Morgan, *Imaginization: The art of creative management,* © 1993, Sage.

Bring the small groups back together and have them share their responses. Typically, humor and creativity will help to defuse some of the more difficult issues, yet these issues will still surface, giving you a better idea of what people are seeing as problems and, more importantly, their perspective of the future. The effectiveness of this tool lies not with the completion of the form, but with the skills of the facilitator in keeping the conversation going and helping people to tell their story. There are always reasons why a particular animal or image was chosen, and the rationale behind the choice is essential to note. Generally, a pattern will emerge, and with the group actively engaged, problem-solving can begin. This same educator group completed the exercise in the following manner:

2 years ago...	swimming in known waters
	a Christmas package all wrapped up
	a tunnel with a narrow destination
	a giraffe overseeing the area
	"the appetizer"
now...	juggler
	amoeba
	Timex watch (keep on ticking)
	octopus (reaching in all directions and grabbing nothing)
	"a full course meal"
5 years from now...	fluid river with many branches
	flock of birds migrating
	space satellite
	wise old owl
	"a smorgasbord"

In this way, the group was able to identify a progression from a singular-focused department with clearly defined boundaries (limitations) through a time of chaos and confusion (no limits now) to a future of continued growth and expansion with direct separation from the merged organization resulting in a community focus.

Using these tools to identify contradictions and creatively describe direction, the educator group we worked with was able to correct some clearly defined problems (no clear role identification, little control over resources) and realize a positive future in a newly merged hospital system.

THE OVERALL VIEW

At this point, we have offered you a variety of survey and assessment tools that are specifically targeted in approach. In summary, we include the overall approach taken by a fellow consultant, Betty Noyes of Noyes & Associates, Ltd., Bainbridge Island, Washington.

Much like the Dream Team approach, Betty encourages three or four people to be deployed on specific missions (perhaps in disguise!) to gather the following facts. It's possible to establish scoring based on your assessment benchmarks. Be creative!

Tool #12 Questions with a System Approach

1. Count the number of patients in the admitting area who are waiting for more than 30 minutes to be registered.
2. Count the number of patients waiting to be escorted from Admitting to the inpatient unit for more than ten minutes.
3. Go to an inpatient surgical unit. Ask a unit secretary for the record of a patient who had blood drawn (not a STAT order) and whose results have been reported. Find out when the blood was drawn and when it was reported on the record. Was it done before the attending physician's rounds? If not, was the laboratory called and by whom?
4. Look at a table of the organization and get a copy of position control by cost center. How many departments have two levels of supervision between the vice president and the supervisory employee with less than 15 employees?
5. Look at the number of administrative manager meetings per month.
6. Compare a copy of the inpatient and outpatient admitting "face sheets." Count the number of redundant data fields.
7. Review each of the Clinical Ancillary Services documentation records. Count the number of data fields that require duplicate information from that appearing on the nursing assessment sheet.
8. Go to an inpatient medical unit during morning or afternoon rounds. Ask the first three physicians you encounter whether (1) the nurses communicate with them about the patient's discharge needs when they are present on rounds and (2) when is the last time she or he was called for new orders due to missed medications or treatments.
9. In a patient room, have a patient or family member count how many different faces enter the room during a given 24-hour period.
10. Count how many simple respiratory treatments are ordered and not provided.
11. Wait for an elevator connecting physical therapy and a nursing unit. Count the minutes.
12. Count the number of trips for physical therapy treatments that did not require major equipment and could have been provided on the unit. Then multiply the number of minutes times the number of trips by the hourly salary of the transporter.
13. How many different consent forms are needed for an average surgical procedure?
14. Count how many people write in the medical record and what percentage of their time is taken in that activity. Multiply that times their hourly salary.
15. Go to a nursing unit on Sunday evening or night shift. Count the number of sheets, towels, and washcloths that remain for patient use during the night.
16. Look at the physician's order sheet for medication or IV orders, then trace the time the medication was actually given. Subtract the two to determine the time for order completion.
17. What is your pet peeve? Put a cost on it!
18. How many calls were made to pharmacy for missing medications in the last 24 hours?
19. Interview the discharge planner, social worker, or utilization review personnel regarding the hours (or days!) patients wait to transfer from unit to unit, from the operating room or emergency department (ED) to a unit, to an extended care facility or home.
20. Ask medical records to review charts for the number of admits or ED visits from patients who have been discharged from an inpatient setting within the last 14 days.

Source: Betty Noyes, Noyes & Associates, Bainbridge Island, Washington.

Success Story: From "Billing and Revenue Focused" to "Patient Focused" Patient Services

We believe the following story, which first appeared in *Successful Restructuring* (Hansten & Washburn, 1996), is an excellent example of a global focus based on asking the right questions in a systematic process. Through a coordinated effort, this small hospital was able to realize significant benefits for both the patient and the staff. Now that's successful redesigning!

Marvin Heskett, Administrative Director of Patient Care at Lebanon Community Hospital, Lebanon, Oregon, a 49-bed rural hospital, spoke with us regarding his community hospital's bold moves to respond to the future of rural hospitals in a capitated health care system.

Last year, a same-day surgery patient traveled to five different departments for two hours to prepare for surgery. The patient (who then understood why we've called clients *patients*) visited imaging, electrocardiography (ECG), lab, registration, and same-day surgery. All those separate departments were revenue focused. "It seemed that no one even thought about the patient." Now, in less than one hour, the patient receives the same services but in the same-day surgery department.

Restructuring meant moving all the outpatient services to the front of the hospital. The laboratory, imaging, physical and respiratory therapy, pharmacy, and same-day care centers became easily accessible to the public. Five new departments took shape:

1. Patient care: nursing and all other clinical departments;
2. Support services: combining billing, information services, purchasing, central processing, and medical records;
3. Quality improvement: includes risk management, infection control, employee health, case management. All these departments function as a report card for the Patient Care Division;
4. Community relations: public relations, fund raising, volunteers; and
5. Plant: equipment and plant, housekeeping, maintenance.

The changes meant that all stakeholders had to be involved. The Board of Directors, physicians, and staff were engaged in planning. Four one-hour sessions were held four times per year to update staff.

To obtain the necessary linkages to survive in managed care, Lebanon Community Hospital has hired its own physicians to provide primary and, most recently, specialty care. This group is linked organizationally to the Patient Care Division. Mid Valley Health Care will be tied with personal computers and local area networks to keep the information flowing. All local physicians will also be connected to this network.

In the Patient Care Services area, Marvin noted that 50 different staff went into an inpatient's room during a three-day stay. They are planning to combine housekeepers with central supply workers to stock rooms and keep necessary supplies on hand while cleaning the patient care areas. Certified Nursing Assistants are being trained to do additional skills such as EKG and phlebotomy as well.

Despite the fact that this has been a "fascinating experience" for Marvin in his role of leading and facilitating the process, he states

▼

"This is what we would have done twenty years ago if we had been given the opportunity."

▲

Section One References

Andrews, R. (1993). *The Columbia dictionary of quotations.* New York: Columbia University Press, 512.

Benner, P. & Benner, R. (1991). Stories from the front lines. *Healthcare Forum Journal, July–August,* 69–74.

Bridges, W. (1991). *Managing transitions: Making the most of change.* Reading, Mass: Addison-Wesley.

Bridges, W. (1980). *Transitions.* Reading, Mass: Addison-Wesley.

Benner, P. (1984). *From novice to expert: Excellence and power in clinical nursing practice.* Menlo Park, Calif: Addison-Wesley.

Garland, G. (1996). Self report of competence. *Journal of Nursing Staff Development, 12*(4): 191–197.

Hansten, R. & Washburn, M. (1996). *Successful restructuring newsletter,* 1(4). Gaithersburg, Md: Aspen Publishers, 6–8.

Herrick, K., Northwest Organization of Nurse Executives, Hansten, R., & Washburn, M. 1993. *From barriers to bridges: Success strategies for high performing teams,* a portable workshop for team building in today's changing environment. Contact Karen Herrick @ 206-285-0102.

Lowe, A. (1996). Reducing variation in patient care. *Journal of Nursing Administration, 26*(1): 14–20.

Lumsdon, K. (1995). The price of doing it over. *Hospitals and Health Networks,* March 20, 80.

Maurer, R. (1996). *Beyond the wall of resistance.* Austin, Texas: Bard Books, 95–103.

Morgan, G. (1993). *Imaginization: The art of creative management.* Newbury Park, Calif: Sage Publications, 32, 184.

Pelled, L. (1996). How to get diverse work groups to work together productively. *Manager's Intelligence Report, April,* 6.

Prim, Roberta. (1993). Communication: Coping with the unspoken dance. *Nursing Management, 24*(3): 33–35.

1994. Work transformation creates a more rewarding role for nurses. *Hospitals and Health Networks, 68*(7): 51.

Reps, P., Ed. (1961). *Zen flesh, Zen bones: A collection of Zen & Pre-Zen writings.* New York: Bantam Doubleday Dell.

SECTION 2

Planning for Success

Worst Case Scenario:
"Letting Go of Patient Safety"

"There are people coming in off the streets to work with us!" "They have no training. And we had no idea what tasks they could do!" "We had 2 days' notice to prepare for the lay-offs and then they all showed up on Monday." "We have to let go of our patient advocacy role, of patient safety."

We were just beginning the first day of a 2-day training program for registered nurses (RNs) learning to work with assistive personnel when we heard these disturbing quotes. The initial phase of the workshop involves the nurses' responses to change and each participant's accountability necessary to make the change successful for him or her. During the discussion, nurses often recognize that they'll have to "let go of" some of the tasks they are used to doing because assistive personnel will be doing these tasks in the future. They may also have to give up the familiar concept of defining quality of care as a predetermined nurse-patient ratio, for example, when they say, *"quality of care means I take care of four patients by myself."* But rarely do we hear nurses state that to continue working, they'll have to let go of patient safety.

In this particular organization, we had not been involved in the process of care redesign nor were we current with the method by which the changes had occurred. Knowing that staff members are often unable to listen to the news of upcoming changes because of their fear, and that some RNs choose not to participate in planning for changes in care delivery (then react in anger when changes do occur), we listened to their concerns about patient safety with a skeptical perspective.

However, in this case, all of the previous allegations were true. The advent of managed care in this area and an impending merger (read: takeover) by a larger hospital drove hospital leaders to react with immediate budget cuts in the form of personnel, with little assessment or planning for the best methods of achieving the savings. The time spent by hospital managers in response to public outcry, revenue from care contracts lost because of quality concerns, productivity loss due to improperly prepared and distrusting staff, and the expensive turnover of untrained assistive personnel mounted up a budget deficit where there could have been some long-term cost savings had planning occurred.

❷ PLANNING FOR SUCCESS

"Life organizes around identity.... This identity chooses what to notice, what meanings to assign, what paths to take. No person or system changes if it cannot see itself in the proposed future. But we change willingly when we believe that change will serve to maintain our core selves."

Meg Wheatley and Myron Kellner-Rogers (1996)

ONE CONSULTANT'S ROADMAP

Betty Noyes, Noyes and Associates Ltd., formerly of Chicago and presently from Bainbridge Island, Washington, shares the principles and roadmap she uses in guiding reengineering projects in health care facilities. She recognizes as a driver for redesign the dissatisfaction we may feel when, at the end of a long hard day, we wish things could somehow be simpler, more logical, for our patients. Reengineering is an opportunity to improve outcomes, in terms of quality and cost, for ourselves and our patients.

The following principles of redesign are those that guide her practice:

- vision of patient focus and cost realities
- patient aggregation: centers of service
- work simplification: find the 20% that is costing you 80%
- decentralization/relocation of services based on patient service utilization patterns
- leveraging of professional staff (skill mix)
- cross training care providers into interdisciplinary work force
- flatten management structure
- quality, service, and financial targets
- involvement of stakeholder
- change management plans
- critical paths/case management

The systems approach Noyes and Associates have found most effective includes the clinical areas and support areas.

Redesign: A Systems Approach

Efficient and effective care requires expert management of patient and information process flow.

The clinical areas are

- Inpatient
- Outpatient Services

- Surgical Services
- Clinical Ancillary: Rehabilitation Therapies, Respiratory Therapy
- Diagnostic Services
- Pharmacy
- Home Care
- Case Management
- Social Services
- Occupational Health

The support areas are

- Admitting
- Registration Scheduling
- Medical Records
- Business
- Offices
- Information Systems
- Purchasing
- Contracted Services
- Housekeeping
- Dietary
- Maintenance/Engineering

The first two phases of her process include the vital planning elements we will be discussing further in this section.

Phase One: *Opportunity Identification*

1. Understanding of current environment (strengths and weaknesses)
   - What are the organization's strategic drivers and desired alignments?
   - What are the cost reduction opportunities, and what are revenue enhancement potentials?
   - Relationships, both internal and external with the community, all providers, and customers
   - Legal constraints
   - Management capabilities and capacity
2. Benchmarking for targets for financial and service standards
3. Formulate vision and targets (strategic, financial, standards of quality service) that can be easily understood and communicated to all
4. Leadership assessment and selection
5. Feasibility analysis of vision and targets

6. Consensus on recommendations for future redesign—change management strategy for both the short and long term
7. Final approval of project plans: includes
   - human resources
   - communication plans
   - measurement tools for all key target areas

Phase Two: *Approach to Redesign*

(Many occur concurrently and may not be in sequential order.)

1. Define scope of service for each segment: What services can be decentralized, eliminated, and/or enhanced?
2. Identify measurable key success factors: customer, financial, interdepartmental service targets
3. Analysis of peaks and valleys of supply and demand
4. Analysis of specific procedures to specific service requirements—work simplification redesign of those specific processes that are key quality and cost drivers
5. Analysis of business and informatics support
6. Employee task analysis: role redesign
7. Management responsibility redesign
8. Implementation timetable:
   - Human resource plan
   - Education plan
   - Measurement plan

Courtesy of Noyes & Associates, Bainbridge Island, Washington.

We'll revisit Noyes and Associate's multipurpose tool used for assessment prior to redesign, systems appraisal during the process as a checkpoint, or as evaluation criteria in the Evaluation section.

VISION OF REENGINEERING PROJECTS: WHAT'S THE PURPOSE?

Why a Vision?

No one will choose to jump through the window of change with energy and anticipation without knowing what's on the other side of the window sill. Further, it's much more difficult to push someone through a window (whether open or closed) than showing him or her the promised land on the other side and allowing that person to choose the direction.

It's not rocket science, but we often note that basic principles of human behavior are overlooked when an organization is experiencing the fervor of a change process. When we ask people to step completely beyond their personal boundaries of comfort, to radically alter their daily work lives—in effect to become a new person—there had better be a reason; and it better be measurable; and it better be a change they can really support, or you'll see behaviors ranging from sabotage to passive resistance rather than whole-hearted commitment. Absolute engagement is necessary for this brand of "out-of-the-box" creativity imperative for engineering a cost-effective system.

The fear present in health care related to reengineering or care delivery redesign is healthy. The fear may be based on inaccurate data, unsubstantiated rumor, or a personal concern regarding potential job loss. But the presence of fear may also point to a real investment in our ultimate mission as health care workers to make a difference in people's lives, to create health where there has been illness, and to guide persons and communities in their own transformation. When health care providers know that there is a purpose, that they are able to count on measurement of the factors leading to success, then they will be able to move beyond the fear and begin to learn the concepts and skills they must possess to be able to move forward with creative change.

Daniel Beckham observes the following about health care: "Nowhere else does the buyer surrender so completely to the seller. Few businesses touch everyone with such inevitability and span across family and friends with such impact. In few other places on a daily basis do talent, thinking, teamwork, and technology matter as much. Seldom do you find as much drama and human spirit packed into as narrow a geography as a modern hospital. In few places do people give as much credence and importance to their interactions as in a doctor's office. . . . Call it what you want, health care is in desperate need of something like what Nike has—a vision that is authentic. It's more than a little frightening that many health care organizations can't seem to connect with anything more inspiring than preparing themselves to accept a capitated dollar" (Beckham, 1994, p. 67).

A study of *The 100 Best Companies To Work for in America* showed that the 100 "Best" companies were visionary and were more than twice as profitable as the Standard & Poor's 500, and their stock price grew three times more quickly, earning 17.69% more return on investment (Lipton, 1996, p. 86). Another study published in the *Wall Street Journal* showed that visionary companies who actually managed with the vision ("walked the talk," so to speak), showed that $1 invested in 1926 in these firms would have yielded $6,356 now, more than six times over the yield of a control group and more than 15 times the general market (Lipton, 1996, p. 84). It seems that people who are excited about achieving a vision they share are more productive, and the company grows.

▼

Clarity of vision allows for decreased fear and immobility, and increased movement toward the intended direction. It's also good business.

▲

What happens when the project's vision and measures of success are ignored? Members of the organization will surmise the worst—greed (an anathema to most health care workers), suspicion that the leaders are lining their own pockets with revenues from the reengineering cost savings. Repeatedly, staff will point to construction projects (for example, a staff member may state, "How did we have funds to remodel the obstetrics unit when my friend was laid off?"), other potential waste in the system, and will often resist redesign efforts with sabotage. You will recognize the list of behaviors that we've seen occur—stretching of acuity points for patient care to ensure more workers for the next shifts, ill time being taken unnecessarily with other staff members having full knowledge of this, and wastage of time and materials through an attitude of entitlement (for example, staff members thinking, "After all, we've worked so hard, and no one appreciates us, so she deserves a day off!").

Honesty, one of the main characteristics necessary for maintaining or rebuilding trust in an organization, can be translated into action by discussing the *true* reasons for planning changes in the system. If generic "improved quality of care" is discussed as being the impetus for reengineering, and yet staff members consistently observe budget "bottom lines" being discussed and managers note that their performance is measured by staffing productivity and nothing else, truth is a missing commodity. The following long-held maxim holds the key: *We measure what we value and we value what we measure.* If we have not yet defined quality of care, or the new improved quality we now intend to achieve, and don't intend to, then fear will again gain a hold on the hearts of those confronted with the process of delivering care without reasonable support. They certainly won't be able to learn how to implement new processes or deal with new workers when immobilized by these emotions.

The best vision, then, whether it is truly cost savings and organizational survival, improved quality of patient care, or a combination of both, is the *real* vision, not one "cooked up" for the board of directors for the yearly stockholders' report. Sure, it is easier to rally round the flag of improved patient care than saving money. But most employees routinely handle limited resources in their own lives (unless they are the fortunate few who donate their paychecks to "The Memorial Hospital Foundation") and can deal with the reality of needing to save their own jobs as well as the organization. And most can smell a false vision by observing the realities of daily work and how efforts are being measured.

Most employees would prefer coming to work daily with an idea of a selected future rather than with no hope of future renewal or growth. As much as we may think human beings resist change, they invite change when it is meaningful to them. Remember the last time you decided to remodel, paint a room, or replace the carpet? Maybe change was planned for boredom's sake, but often change is planned because of perceived problems with the current status. The process to correct the current situation may have taken longer than anticipated and may have been rigorous work, but the longed-for potential beauty and functionality of the remodeled room kept you going. In redesign efforts, most employees are anxious to change the things that bother them. The planned change should allow staff to envision a system that will work better for them and their patients.

▼

Be honest, clear, and consistent when discussing the true vision of a reengineering process. If the purpose is really saving money, then let people know what decreasing costs will do for them and why it's necessary. If it's quality that you hope to achieve (or a combination of the two), discuss what "quality" means, and how it will be measured.

▲

Employee Involvement in Creating the Vision

The idea of care delivery redesign or reengineering entails changes in the processes and ways we deliver services (care) with the purpose of making dramatic improvements in overall performance of the organization. Most individuals in the organization, whether in management or staff positions, prefer a workplace in which systems and individuals work together effectively, if they can visualize that possibility. People working at the "front lines" have many ideas about how resources could be saved as well. Ask them what they'd like to see happen and how this would best be achieved.

For example, employees will often have some detailed and descriptive benchmarks for quality, such as the following:

- getting medications to patients within 2 hours after they are ordered;
- having clean beds and rooms available to place patients when they are admitted from the emergency department (ED) and desperately need a place to lie down and be treated;
- receiving assistance as needed from coworkers from all disciplines without complaints or "sandbagging"; and
- making sure patients will be able to cope in their home situation with all of their discharge instructions.

When we work with physicians, we ask them what they'd like from a facility, and we hear that quality to them means the following:

- receiving calls from the nurses when necessary;
- patients not complaining about care they didn't receive (or care they received instead of the intended person) because these mistakes would not happen; and
- an organized setting so that they can do their jobs effectively.

What do customers want? Health care workers sometimes respond that it doesn't matter what patients want, they can no longer provide for them the "hotel" amenities that they think many patients expect. However, a survey of 2,000 patients from

17 hospitals reports that the "service reported to be needed at least once by almost every patient was participation in making decisions about their care" (Minnick, Young, and Roberts, 1995). Consumers now want someone to help them navigate through the system, and they want to be involved in deciding what is to be done. Rapidly diminishing are compliant comments such as "Yes, doctor, just do whatever you think is best."

Quality to patients may mean the following:

- getting physical needs met;
- getting pain relieved; and
- getting information to guide them through the present and into the future

Employees who are involved in determining the vision and success measures for reengineering projects relish asking patients what they want beyond the amenities that some staff members believe they may want. Patients knowing how to care for themselves after discharge is more important and reflects the true mission of health care, rather than whether every meal was piping hot from a gourmet kitchen.

▼
Multidisciplinary involvement in definition of quality is an important first step in clarifying the plan for the project.
▲

Commitment is necessary to make the project work, and it starts with involvement in determining the vision. When we participate, we begin to be involved enough to believe that we can make a difference. When we have been a part of decisions, we then possess a psychological ownership that becomes commitment. To put it in more common terms, how many of us change the oil in a rental car, or put in a new lawn and shrubs outside our hotel rooms?

To illustrate the importance of participation, attempt to replicate a recent study of human nature in which two groups of 20 people had been offered lottery tickets. Each individual in group A was given a lottery ticket. Each individual in group B *chose* a lottery ticket from the stack. When asked to return the tickets, those in group A willingly returned them for the ticket price of $1. Group B valued their tickets so much more highly that they asked for at least $4 per ticket (Langer, 1995, p. 4).

The participation that leads to commitment is individuals' personal investment of time in their own preferred futures. They are then able to connect with the vision and share the operational knowledge necessary to reengineer work processes, control costs, and improve quality. True success of any organization can be achieved when the behaviors of all reflect a consistent alignment of actions with the purpose.

▼
As many employees as possible must be involved in defining the vision and measures of success for the project.
▲

SUCCESS STORIES AND TOOLS FOR ESTABLISHING WORK TEAMS AND VISION

There are any number of tools and processes that are available to help personnel break away from daily norms and see a positive potential. These processes can be combined or individualized as needed for your organization. Several important practical points are necessary to keep in mind, such as those presented in the following box:

Principles for Establishing a Vision

- Plan a retreat away from the organization, and get rid of pagers or other interruptions. This process must be seen as important by all participants and must be supported by upper management through availability of resources (for example, outside site, coverage for participants).
- Be certain that all important stakeholders will be there. Include union leaders, representation of all departments, managers, staff, educators, and board of directors.
- Before the retreat, assign reading of articles regarding change processes, and mail packets of assigned reading to the participants' homes. Include mission statement, the present market status of the organization, local health care projections, and relevant budget data.
- Use assessment tools (see Section One on assessment) to encourage thought about issues before the workshop. Analysis of the data may be completed before the retreat, so that a composite of workgroup answers is available to save time.
- Come prepared with documents such as the mission, values, and organizational vision.
- Use games and visual and audio stimuli to "free up" the right side of the brain.
- Be practical! If the retreat "swerves off into the woods" and never gets to the real point *(how the preferred future vision will help the participants deal with real issues that prevent them from doing their jobs),* they may feel like they've just been to camp, singing "Home on the Range" around a campfire.

Planning/Visioning Process

The following narrative describe the use of the worksheets (Tools 13 and 14). They can be mixed or matched according to your organization's needs.

1. Establish planned outcomes and ground rules for the work group. Sample outcomes may include the following:
   - At the end of the retreat, the group will define the preferred future for the organization in terms of quality measures.
   - Problems that surface will be assigned to interdisciplinary task forces for development of specific, time-limited action plans.

   If the group is being asked to find methods of saving a certain amount in the next budget year, then outcomes may include the following:
   - Group will define 10 major areas of overlap, waste, or potential savings in systems change that will accomplish the objective. At the end of the day, task forces will have been formed with specific missions.

2. Develop a process by which each individual considers the following:
    - why he or she is doing what he or she is doing (how this purpose works with the organizational mission);
    - how this fits with the mission of the organization presently;
    - what doesn't work in his or her current job;
    - what major problems inhibit that mission from occurring;
    - what he or she would like to see the organization be like in the future (What would it look like? Sound like? Smell like? What would make him or her the most proud?); and
    - how you would define quality from his or her perspective, from other consumers' perspective?
3. Proceed with specifics according to previous outcomes—groups identifying areas of overlap, waste, recurring problems that reflect quality issues.
4. Use a format for action planning with outcomes—action planning form or performance outcomes agreement will assist groups in completing the planning while considering outcomes, timelines, and resources.

Discussing Values

A warm-up for your retreat or workshop may include an exercise to help participants get in tune with their own values and how they fit with those of the organization. This tool can also be used as a beginning point to develop organizational shared values. In this sample, we have included the organization's existing values as well as other common values. Participants are asked to first circle their ten most important values. The facilitator then asks them to narrow their choices to 5, then 3, and finally, two. Once each participant has selected his two priority values,; the facilitator calls out each value on the list, asking participants to stand when one of their two values is named. This process continues until all are standing. The top 5 values (those with the most votes) are then compared with the organizational values. This worksheet refers to William Bridge's discussion of the "4 Ps" of making transition work: The 4 Ps are the *purpose, picture, plan, and part*, those issues that must be clarified for all individuals in the organization to make a change successful (Bridges, 1991, p. 52).

We thank Bill Grace, Executive Director of the Center for Ethical Leadership, Seattle, Washington, for allowing us to use this example.

Tool #13: Planning/Visioning Process

I. Outcomes planned:

Why do I come to work every day? (Why do I do what I do?)
How does my job fit with St. Joseph's mission?
What doesn't work for me in this job is....
What major problems across the medical center stop the mission from being achieved?
In the future, I'd like to see the following:
To me, quality means....

Tool #14: Discussing Values

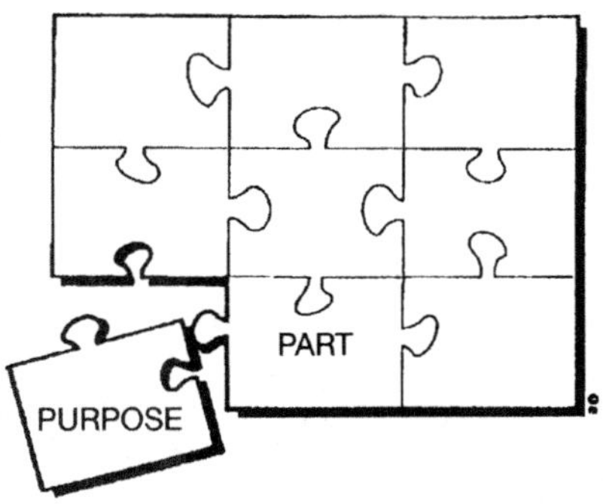

VALUES: YOUR PURPOSE AND PART

PEACE	INFLUENCE	FAMILY
WEALTH	HEALTH	TRUTH
HAPPINESS	DIGNITY	WISDOM
SUCCESS	GENEROSITY	STATUS
FRIENDSHIP	JOY	FAIRNESS
FAME	LOVE	SAFETY
HONESTY	RECOGNITION	COMMITMENT
POWER	TRUST	INNOVATION

Courtesy of Center for Ethical Leadership, Seattle, Washington.

Defining the Purpose of the Organization or Department

This tool can be used as a preparation for planning reengineering processes or to begin interdisciplinary team building. Members of the group fill out the blanks individually first, then follow up with group discussion and consensus building. Clarification of purpose will lead to determining the vision of the project.

Although it may seem that the answers to the blanks on the following tool are self-evident, we find this is not necessarily so. In one organization, we noted that an ED was struggling, especially during reorganization. Turnover of respected staff was high, interdisciplinary conflict reigned, and patient satisfaction surveys showed little satisfaction. Beginning a process to determine the causes of the turmoil, we spent several hours with the ED team members to facilitate their determination of their true team purpose. We discovered that the team purpose was at the root of the debate. One faction held that "Our ED is a safety net for our community." Those individuals took time to talk with patients and connect them with appropriate social service agencies that would meet underlying needs. Another faction believed that "We are a trauma center." They thought that members of the former group were lazy and unfit to be critical care providers. When patients came for assistance with less than a full-blown emergency, patients were chastened by the second group for using emergency services when they could have waited for office hours. When the entire department identified the main purpose of the ED, then relationships began to be repaired and patients felt they were treated with respect.

At any time during a transition process, this tool can be used to clarify points and to keep on track. Are physicians members of the team? If so, how do we interact with them? Are the patients and their families also a part of the team? Do we ask them to be involved in determining their care? How does the community interact with us? Do we have other departments delivering support services that see themselves as unimportant and uninvolved? If they saw themselves as members of our team, integral to the patient's successful outcomes, would they act any differently?

Tool #15: Defining the Purpose of the Organization or Department

TEAM PURPOSE

Who are the members of this team and what is it called?

____

____

____

____

What does/will this team provide?

____

____

____

____

To whom is this service or product provided?

____

____

____

____

What could be the most significant accomplishment of this team?

____

____

____

____

Purpose:

____

____

____

____

____

____

____

Putting Together Purpose and My Value to the Organization

You will note similarities with Tool #13 and this tool. Each individual is asked to fill in each ticket with either a picture, or a phrase or two that will illustrate the issues he or she is planning to deal with in this retreat. Using pictures or phrases sometimes allows for increased creativity and true sharing of the emotions that are driving behaviors in the workplace. In the first tool the leaders brought predetermined outcomes with them and asked for the participants to define quality. In this rendition, we are searching for participation in developing the future vision and connecting that vision (and potentially the reengineering process) with solving the problems that are inhibiting each individual from doing his or her best job.

Tool #16: Putting Together Purpose and My Value to the Organization

Why I come to work:

What skills and qualities do I bring to add value to this organization?

These issues or problems prevent me from doing my job effectively:

This is how my department looks today:

This is what I'd like our organization to look like in 2 years:

Using Visual Imagery

We have included the train metaphor with some groups as a part of their planning process. Filling in the blanks on the train and in the environment surrounding it allows for discussion of the strengths, weaknesses, threats, and opportunities present in the current health care environment that will be affecting your redesign project.

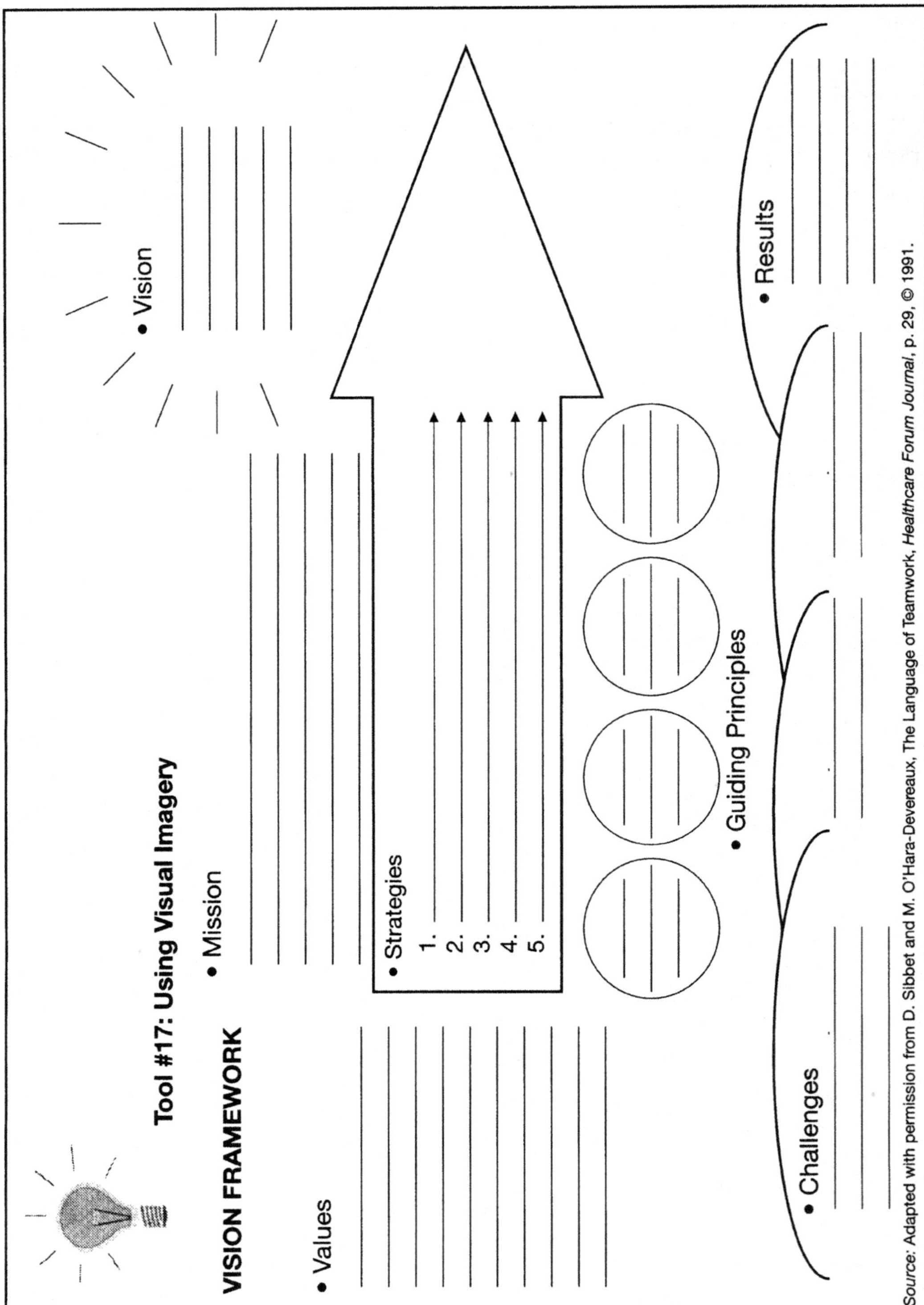

Source: Adapted with permission from D. Sibbet and M. O'Hara-Devereaux, The Language of Teamwork, *Healthcare Forum Journal*, p. 29, © 1991.

Sample of Vision Framework from Norman, Oklahoma

One unit's vision was developed by staff, has been reproduced on T-shirts and patient orientation pamphlets, and exists on the wall behind the central nurses' station. The process involved in creating it, as well as the positive values this logo represents, exemplifies the mission of 5N (Five North), a medical/surgical unit at Norman Regional Hospital.

Tool #18: Sample of Vision Framework from Norman, Oklahoma

Courtesy of Norman Regional Hospital, Norman, Oklahoma.

Legacy Patient-Focused Vision

This example shows how Legacy Health Systems, based in Portland, Oregon, began its restructuring and redesign projects. Throughout this toolbook, you will be reading more of the Legacy story.

PATIENT-FOCUSED CARING—Legacy Health Systems

The vision:

We at Legacy promote an optimal healing environment for patients and families. With the patient as the central focus, interdisciplinary teams will collaborate to provide efficient care, and meet customer expectations for quality and value.

The purpose of patient-focused caring is to identify processes and design systems for how we provide care that does the following:

- focuses on patient needs and expectations;
- increases efficiency; and
- maximizes the use of staff resources and abilities.

The goals are the following:

- increased staff time with direct patient contact;
- decreased wait time and travel time for patients and staff;
- improved cycle time of diagnostics and treatments;
- increased individualized patient care; and
- greater satisfaction for patients and their families, staff, and physicians.

The Patient First demonstration units (4C medical, 45 surgical, Kern critical care, and Pediatrics) designed, implemented, evaluated, and modified processes and systems using these goals. We took what we learned from the demonstration units and now, as we move forward, our focus is to implement patient-focused caring into the way we work, using the four core values of the Legacy.

The patient-focused caring staff will work with each unit to incorporate patient-focused caring into its operating plan. Each unit will be assessed for where it is on the pathway to patient-focused caring, and a plan will be developed and evaluated.

Tool #19: Legacy Patient-Focused Vision

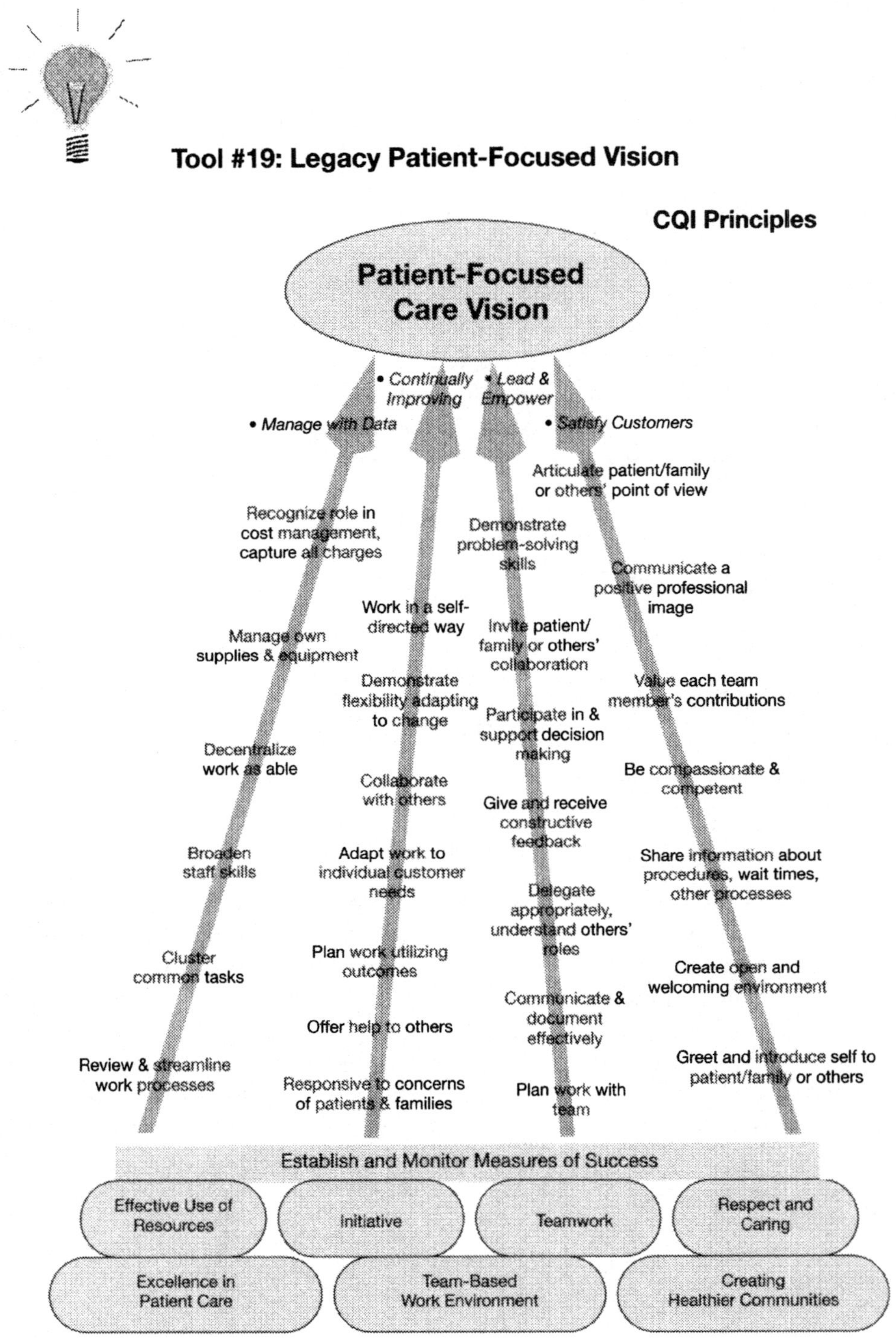

Courtesy of Legacy Health Systems, Portland, Oregon.

STRATEGIC PATHWAY #2—HOW WE WORK—Legacy Health Systems
PATIENT-FOCUSED CARING IMPLEMENTATION PLAN

Unit Based Steps/Components: 3- to 4-month process

- Unit Assessment: Current Status
  - Manager readiness
  - Level of shared practice structure
  - Level of team's structure and interactions
  - Skill-mix level
  - Patient activity data base
- Design Implementation Plan
  - Timeline, responsibilities
- Develop Shared Practice Council Structure
  - Practice Council/Subcommittees
  - Patient Care Congress tie-in
  - Team behavioral expectations and accountability
  - Manager and staff development and orientation
- Practice Council To Work on Patient-Focused Caring Concepts
  - Review of data:
    - Customer satisfaction
    - Unit activity
    - Patient acuity
    - Use of supplies and equipment
    - Patient aggregation
    - Financial data
    - Key customers and services provided
    - Service quality issues
  - Review and implement measures of success
  - Team structure and skill mix and scheduling
  - Space planning and decentralization needs
  - Physical improvements
  - Unit-specific work processes
  - Charge structure implementation
  - Improved patient and family involvement
  - Unit communication and coordination
  - Ongoing monitoring methodology
  - Review tools and resources needed
- Training Tool Box
  - Continuous quality improvement (CQI) basics
  - Change management
  - Conflict resolution
  - RN professional development modules/video
    - RN practice in a changing health care environment
    - Delegation
    - Outcome planning (task assignments, shift report, patient interviews)
    - Giving and receiving feedback
  - Certified Nursing Assistant (CNA) module
  - Computer training
  - Body mechanics
  - Cultural diversity
  - Team building
  - Shared practice council development

Courtesy of Legacy Health Systems, Portland, Oregon.

TEAMWORK TOOLS

The following tools begin with the vision and purpose of the redesign project and add practical tracking features.

Performance Outcomes Agreement

As presented in our *Successful Restructuring Newsletter, Vol. 1(2)* (Hansten & Washburn, 1996), this format can be used for individual performance improvement planning, or in planning and tracking the progress of various task forces or work groups used in reengineering projects.

The template we've included (adapted from work by Beck and Yeager, 1994) has been customized to specific needs in many organizations, and has been used effectively for evaluating standing committees and keeping them on track. The advantage of this tool is that it assists planning teams in being clear and organized about their purpose, outcomes, and progress. We are focusing on the following concepts essential for the planning of projects as well as providing feedback to individuals and groups during organizational development. The following ideas are fundamental:

- The 4 Ps (**p**urpose, **p**icture, **p**lan, and **p**art) for managing transition (Bridges, 1991, p. 52). In this tool, the individuals or group must understand the purpose of the task force or the purpose of their job, understand what success "would look like" and the more detailed expectations that are inherent in achieving success, discuss a plan for getting there, and understand what each person's part will be.
- The 4 Cs (**c**ommitment, **c**hallenge, **c**ontrol, and **c**onnection) of thriving in changing organizations (Scott and Jaffe, 1989, p. 19). The individual or group must make a commitment to the purpose of the project or his or her role, as well as commit to the projected dates and targets. A leader must commit to his or her role in providing adequate resources to make the task force's work productive or to assist in providing educational opportunities or tracking for the individual's performance to improve. Challenge is inherent in the act of addressing the need for change and embracing it as a growth experience rather than an exercise in blame. Control is present in the choice made by individuals or group members to identify steps they would take personally to make the purpose come to fruition, and in the presence of critical checkpoints. Connection is essential in the process of discussing who will be doing what task or step and what each group member needs in terms of support from the leader and each other.

In example one, you're putting together a quality task force to determine why there have been patient complaints, and to create some potential solutions for the problems, to be brought to the department meeting for discussion and approval next month. To begin the first meeting, the group would name itself, dating the form. It's essential for the leader to clarify the more global, energizing purpose, to ensure high quality patient care. The group would clarify its goal, which would be "to determine reasons for increasing number of patient complaints and create possible solutions."

As a leader, you may delineate your expectations: "1) come up with two to six possible reasons, 2) match those reasons with solutions, and 3) be ready to report in written and verbal form by the date the department meeting will be held—May 10th." If expectations are unclear, the task force's progress will be obstructed. Much time is often lost during discussions of "What does he or she really want us to do?" You rarely get what you want without asking for it!

The task force would then discuss the steps needed to achieve its goals. These may include the following: 1) review the existing patient complaints; 2) compare these with past complaint data; 3) gather thoughts from other team members regarding the origin of these complaints; 4) group main type of complaints; 5) brainstorm to determine possible solutions; and 6) review the literature for ideas from other organizations; and so on.

To be effective in achieving the goals, teams require clear discussion regarding the role of the department leader and availability of resources. We often note the presence of groups' undisclosed expectations regarding these issues. Does the group need additional time to complete the process? An "OK" to use the on-line library or on-work time? Secretarial or typing resources? How much support and direction do team members need from the manager? Discussion of these issues should be reciprocal among the managers and leaders, and task force members.

Critical checkpoints also may be unstated, and therefore, unobserved. If the manager is concerned about hearing from the group a week before the staff meeting so that he or she can determine the amount of time needed on the agenda, a date and time should be included in that area of the form.

In example two, consider the process necessary when counseling a staff member about his or her chronic tardiness. The performance outcomes agreement can be used to assist the individual in being clear about expectations from his or her leader. For example, it is essential that Sally comes up with the steps to solving the problem herself. In this case, the employee has determined that she has a long history of being late (all her life) and that it would help her if the other staff and managers make positive comments to her when she is on time. (The staff and manager may not decide this is a reasonable request, but certainly that can be negotiated!)

Tool #20: PERFORMANCE/OUTCOMES AGREEMENT

Employee/Group Name: Date:

Goal/Purpose:

Expectations:

Steps to Achieving the Goal:
1.
2.
3.

Leadership Style/Resources

Resources Needed:

Support Needed: High ———————— Low
Direction Needed: High ———————— Low

Critical Checkpoints: Date:
1.
2.
3.

continues

Tool # 20—Example 1

PERFORMANCE/OUTCOMES AGREEMENT

Employee/Group Name: Date: 2/20/97
Patient Complaint Task Force

Goal/Purpose:
Overall: Ensure high-quality patient care, as defined by patients.
Determine reasons for increased patient complaints; create solutions.

Expectations:
1. Come up with two to six possible reasons, with matching solutions; report verbally and written to large group by May 10th.

Steps to Achieving the Goal:
1. Review existing complaint data.
2. Compare with past data.
3. Gather thoughts from others on team.
4. Group types of complaints and look for patterns.
5. Brainstorm.
6. Review literature or talk to other agencies who have dealt with this.
7. Work on solutions (?subgroups?)
8. Type up for meeting and present.

Leadership Style/Resources

Resources Needed: Help from unit secretary for getting med records.
On-line library

Support Needed: High ——————————X—— Low
Direction Needed: High ——————————X— Low

Critical Checkpoints:	Date:
1. Report progress to department manager	3/7/97
2. Discuss project and complaint results with staff at staff meetings	3/15/97
3. Report to large group	6/10/97

continues

Tool # 20—Example 2

PERFORMANCE/OUTCOMES AGREEMENT

Employee/Group Name:
Sally Jones

Date: 5/20/97

Goal/Purpose:
To promote high quality of patient care and responsible use of resources, all staff must be present at 19:00 for shift report to communicate important information.

Expectations:
Each staff member who is assigned to be present at 19:00 will be present then and ready to work, ready to listen to shift report.

Steps to Achieving the Goal:
1. I will need to leave for work before traffic rush hour.
2. I will bring coffee from home rather than wait in line at the espresso bar or get my latte on break.
3.

Leadership Style

Resources Needed: None; would like lots of positive feedback

Support Needed: High ——————X—————————— Low
Direction Needed: High ——————————————————X— Low

Critical Checkpoints:	Date:
1. Review progress with leader	6/10/97
2. Review progress at annual performance review	8/20/97

Source: Reprinted from R. Hansten and M. Washburn, *Successful Restructuring Newsletter,* Vol. 2, No. 1 © 1996 Aspen Publishers, Inc.

Action Plans: A Simple Tool for Tracking

This tool (Tool #21) will help make sense of the sometimes confusing planning process when beginning a large project. Breaking down the parts of the project into steps and each task force's charge into reasonable pieces will help members have faith that they will reach their goals, even when it seems overwhelming during the process.

For example, when an interdisciplinary group met to begin redesigning the care delivery system in the perioperative area, several individuals were anxious to redesign the roles of the personnel present in assistive roles. After brainstorming about what a new "multiskilled" individual might do, they began a process by which each individual was assigned certain duties between meetings. Their entire process may take up to 6 months, including writing the job descriptions, but it began with such action steps as the following:

1. Interview present orderlies, instrument room personnel, and surgical assistants to determine when they have extra time, what they do now, and what they would like to do in a redesigned role. (For example, Patty will need 16 extra hours on clock, beginning now, to be done by the 2/24 meeting.)
2. Gather and read present job descriptions for overlap (for example, Greg by 2/24 meeting).
3. Observe flow of work for these individuals (for example, John, during charge nurse role daily, by 3/5 meeting).
4. Talk to other staff involved in perioperative care in metro area regarding roles. (Jamaal will do the telephone calls during down time during evenings or get approval for extra time, ready by 3/5.)
5. Review literature regarding new roles elsewhere (for example, Angie, librarian, report ready by 2/24).

This tracking can be continuous and consecutive, and the form can be adapted to your own purposes, adding or deleting essential data, as has been done in the following success story.

Success Story

Patient-Focused Care Work Plan 17 West, Legacy Health Systems, Oregon

The following work plan is an example of how a surgical unit began to tackle areas needing improvement after the initial patient-focused care plan had been instituted. (See patient-focused unit work plan.)

Tool #21: Action Plan

Date of Plan:

Goal or Outcome:

Planned Dates					Actual Dates	
Begin	End	Action Steps	Who	Resources	Begin	End

PATIENT-FOCUSED CARING UNIT WORK PLAN

UNIT: 17 West
DATE: 7/31/96

MANAGER: Nurse Manager (NM)
PFC SUPPORT: Patient Focused Care Specialist (PFCS)

AREAS FOR DEVELOPMENT	PLAN	WHO*	WHEN	MONITORS—WHAT AND WHEN
TEAMWORK				
Patient-Care Council (PCC)	1. Form task force to identify PCC structure for unit, recruit or select members for PCC	NM, PFCS	mid August	
	2. Formation of PCC and subcouncils	Task force		
	3. Conduct all-day training session for new council members	OD, PFCS	Sept–Oct	
	4. Begin PCC meetings (team charter, ground rules, communication plan, setting priorities. . .)		October	
Roles and Responsibilities	1. PSA Integration and team building sessions	NM	Aug. 26–28	
INITIATIVE				
Collaborative Practice	1. Cardiac Surgery Collaborative Practice Issues: Portable CXR POD 3 Use of PAS for OHS Standard of Care: OHS patients	CNS, NM		
	2. Cardiology Collaborative Practice Standards of Care: Invasive Procedures	CNS, NM		
	3. Surgeon's office Cardiac Rehab communication, hands-off issues, how to know more about the patient ahead of time, other	PCC		
EFFECTIVE USE OF RESOURCES				
Decentralize Nursing Station	1. Move charts to writing stations Need: Jobar chart racks, Holders for stamper plates	PCC		
	2. Develop remote computer work stations Need: Phones, Computers moved, Printer, Addressographs, Paper racks, Desk organizers	PCC, USs		
	1. Develop MTs as single source with log to track all broken equipment and seeing to repair	MTs	Now	
	1. Develop ability to do all of the EKGs on the unit Need: EKG machine, Train MTs, others	NM CM, NM, PCC		
	1. Broaden access to kitchen			
	2. Explore options for patient and family lounge	PCC		
	3. Business cards for the unit	NM		

*NM = Nurse Manager; PFCS = Patient Focused Care Specialist; OD = Organized Development Department; CNS = Clinical Nurse Specialist; US = Unit Secretary; MT = medical technician; CM = cardiopulmonary manager.

Courtesy of Legacy Health Systems, Portland, Oregon.

ORGANIZATIONAL COMMITMENT TO SUCCESS

What resources are necessary to fulfill the plan?

We have worked with organizations that have spent millions on reengineering consultant groups to begin the process, hundreds of thousands of dollars on staff education and retraining, and undetermined amounts in salaries for planning or implementation teams. We have also worked with organizations that have attempted to "limp along" on the "economy plan," attempting to use in-house resources by sending someone to a workshop somewhere (always out of state). Although often "we get what we pay for," there does not seem to be a uniformly direct relationship in terms of dollars spent and project results. In general, however, those organizations that have carefully analyzed, planned, and aligned resources with intended results are the most successful in achieving intended outcomes. As unnecessary as it may seem to state the following truth, we've noted it bears repeating: Those organizations that are unwilling to provide the necessary resources will not achieve their intended outcomes.

Illustrations of these points comes from our experience: When the goal was for RN staff members to learn supervisory and delegation skills, but the RNs were not trained, there was evidence of increased illness time, overtime, and complaints from patients and physicians of negative behaviors and "attitudes." Assumptions had been made by the planning task force (made up of experienced RNs who had worked in team configurations in the 1960s and 1970s) that everyone knew how to delegate and supervise others. This assumption (not based on actual assessment of existing skills) encouraged increased resentment, errors, and mistreatment of assistive personnel and other publics.

In another organization, it was assumed that the interdisciplinary shared governance task leadership group would take on the planning of care delivery redesign. Nothing happened, and there was a flurry of finger-pointing and scape-goating behavior among team members when executives asked for results. The group was new, had not had training in reengineering principles, and was overwhelmed with new, additional job duties. The necessary person-power and time had not been requested nor taken.

Underpinning the resources necessary for planning and implementation of the transition plan are the human resources necessary to carry out daily patient treatment. A resource that seems to be forgotten when care delivery redesign is planned to prepare for managed care, with the only focus being financial outcomes, is evaluation of the necessary numbers of the necessary skill levels of staff to implement care. When employees repeatedly state that they are unable to get the work done, it is time to do further assessment. There may be the correct number of professional staff and assistive personnel, but critical to the success of the new system is the ability of the patient care leaders to implement new roles and to focus on patient outcomes rather than tasks only. Also necessary is the use of critical thinking as inherent in professional roles, so that RNs can coordinate and lead the process of patient care, for example. Assistive personnel and allied health professionals must be able to perform their roles as assigned and directed, and know when to report appropriately. It is also possible that there is *not* the correct number or skill type of staff available for optimal patient care. Assessment (or evaluation) of the numbers and type of human resources necessary will be discussed in the evaluation section of this book.

▼
Resources must be assigned in sufficient quantity to support achievement of intended outcomes.
▲

People Resources for Planning

Success Story

MultiCare Medical Center in Tacoma, Washington, developed effective plans for work redesign. Diane Cecchettini, vice president of patient services, and Mary Ellen Swatta, Operations (OPS) improvement team leader, have contributed the following information:

The work redesign process began at MultiCare Medical Center, a tertiary, multihospital metropolitan system, in 1991. Within 15 months of planning and preparation, the design was initiated. As a result of the 4-year plan, 32 million dollars were saved, turnaround times were improved, more time was spent with patients, and fewer individuals interacted with the patients (see the evaluation section).

Initial efforts centered around inpatient-care delivery systems. Care models on all inpatient units were redesigned concurrent to patient flow and ancillary service delivery. Critical to the success of MultiCare Medical Center was the staging of the activities, because a seemingly minor change in any part of the system has profound effects on other parts. To minimize the disconnects, we found it imperative to evaluate support and adjunct systems as patient care systems are created. This was accomplished by using the "operations team" to maintain connections, review recommendations, and provide endorsement before forwarding recommendations for steering committee approval.

The initial organization of redesign activities centered around teams of participants. Each task force was provided direction, which we call "scope," financial targets, and timelines. The service targets were provided in a broad definition and each task force refined the measures as it began its activity.

The project team is the heart, soul, and conscience of the redesign projects. This group closely monitored progress, set targets, provided resources, and supported forward movement. It consisted of the vice president of patient services and human services, project director and analysts, operational directors of the nursing departments for each hospital, and eventually, the individuals supporting the clinical efficiency effort. This group remains to provide overall direction and prioritization to improvement projects.

The steering committee included the medical staff leadership, the CEO, vice presidents, and finance and project directors. After the second year, the steering committee delegated approval authority to the OPS team.

The OPS team included operational directors from both hospitals. The function of this team is to make connections, identify implementation issues, smooth the implementation, and challenge findings. It has been effective in its role and is one of the few meetings that is 100% attended. It became the key communicator forum for change.

By the time Care Models II emerged (about 2 years into the process), it was time to decentralize the activities. The nursing leaders from each hospital co-chaired the activities. The clinical director from each patient-care unit assembled a unit-based

Organization

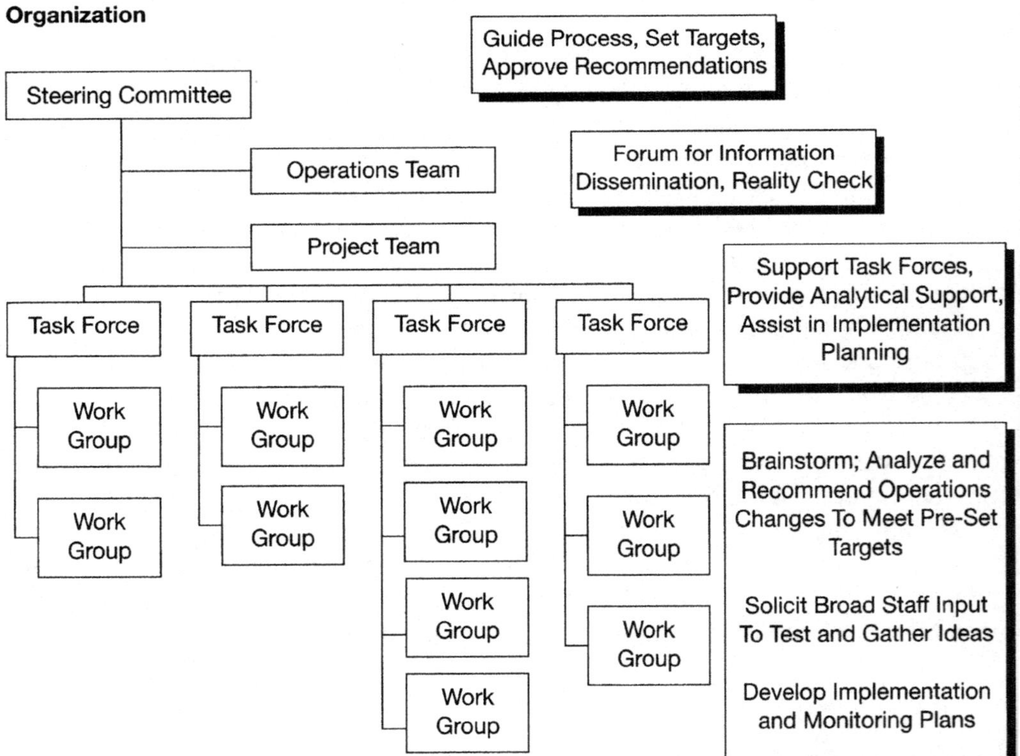

Courtesy of MultiCare Medical Center, Tacoma, Washington.

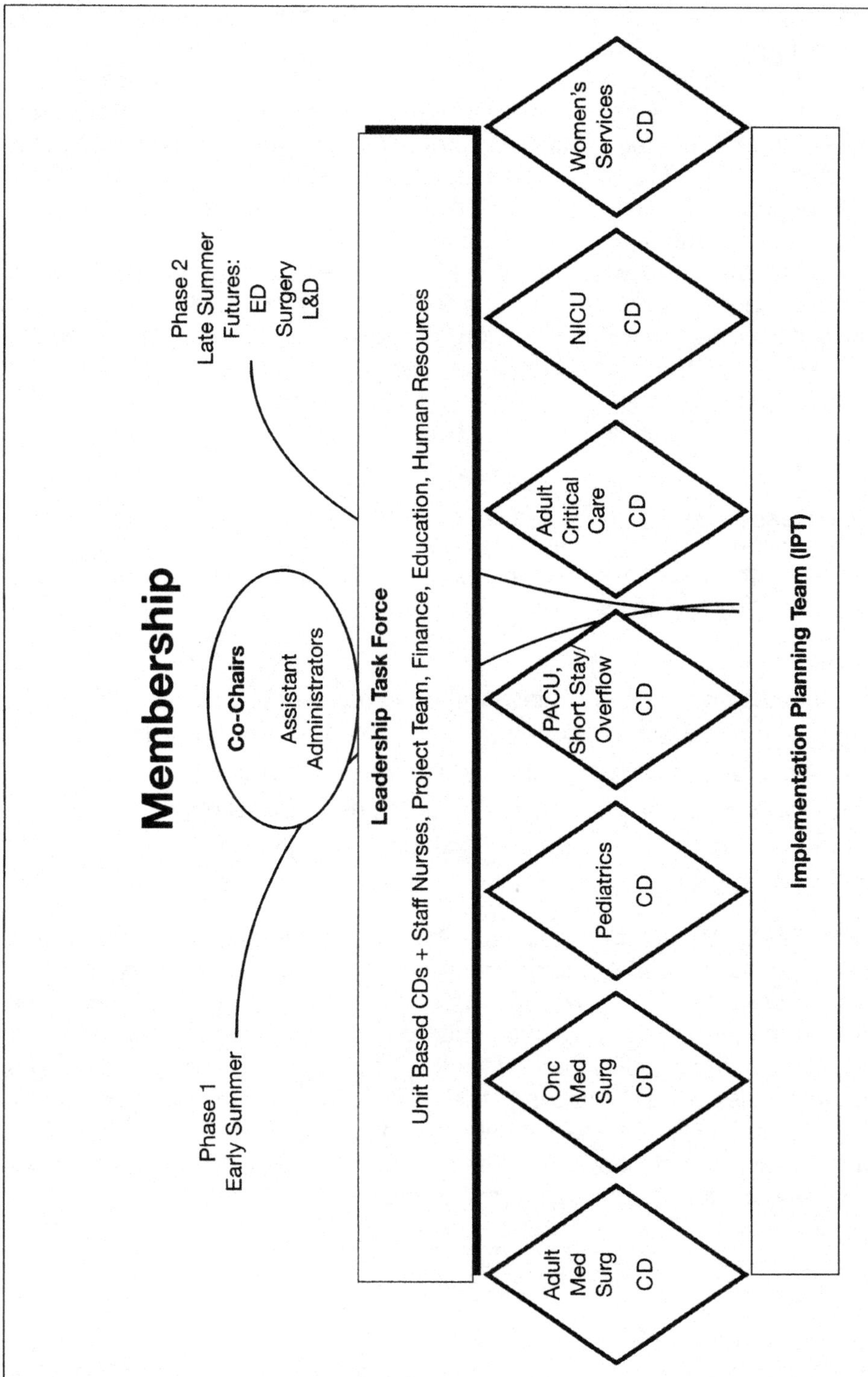

Courtesy of MultiCare Medical Center, Tacoma, Washington.

team effort to re-evaluate the original care model and make recommendations for additional changes.

At the same time, we had learned the value of beginning implementation planning at the time of design and used an implementation planning team to produce education plans, quality monitoring indicators, procedure changes, equipment evaluations, and other details. The team began to develop implementation tools as the design team began to define recommendations. This has been an effective way to ensure a smooth implementation and has been used since 1994.

Each team's membership was determined by a stakeholder analysis, in which groups selected those that would be, or could be, affected by the changes. Key individuals and groups, critical information, and opportunities for communication become evident. When those who may be affected by the change are identified and involved, not only is the end product better, but the likelihood of resistance, disruption, sabotage, and/or just plain misery, is reduced.

Educational Resources

When planning the necessary resources for education of staff in the transition process, ask the following questions:

- Is education necessary?
- What outcomes do I want to achieve with the educational process?
- What assessment data indicate that this type of education is needed?
- Will education really solve the problems or needs I have identified?
- What type of process will best be suited for the educational objectives?
- How will I measure the effect of the educational process?
- How much will it cost?

Cost and benefit data are available but difficult to apply directly, because each organization's personnel and existing resources are so variable. A study of 12,000 publicly traded companies that had undergone restructuring measured the impact of education in the form of skills training, coaching and mentoring, cross-functional teams, job rotations, and quality circles. These yielded within 1 year, per employee, $27,000 more in sales, $3,814 more in profits, and $18,641 more in market value, or a total of $107,000 increase in market value per employee over time (Collingwood, 1996, p. 18). Knowledge of what outcomes can be achieved with training will assist in planning the education budget resources to match the needs.

Outsourcing

Some organizations have run amok in eliminating line management and in early retirement programs in pursuit of short-term savings, so that experienced workers and layers of management have been omitted. In some cases, we heartily agree that some organizations have historically multiplied "supervisory" or staff development roles, so that front-line workers felt overwhelmed with the number of people analyzing and judging their performance. Occasionally, we've noted that organizations have avoided counseling those who have chosen not to keep up with their professions and weigh down the organization so that early retirement of some individuals is a positive option for all involved. However, in many cases, the most experienced and wise leaders are now absent, and in-house resources are lacking. An organization may need short-term consultant assistance to provide an outsider's viewpoint and to keep the process on track. In our consulting experience, we note that many organizations who call us in for a 1-day "teambuilding" session would have benefited in terms of time and dollars saved had we been called in earlier during the process to identify a few areas in which alterations of the plan could have saved resources. For example, a hospital asked us to work with an interdisciplinary patient-care team. As we evaluated the job descriptions, we noted that some of the tasks in the job description of a licensed practical nurse (LPN) were forbidden by that state's law. However, all the staff had been educated in these new roles and had been implementing them for some time. Retraining would be necessary, and distrust of the process and administration would be rampant.

Occasionally, a consultant team can provide an outsider's viewpoint and a "wake-up call" to those individuals who have been reading *Good Housekeeping* or *Field and Stream* magazines rather than their professional journals or keeping up with their profession in other ways, and believe that the changes in their organization are being made by the sadistic administration. Often, staff will not listen to an in-house trainer who is inexperienced or who has a reputation for being "out of touch." Consider the salary time spent for developing training resources and whether the cost of an individualized or packaged approach may be more cost-effective for the results achieved. The skills of a good facilitator can improve the speed and effectiveness of the process greatly.

▼

Use internal resources when possible and when the quality of expertise will be reflected in the desired results.

Use outside consultants or trainers when they will achieve the desired outcomes in a more cost-effective manner.

▲

Timelines

When planning the project timeline, there are no hard and fast rules. We have worked with organizations that placed a 2-month time limit on the planning process, and a 6-month limit for implementation of plans. We have worked with departments that have taken 3 years to plan before implementing the first training and implementation phase of a project. Reactions of individuals range from "What!

We are implementing this project *already*! I haven't had time to mentally prepare myself!" to "Let's just *DO IT*! Why all this excruciating waiting?" no matter how much time is taken. Occasionally, timelines are kept short and specific because of set environmental agendas (such as new state reimbursement regulations impacting the budget or a merger). Keeping in touch with the pulse of the organization will allow members of the development and planning teams to judge whether timing is correct. The following few guidelines may assist in determining the timeline:

- Allow for enough time to communicate the impending vision and plan in as many ways as possible—in meetings and in written communications.
- Be certain all individuals have had ample opportunity to respond with concerns and ideas.
- Determine if research time may be necessary for committee members to call other organizations and to research the literature for ideas.
- When individuals or groups say, "Let's get on with it!" or "What's the hurry?" evaluate their concerns carefully for practical implications. Pay attention to rationale and what's behind it. Behavior can be driven by attempts to avoid making the changes or to avoid discussing the issues.

Timelines at MultiCare Medical Center

MultiCare Medical Center in Tacoma, Washington, shares the following timeline (contributed by Diane Cecchettini and Mary Ellen Swatta), describing that initial efforts centered around inpatient care delivery systems. First, care models were redesigned concurrent to patient flow and ancillary services delivery. The staging of activities was critical to their success.

1992 ——→ *1995*

1992–1993	*1994*	*1995*
• Care Models	• Second-Generation Care Models	• Second-Generation Care Models
• Inpatient and Ambulatory		
• Patient Flow		
• Supply Chain Management		
• Ancillary and Support Services	Clinical Information Systems:	Core Processes:
• Products	• Billing Cycles	• Registration
• Pharmacy	• Data Systems	• Documentation and Coding
	• Medical Records	• Revenue Optimization
		• ED Paperflow

Courtesy of MultiCare Medical Center, Tacoma, Washington.

For further examples of timelines, please review the CHMC planning case study at the end of this section.

MANAGER AND STAFF ROLES IN PLANNING: THAT MEANS EVERYONE!

Managers, a group that may be in need of protection as an endangered species, face multiplying job duties. Staff, reading the newspapers and hearing local or national trends regarding lay-offs, coping with a shift in thinking from life-long employment to employability and increased cross-training, find themselves asked to participate in reengineering efforts without prior experience in leadership of teams and supervisory skills. The situation for all employees in health care can be one of distortion of a world that was at one time routine, resulting in distraction and distress about personal ability to succeed in the new world.

All groups and individuals are groping their way into the future, yet the input of those at the front lines, and that of managers who may see the bigger picture and may have more experience to share, is essential to developing the most effective health care systems. We also know that there is an increasing potential for conflict during the transition process. Making certain that *all* necessary groups are involved in planning and implementation of the process is essential for successful outcomes. Note the following circumstances in which negative sequelae have occurred because of an imbalance of participation:

- In pursuit of the "fruits of empowerment," staff without prior experience in such areas as running meetings, working within a budget, planning for work groups, and using leadership skills are given a task—reengineer the care delivery system. Managers keep a "hands-off" approach and then become angry because the staff can't seem to get the tasks done, and spend all their time complaining about issues such as staffing or personal behaviors of individuals on the team.
- Nursing, pharmacy, housekeeping, and dietary services seem to be working together on designing a new method of patient-focused care, with new roles being developed. However, no one thought staff in the radiology department or the physicians would care too much about the project, and thought they would "bring them in when it's done." The nurses in the inpatient units quickly began talking about all the changes, especially the plan to do multidisciplinary care mapping. "Guess you'll have to talk with that other cardiology group, Dr. Jones! Won't it be fun to look over these standard orders and come up with a routine plan? Should save us all time, don't you think?" Imagine their surprise when Dr. Jones responds: "Cookbook medicine! I knew it was coming! Why aren't we, the doctors, involved in the planning?!"
- Some serious errors were encountered when we were completing an on-unit assessment. The errors may have been life-threatening had they not been intercepted by another staff member. We are told by yet another member of the staff that this kind of performance has been the norm for months, and the manager,

although aware, had not dealt with it. When the manager was asked, she stated she didn't really know what was going on and hadn't seen a patient for months, unless there was a specific complaint. "I can't do anything about it; I have to keep within the budget. I can't afford to fire anyone, we are too short-staffed," she said. Keeping herself out of the loop and locked in an office making calls for additional staff, her hands-off attitude allowed her to be hand-cuffed to the budget. A new manager who had not sought out additional management training, overwhelmed and uncertain in the midst of care delivery redesign, had become a glorified staffing clerk and bookkeeper.

We are observing managers who have such large spans of control that they are unclear about their personal missions or their accountability for outcomes. They become far-removed from the realities of the front lines, expecting staff to solve their own problems without the necessary leadership. Managers must focus on those budget numbers and variances, because numbers are clean and precise and sometimes seem more easily controlled. Managers and staff are not offered, and sometimes do not search for, the necessary skills for leading or participating in change processes. Managers, becoming removed from the messy fray, wait for staff to come up with the answers without checking on progress. Staff, wading through ineffective meetings, become frustrated with lack of progress, become disenchanted, remove themselves from participation, and become disenfranchised. During the chaos, the pivotal input and participation of colleagues from other disciplines are overlooked. Follow these guidelines:

- Involve people that could be affected in the potential changes. MultiCare Medical Center found it profitable to spend time discussing and determining stakeholders, discovering that this exercise reduces resistance and produces a better planned process.
- Be certain managers are aware of the progress of groups and can participate as necessary to guide, coach, and provide resources.
- Every meeting and every group must reiterate its mission or task at each meeting. Discussion and measurement of progress must be a part of each meeting.
- An oversight group should exist to steer the progress of the project from an organizational perspective. This point is essential and often missed when departments focus on their own work and budgets from a narrow perspective, losing sight of the "patient centeredness" of their mission.

For managers, the following checklist may assist in "getting a handle" on what you are doing and help you feel some sense of accomplishment. (Many managers who have left their jobs have shared that they may have stayed if they could have seen that they were making a difference.) Use of this tool may also help clarify your role in the reengineering efforts. Remember not to focus on tasks, but to focus on the outcomes for which you are accountable.

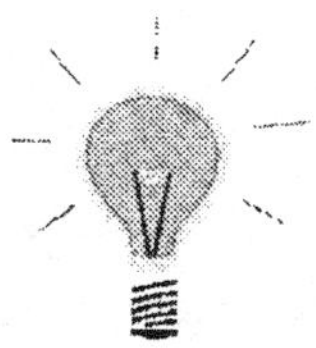

Tool #22: Checklist for Planning Time for the Manager

Fire Prevention

❑ Plan time apart to refocus and think.

❑ Jot down what you've accomplished. What outcomes have you helped occur? (If necessary, review your job description or goals for the year and what you've been doing. Give yourself credit for what's been done.)

❑ Evaluate and rank problem areas and trends, reviewing the progress of planning groups or task forces in the reengineering efforts. Prioritize their issues and whether you need to take action in relation to the following:

- overall pervasive nature of problems or issues;
- those that are most important to those you serve;
- those that deliver the most potential benefit toward achieving outcomes and are sequential in terms of the transition process;
- those that are quickly solved or unraveled into easily resolved portions;
- those issues that are easily delegated; and
- recurring complex issues that must be resolved once and for all because of potential negative effects on outcomes.

❑ Decide what you are going to do to resolve priority problems. Decide how to get others involved, sketching out a rough plan.

❑ Decide what to delegate, do, or ditch (the three Ds).

❑ Mark your next planning session in *ink*.

Source: Adapted from R. Hansten and M. Washburn, *The Nurse Manager's Answer Book*, pp. 117–118, © 1994, Aspen Publishers, Inc.

SHARED GOVERNANCE COUNCILS, SELF-DIRECTED TEAMS, AND UNION COMMITTEES: ROLES IN PLANNING

In the 1980s and early 1990s, we began to observe an increase in use of teams throughout business as well as in health care. In 1989, more than 50% of Fortune 500 companies were using, or planned to use, self-managing work teams (Hackman, 1992). Shared governance for RNs became a valuable recruitment and retention tool (Westrope et al., 1995). True empowerment of those at the point of service yields measurable results: we observe improvement in productivity by 30% to 50% when self-managed teams are used rather than the previous work configuration (Wellins et al., 1992). If teams such as shared governance councils already exist in your facility, it can be most effective to use the groups already in place and functioning well within your organization for the planning and implementation phase of the project.

Begin by evaluating the effectiveness and scope of responsibility of existing teams before adding on new charges. In our experience, some "shared governance councils" were effectively making decisions and creating reasoned solutions for emerging unit and interdepartmental problems. Others were functioning as poorly attended discussion groups for "rubber-stamping" management decisions that had already been made at the executive level. Certainly not all groups of staff are prepared to assume effective self-management. As Richard Hackman discusses in his landmark publication, "The Psychology of Self-Management in Organizations," the following certain conditions must exist for workers to be fostered and empowered:

- clear engaging direction;
- an enabling structure;
- a supportive context;
- expert coaching; and
- adequate material resources.

Several of the following behavioral signs must be evident to provide clues to managers that personnel are ready to be integrally involved in organizational planning and decision-making:

- intense feelings of personal responsibility for group outcomes;
- members monitoring their own performance continuously and taking corrective action on their own;
- group members actively seeking guidance and the resources they need; and
- taking initiative to help others improve their performance (Hackman, 1992).

If your existing teams are not exhibiting these kinds of qualities, or if preexisting conditions are not apparent in your organization, plan to provide the direction, support, and coaching needed, as well as the material resources. Include committee members' development as a part of your plan.

▼

Existing groups may be used to develop plans for redesign, or new groups may need to be developed. But, be certain to evaluate for the qualities necessary to achieve success. Where qualities or resources aren't present, plan to provide the necessary education or coaching.

▲

Legacy Health Systems shared with us the development of their shared governance system as a part of the patient-focused care project. We thank all the individuals who were involved for the following example of how reengineering and systems analysis can help develop staff for decision-making. Note that the Patient Care Councils have become the evaluators of the process of patient-focused care implementation and their role will be discussed further in the evaluation section.

Legacy Patient Care Council Development Process

Patient-Care Services Division

We combined our internal resources and expertise of organizational development staff, clinical nurse specialists, patient-focused care staff, nurse managers, directors, and vice president for an all-day retreat. The retreat was focused on what shared governance would be for the patient care services division. We decided on areas such as a common name; what to call "it"; the purpose, the parameters, the areas of focus, and resources required; the quality measurements; and the roles and responsibilities.

Unit Level Development

The patient-focused caring specialists have begun to work with each of the inpatient nursing units as they conduct their patient-focused caring assessments to develop or relook at a patient care council (PCC) structure. This process is begun by forming a multidisciplinary task force that reviews the division parameters and perceptions of shared governance, examples of other councils, current issues, committees, and unit needs, and then forms the specific structure and parameters.

The task force then communicates its recommendations to the rest of the staff members and recruits for PCC participants.

The new PCC (and/or subcouncils) members are then identified and an all-day training session is then provided. The new council members learn basic meeting and planning skills, continuous quality improvement (CQI) tools, and techniques. They also begin to develop a team vision, charter, ground rules, roles and responsibilities, communication mechanisms, and agreements.

The patient-focused caring specialists then continue to support the unit PCCs as they work toward implementing patient-focused care (PFC) recommendations and vision.

Purpose

The purpose of the Patient Care Council is to facilitate direct involvement and accountability of all staff in planning and implementing practices that improve the quality of patient care. The Patient Practice Council also provides integration and alignment among units and departments in fulfilling the organizational goals of Legacy Portland Hospitals.

Parameters

- The scope of decision-making is clearly defined (whether it is consensus, voting, etc.).
- The manager's level in the decision-making process is determined (for example, veto privileges).
- Manager defines boundaries for decision-making, budgetary constraints, and other issues as defined.
- Ground rules need to be established for behavioral expectations of council members.
- Methods of communication need to be addressed to "get information out" to staff about decisions of council.
- Roles of all council members are understood and each member is accountable for that role and associated work assigned.
- Impact of decisions on other operating units needs to be fully understood.
- Manager attends all meetings to provide guidance and identify resources.
- Selection process for council members must be clearly defined.
- Council is understood to be the decision-making body for unit operations within budgetary, regulatory, licensing, and organizational policies and procedures.
- All decisions are based upon data using CQI principles.

Roles and Responsibilities

Manager

- Set, define, and monitor clear parameters.
- Encourage risk-taking.
- Share responsibilities and accountabilities with staff.
- Share information.
- Serve as facilitator and resource, not rescuer.
- Prepare and provide staff with skills and knowledge needed to succeed.
- Be an active member of the council.

Council Members

- Take responsibility for getting information and passing it on to others.
- Be a role model for others.
- Participate in problem identification and resolution.
- Actively participate in the implementation of decisions.
- Own and support council decisions.
- Be patient with the process and focus on the outcome.
- Commit to work as a team.
- Take risks and get involved.
- Focus on the patient as the primary customer.

Staff

- Trust the work of peers.
- Give feedback directly to peers.
- Focus on the patient as the primary customer.
- Maintain accountability for actions and communications.
- Contribute to problem identification and resolution.
- Respect and work with the council as the operating structure.

Director

- Help establish clear parameters, depth, scope, and vision.
- Actively support the council(s).
- Recognize and acknowledge the efforts of others.
- Respect and work with the council as the operating structure.
- Give units permission to make mistakes and time to learn.

Clinical Nurse Specialist (CNS)

- Be an active member of the council.
- Provide education regarding CQI, patient satisfaction, and practice issues for staff.
- Assist with implementation of decisions.

Courtesy of Legacy Health Systems, Portland, Oregon.

Union Committees

Union involvement with restructuring efforts has become adversarial (or at least strained) in many areas. However, at Allina Health Systems in the Minneapolis area, the establishment of a clear vision and operating principles allowed for labor–management teams functioning so well that when restructuring necessitated closure of one 800-bed hospital, affecting 1,800 employees, a jointly managed placement process resulted in placing all but 100 employees at other institutions, with a cost savings of at least 5 million dollars. The public and employee trust generated by this effort was phenomenal, decreasing fear of lay-off and improving employee involvement and quality of worklife. (See Allina Labor Management Vision.) We'll discuss their success in more depth and how they achieved it in the evaluation section of this book.

PLANNING: CREATION OF ROLES

Throughout all areas of the health care system, groups are working on developing new roles, new types of assistive personnel, and new care delivery systems, with or without the assistance of outside consultant reengineering groups. Occasionally, asking the right questions during the planning process will save time, money, and aggravation. We offer the following insights for groups engaged in this process. The following process reflects our observations of some issues that haven't been considered before implementation of systems, often with negative consequences.

Allina Labor Management Vision

Allina's vision is to be the recognized innovator in community health improvement. Allina's employees are its most valued resource in realizing this vision. To achieve this, unions and management will form strategic partnerships to anticipate, provide and affordably enhance the health of people living and working in the communities we serve. The partnership is based on a foundation of mutual trust and respect among employees, unions and management. The relationships are characterized by cooperation without compromising the integrity and distinctive roles of the parties. This partnership will provide a strong foundation for making Allina highly competitive and will enhance the dignity, respect and professional growth of Allina employees.

The following values will be inherent in this partnership:

- Allina will ensure a work environment which attracts and retains the best employees, recognizing their value and motivates them to excellence in their work. This includes opportunities for professional and career growth, improved job skills, enhanced satisfaction and employment assurances. Allina will be recognized as the health care employer of choice in the local area.
- Within the shared vision, values and strategies of Allina, the individuality of each of the labor unions, and Allina's various facilities and operating units will be acknowledged and respected.
- Union leadership will participate in shaping the strategic direction of the company.
- Administration and union leaders will have shared responsibility and accountability for leadership in providing quality, cost effective patient services and care. As improvements in quality and productivity are planned, implemented and evaluated union leaders and administration will provide support and guidance to employees and managers.
- Work will be designed through collaborative processes by management and employees so that expertise from all parties is utilized, ensuring the optimum value in the organization's services. Decision making will be based upon appropriateness, effectiveness, and efficiency.
- Unions will understand and respect the business requirements of Allina's operating units; management will understand and respect the organizational requirements of unions.
- Unions and management will jointly support the employees in gaining an understanding of health care economics and how it impacts Allina's short and long term decision making.
- Labor/Management agreements will reflect the needs of the parties for long term stable relationships with the goal of arriving at them through mutual methods.
- Both parties recognize that change will occur and must be confronted creatively at all levels. Unions and management will partner to anticipate and plan for the changes that will impact employees and the work environment creating opportunities that support them through all stages of their career.
- Employees will have an ability to influence resource allocation and utilization, consistent and creative rewards and recognition, involvement in all levels of decision making and consideration of the employees unique life situation.

Finalized 1/9/96

ALLINA
HEALTH SYSTEM

Courtesy of Allina Health System, 1996, Minneapolis, Minnesota.

Tool #23: Planning for Care Redesign Checklist

❑ Determine the characteristics of an *optimal* care delivery system. How will you spell success?

❑ What kinds and quantities of patients need care, within which levels of quality, and by which standards? How would all personnel be used? Refer to your mission and vision.

❑ Think about which parts of the current care delivery system work well and should be preserved. For example, if RNs are able to supervise other personnel while they coordinate care with other disciplines, write that down as a non-negotiable constant.

❑ Decide which aspects of the current care delivery system aren't working as well as could be expected. Do the nursing assistants have "down" time with nothing to do? Are the RNs overburdened with heavy lifting and other patient care duties without help? Are physicians confused about who is taking care of whom?

❑ Record your "givens" in terms of budget, personnel resources, educational systems and types of care being delivered. Once you've recorded constants, challenge them.

For example, if any of these are stumbling blocks, think about creative methods of changing them. Also, if your personnel budget seems too low for the required level of staffing coverage, plan to reallocate financial resources based on potential revenue. Check out whether your system is considering the budget as a whole (based on managed care reimbursement) or remains locked into fee-for-service mentality. Consider how to deliver the same "amount" of care less expensively. Think about other ways of educating staff about different roles if your educational department isn't able to help you. Can your unit add a service for less acute patients to the current complement and spread the acuity differently? If you need more staff for desk coverage, would two nurse assistive personnel equal one tenured RN salary, or would one secretary do the job? Would turnover of assistive personnel cost more than the status quo? What does the area's job recruitment market look like? Don't plan to hire LPNs and licensed vocational nurses (LVNs) if none are available.

❑ Think now about the details of what happens during each shift in your department. *Now* is the time to *be there*—on each shift and on weekends—to observe and ask questions.

continues

- ❑ Which tasks or processes aren't being done as well as you'd like them to be? (Look at unusual occurrence reports, errors, complaints, and staff input.)
- ❑ Which staff are doing tasks that someone else could or should do? Do any of the job descriptions contain overlapping functions?
- ❑ How are people rewarded and for what behaviors? Does talking together while walking down the hallway seem to be more rewarding than performing care? Are tasks being seen as the most important? Is short-term outcome planning or long-term planning for the patients discussed?
- ❑ What duties are occupying staff time? What do they see as redundant roles or tasks?
- ❑ Examine the details of your department as they relate to the type of patient: Are the post-surgical patients being scheduled for physical therapy at the same time? Do the respiratory therapists (if you are lucky enough to have them) make rounds at certain times and wait with a cup of coffee while the treatments are being done? Is chemotherapy spaced throughout the shift or is it heavier from 4:00 to 8:00 PM? What happens during each shift will help determine the work flow and need for overlap or different types of personnel.
- ❑ Who do you want to manage the patient throughout his or her care? Will it be a primary nurse, a case manager, or whoever happens to get assigned to the patient during the next few shifts? Determine if or how you would like to see professional nursing influence the outcomes of the patient and coordinate the care. Or, will you expect social workers to monitor patient progress throughout the continuum?
- ❑ How will physicians, nurses, and other health care professionals communicate? Will you use rounds, communication sheets, the chart forms, or multiple phone calls?
- ❑ Determine the transport issue as a department within your organization. Who does the transport of supplies, people, equipment, and mail? Some facilities are beginning to use robots for some of these. If you can't find a warm body, use a cold one.
- ❑ Who is best able to provide cleaning and other environmental services? Will every individual on the team consider this as a satisfying part of his or her role?
- ❑ What specifics in technology affect your service and the care delivery? What do you anticipate happening with that technology in the next several years?
- ❑ Find several tasks that can be eliminated and duplication of effort that can become a single effort.
- ❑ What work is more efficient using two people?

continues

- ❑ Collate the information reviewed previously in a cogent format for committee discussion.
- ❑ Collect and review articles about different care delivery systems to further enhance your creativity; contact facilities that have tried new ideas and get the real story from them. All disciplines of staff should be involved in this exploration. Be certain that group members who are doing the planning talk to those on the front line that are truly experiencing the system. On-site observation, if your facility can afford it, works best.
- ❑ *Don't* duplicate a plan from a workshop or article and decide it's the perfect system for you. *Any care delivery system must be adapted to your own organization and department.* Change only those things that need to be changed, and be sure you can articulate a good reason for doing so.
- ❑ Be certain your care delivery system framework reflects the intended outcomes you've planned, and that all disciplines are involved.

Source: Adapted from R. Hansten and M. Washburn, *The Nurse Manager's Answer Book*, Aspen, pp.190–194, © 1994, Aspen Publishers, Inc.

A corollary part to the overall planning of care delivery restructuring is the creative use of assistive personnel. The following tool is a checklist developed from our experience in observing all types of assistive personnel being developed in various facilities. Creative, hybrid combinations of several of the more conventional roles are being developed, in addition to the "patient care assistant" type of job. Respiratory therapists have added skills as have phlebotomists, nursing assistants, and emergency medical technicians (EMTs) or medical assistants. In some orthopedic departments, a physical therapy assistant may be trained to do nursing assistant work, some secretarial duties, and also perform the role of a cast technician in the outpatient or emergency departments. Occupational therapy assistants, pharmacy technicians, and rehabilitation aides are seen throughout the continuum of care. As roles are developed, however, it's important to be certain that these valuable people, flexible workers of the next millennium, don't become facility "Frankensteins"! Poorly planned personnel changes are not only painful to that employee group, but to the other team members as well. These role creations can become nightmares at the executive level as well if you've interpreted state regulations improperly.

Tool #24: Planning for Assistive Personnel

- ❑ Take a look at the tasks now being performed by RNs, pharmacists, and other professionals. Which tasks could be given away to someone else while preserving the professional's ability to supervise and be accountable, allowing for the necessary time for evaluating the patient and using professional judgment?
- ❑ Determine which basic skills are needed for the type of service you provide. For example, if you manage an intensive care unit (ICU) with many patients on ventilators, respiratory therapy skills may be the best basis for cross-training. If you are working in a subacute facility, you may wish to cross-train a combination of workers, such as physical therapy aides, nursing assistants, hygiene aides, and recreational therapy assistants.
- ❑ *Reread your state practice acts*! We note that many states have some older statutes that may conflict with newer laws, and that some individuals (such as surgical technicians and some medical assistants) have never been defined. Ask what certification and/or licensure is needed for all the duties you'd like performed. Consult with your state licensing boards and/or departments of health and talk about your plans. Many states, as well as the National Council of State Boards of Nursing, continue to wrestle with emerging issues and are issuing new position papers. Be clear to all planning committee members that, in your organization, you do *not* ask people to do procedures for which they are not trained or certified. Individuals on the team must be aware that they are not authorized to take on duties beyond their revised job descriptions or competency levels.
- ❑ Before you embark on a training program, assess your professional staff's ability to delegate clinical skills and remain accountable for the care of the patient. Delegation and supervision ability may seem basic to those who have had experience with these, but we repeatedly observe that many professionals do not wish to take on this type of professional accountability. Education will be needed for those who are supervising and coordinating the personnel or multiskilled workers you may be using.
- ❑ Those at the point of service will have the best idea of how well a proposed skill-mix transition will work. Planning group members may wish to work a shift as a certain type of worker to determine whether the planned role will fit in with the work flow.
- ❑ Once the roles are planned, develop an easy-to-use skill template for team members to refer to again and again. (See the section on intervention.)
- ❑ Members of management and the planning group must be involved and present when the new workers are beginning to be used.
- ❑ After the new assistive personnel have been working in your department for several weeks, hold meetings to again discuss the roles and clarify questions. Ask each group, "What do you wish your RN understood about your job as a patient care assistant?" and vice versa. Clarify what each group expects of the other regarding duties, communication, and methods of feedback and supervision. (See role clarification tools.)

Source: Adapted from R. Hansten and M. Washburn, *The Nurse Manager's Answer Book*, p.194–197, © 1994, Aspen Publishers, Inc.

Success Story

Griffin Hospital in Derby, Connecticut

As we discussed in Hansten and Washburn's (1996) *Successful Restructuring Newsletter* Vol. 1(3), Griffin has earned the award as the best health care environment in the country, according to the Center for Healthcare Design. It has achieved success with patient satisfaction, decreased length of stay, and greater professional satisfaction. A portion of its design includes a multiskilled technician role. Selections from the job description are included in the following.

Griffin Health Services Corporation
Griffin Hospital
Job Description Multiskilled Technician

Main Function: The multiskilled technician (MST) will perform or assist in routine and "stat" blood draws, electrocardiograms (EKGs), limited physical therapy, respiratory therapy modalities, and assist in the care of patients under the supervision of an RN. When required, he or she will assist other MSTs on other units in drawing blood and taking EKGs.

Job Relationships:

Accountable to: unit clinical director

Responsibilities and Duties:

Job Knowledge

I. Completes assigned tasks and job responsibilities in a timely manner without compromising care and safety.

II. PHLEBOTOMY

A. Follows standard precautions and, as per procedure, draws blood samples ordered as routine and stat
B. Correctly enters information in computer to obtain accurate label

(Performance will be observed for competency at least annually by qualified phlebotomist or designee appointed by department director.)

continues

III. EKG

A. Obtains EKG ordered routine and stat, as per procedure
B. Correctly enters information on EKG printout

(Performance will be observed for competency at least annually by qualified EKG technician or designee appointed by department director.)

IV. RESPIRATORY CARE

A. Accurately sets up oxygen equipment and performance incentive spirometry treatments
B. Documents actions as required in the patient's record
C. Processes required paperwork
D. Performs daily oxygen rounds

(Performance will be observed for competency at least annually by qualified respiratory therapist or designee appointed by department director.)

V. PHYSICAL THERAPY ACTIVITIES

A. Carries out range-of-motion (ROM) exercises consistent with training
B. Safely ambulates patients consistent with training

(Performance will be observed for competency at least annually by qualified physical therapist or designee appointed by department director.)

VI. PATIENT CARE

A. Assists in the patient admission process
   1. Obtains and records vital signs, weight, and height
   2. Collects, labels, and stores patient valuables
   3. Orients patient and significant other to TV, phone, nurse call system, bed operation, and, when appropriate, to view care, visitor kitchen, and resource room
B. Assists in patient-discharge process
C. Assists in patient-transfer process
D. Assists in the preparation of expired patient
E. Identifies stock needs and restocks supplies in patient care area, carts, utility room, etc.
F. Obtains and records vital signs
G. Collects specimens, for example, urine, stool
H. Feeds patients or assists patients in feeding
I. Records liquid intake as required
J. Provides patient with water and nourishments

continues

K. Assists in distribution and collection of dietary trays and does so in a timely manner
L. Demonstrates an awareness of patient rights
M. Accepts and completes other duties as assigned
N. Assists with the orientation of new personnel as assigned

VII. PROFESSIONAL RESPONSIBILITIES

A. Sick time is within Griffin Health Services objective (5 occurrences/year)
B. Provides proper notification for sickness, absence, and tardiness
C. Consistently demonstrates those qualities as stated in the employee philosophy
D. Knows where to access information regarding hazardous materials
E. Demonstrates initiative (doesn't need to be told)
F. Complies with nursing division staffing and scheduling policies and procedures for weekends, holidays, rotation of shift/units, etc
G. Checks communication system for individual and/or organizational messages daily
H. Attends three MST meetings yearly
I. Attends 6 department staff meetings yearly
J. Attends all mandatory inservices
K. Attends four hours of continuing education yearly
L. Maintains professional activity summary

OUTCOME OF PREVIOUS YEAR'S GOALS: ______________________

____

____

Goal-Setting/Learning Needs	Method of Accomplishment	Time Frame

CLINICAL DIRECTOR'S COMMENTS: ______________________

____

____

EMPLOYEE COMMENTS: ______________________

____

____

Courtesy of Griffin Hospital, Derby, Connecticut.

Success Story: Columbia Northwest Medical Center's Dream Team

The following case represents the whole picture of how planning works well when all the principles we've discussed have been effectively implemented. We again refer to Columbia Northwest Medical Center in Tucson, Arizona (see the section on assessment) and the Dream Team—a group of leaders who questioned the status quo and asked, "Does restructuring enhance approaches to managing patient care delivery?" The ensuing information was previously published in our *Successful Restructuring Newsletter,* Vol. 1(2). We thank Dorothy Sawyer, RN, MN, Chief Nursing Officer, Columbia Northwest Medical Center, Tucson, Arizona.

Getting the Word Out

The Dream Team published a newsletter, updating the staff on its progress, and held frequent employee forums to increase staff awareness of patient-centered care. The following excerpt from one of the newsletters explains the vision and the guiding principles:

> Some people ask "why" when confronted with the possibility of change and yet others ask "why not." Yet, in this age of dwindling reimbursement and managed care, it benefits all of us in health care to reevaluate our efficiencies and effectiveness as caregivers. The Dream Team hopes that by providing a clear vision, we can all work toward creating a patient-focused environment that better manages costs and increases our quality of care.
>
> Patient-Centered Care
> Vision Statement

Guiding Principles

1. Ensure caregiver access to needed services and resources to deliver care.
2. Refocus from the traditional nursing unit perspective to the patient care unit perspective and reinforce the multidisciplinary approach to patient care.
3. Improve system efficiency.
4. Encourage independent staff thinking and innovation in the redesigning of patient care systems.
5. Increase customer satisfaction (patients, physicians, employees, and payers.)
6. Strengthen interdepartmental communication.
7. Incorporate the redesign of patient care into the existing hospital-wide performance improvement process.
8. Ensure that caregiver tasks and responsibilities match caregiver skill levels.
9. Demonstrate cost effectiveness.

Columbia Northwest Medical Center supports a "demonstration unit" project that will be implemented house-wide within a predetermined time frame. The demonstration project will restructure the work environment to create efficient, cost-effective, service-oriented, quality care while focusing on employee satisfaction.

The Implementation Plan

With a demonstration chosen, and work begun, the role of the team shifts to that of an advisory council. "These seven are the redesign experts inside our institution—they are the glue that keeps this thing ticking, and allows consultation to other departments," says Dorothy Sawyer, Chief Nursing Officer. Their acronym has evolved to reflect these changes in role: **D**ynamic **R**edesign **E**nhances **A**ctions between **M**ultidisciplines. The team will continue its work until patient-centered care principles are universally applied in Columbia Northwest Medical Center systems.

Purpose of Advisory Council

- Coordinate information.
- Inform hospital of new projects and ongoing progress.
- Provide resources and guidance (conscience).
- Maintain a reality-based perspective regarding feasibility and financial responsibility for projects.
- Encourage continuous progress for monitoring and measurement.

Responsibilities of Advisory Council

- Integrate news into a hospital-wide newsletter.
- Meet monthly to review submitted work redesign proposals.
- Review ongoing performance improvement projects for progress and measurement.
- Advise departments that are considering a project but not sure how to proceed.

Within 1 year, all department directors along with members of their department will be asked to attend at least one advisory council. The intent is for individuals to disseminate information to their departments, to be aware of the overall progress of the hospital-wide program, and to share their ideas and perspectives.

The Work Redesign Project Worksheet

There are times when members of a unit may decide to make changes for improvement, not realizing the potential impact on other departments. To eliminate this potential, and to reduce duplicated and overlapped efforts, the Dream Team created a tool for project review. Departments considering change present a completed worksheet to the team for review and advice. (See the work redesign project worksheet.)

DREAM TEAM COLUMBIA NORTHWEST MEDICAL CENTER

Work Redesign Project Worksheet

The Opportunity for Improvement:

Project Name: ______________________________

Contact/Team Leader Name: ______________________________

Dept. ______________ Ext. ______________ Start Date: ______________

Team Members:	Department:
______________	______________
______________	______________
______________	______________

1. What effect will the proposed redesign have on other disciplines?

Disciplines	Effect
______________	______________
______________	______________

2. Does the proposed redesign promote patient-centered care? Yes ___ No ___
3. What are the direct benefits of the proposed redesign?

4. Is the proposed project cost-effective? Yes ___ No ___
   Explain:

5. How was this opportunity identified? (Please provide supportive data.)

6. What are the proposed time frames for this redesign project?

7. After implementation, how will this redesign project be evaluated?

8. Identify any negative outcomes or results.

Courtesy of Columbia Northwest Medical Center, Tucson, Arizona.

PLANNING CASE STUDY: CHMC, SEATTLE, WASHINGTON

Jaleh Shafii and Mary Chmelik shared with us their experiences in planning for the Children's Hospital Reengineering Project. Children's Hospital and Medical Center (CHMC) is a 208-bed tertiary regional pediatric medical center and teaching hospital in Seattle, Washington. As co-pilots of the process, they navigated one of the best planned projects we have been fortunate to experience as consultants and trainers. The following was written by Jaleh Shafii and Mary Chmelik. You will note that introductory materials were discussed in the section on assessment.

Redesigning the Process Stage

The stage of redesigning the process focused on preparing the current environment for the actual integration of a skill mix model. In this stage, there were the following three areas of focus: 1) designing the skill mix model by patient care unit, 2) identifying impacts in relation to the current environment, and 3) creating a structure to address the impacts.

Designing the Models

Seven units at CHMC were redesigned to incorporate a skill mix. The skill mix model was individualized by each unit based on the specific needs of its patient population.

The models were individualized by type of assistive personnel (special care provider or SCP) and type of RN:SCP partnership. The types of SCPs included nursing assistants (NAs), LPNs, surgical technicians (STs), and respiratory therapists (RTs). Types of partnerships were either paired (one RN to one SCP to care for 5 to 10 patients) or shared (one SCP shared between two or more RNs to care for a group of patients). For example, in the acute care surgical unit skill mix model, an RN was paired with an LPN to provide care to a patient population that requires the frequent

CHMC Skill Mix Models

Paired Models: One RN: One SCP

- Acute care medical and rehabilitation units pair a nursing assistant with an RN to provide care for 5 to 10 patients.
- Acute care surgical unit pairs an LPN with an RN to provide care for five to seven patients.

Shared Models: At least two RNs: One SCP

- Emergency department and the postanesthesia care unit (PACU) patient care is provided by a mix of NAs and RNs.
- Operating room provides patient care with a mix of surgical technicians, LPNs, and RNs.
- Critical care units provide patient care with a mix of respiratory therapists and RNs.

Source: Copyright © 1996, Children's Hospital and Medical Center, Seattle, Washington.

administration of IV medications and higher level technical care. In the critical care unit model, an RT with NA registration is in a shared partnership with two to three RNs to deliver care to patients with more intensive nursing and respiratory needs. The NA registration enabled the RT to share basic care tasks with the RN. In all of the models, RNs delegated tasks to the SCP while still retaining overall accountability and responsibility for the nursing care provided.

Identifying the Impacts

The current nursing model at CHMC was primary nursing with a predominately all-RN staff. The challenge existed in adapting the current environment to accommodate the change to a skill mix model. The change impacted both personnel and systems. Personnel impacts included the following: a) designing clear roles for the RN and SCP, b) developing training programs to prepare each staff member for his or her new role and responsibilities and how members would work together in a partnership, and c) informing the entire health care team of the changes. System impacts included the following: a) redefining processes (for example, shift report), b) updating documentation forms, and c) measuring the effects of the changes. The identified impacts generated a long and interdependent list of activities needing to be addressed before implementation.

Creating a Structure

The next step in the redesign process was to create a systematic and thorough approach to address the interdependent activities. The approach selected was a combination of project-management methodologies borrowed from the business industry and adapted to the health care environment. The methodology offered a comprehensive, coordinated, outcome-based approach. The methodology included initiating a project, developing a project plan, and building and managing effective teams.

Initiating a Project

Initiating a project required establishing goals, determining resources, and identifying potential constraints. The purpose of the project was translated into specific and measurable goals. The goals identify what needs to be accomplished and provide directional guidance (Quigley, 1993). The following goals identified for the CHMC skill mix project were based on the results of the work sampling study (see the section on assessment):

1. Increase the time RNs spend in licensed activities, in acute care units, from 58% to 70% and in critical care units from 64% to 70%.

2. Institute the unit-specific staffing models (for example, in acute care units, 1 RN:1 SCP provide care for 5 to 10 patients).

The personnel resources for the project were solicited by the unit managers. Representatives from areas affected by the change participated. Altogether, there were 92 staff members representing all levels of the organization. The majority of the participants were staff nurses (64%); the remainder were managers (21%), clinical nurse specialists (10%), and human resources staff and respiratory therapists (5%). The participants were assigned to work teams that created the systems and processes necessary to integrate a skill mix.

The major constraint identified was time. With seven units requiring implementation, it was necessary to phase-in each unit in a coordinated and sequential manner. Units were phased-in to avoid implementing during seasons of peak census swings. The acute care medical unit needed to begin implementation in mid-July to ensure completion before the busy respiratory season of winter. To accommodate this first implementation target date, redesign for that unit had to occur within a 10-week period. With the goals defined, the resources determined, and the constraint identified, the project was initiated.

Developing a Project Plan

With the project initiated, the next step in the project-management structure was to create a project plan. In the CHMC project plan, the previously identified impacts of change were organized into the following categories: SCP integration, role development, training, policy and procedure, service parameters, and communication. Each category was further broken down into focused and achievable activities with assigned duration (see the RN Skill Mix project table). In the initial project plan, there were nearly 200 individual activities. To manage the various concurrent activities and resources of the project plan, project-management software was used. This type of software provides a ready-made structure for organizing, updating, and tracking activities.

In addition to the plan, two other tools facilitated the management of the project. The first was a status report, which summarized the weekly progress project (see the project status report). The content was organized by current, completed, and future activities. It served as a communication tool among participants of the project.

The second tool was the issues tracking log (see provided example). It provided the method to record and monitor issues that occurred as the project progressed. The issues remained on the tracking log until further action could be determined. Some issues were added to the project plan as activities; other issues were resolved. These tools ensured accurate information sharing, which was essential for completing the work within a defined time frame.

RN SKILL MIX PROJECT
SCP INTEGRATION ACTIVITY TEAM
PROJECT PLAN

ID	Task Name	Duration	Start	Finish
1	**Develop SCP Job Description.**	**23d**	**5/8/95**	**6/7/95**
2	Gather job requirements for all process areas.	5d	5/8/95	5/12/95
3	Clarify licensure and competency requirements for each type of SCP.	5d	5/8/95	5/12/95
4	Determine if any impacts on unions exist.	5d	5/8/95	5/12/95
5	Develop standard format for job description.	5d	5/8/95	5/12/95
6	**Create job description for NA.**	**16d**	**5/15/95**	**6/5/95**
7	Write "draft" job description.	5d	5/15/95	5/19/95
8	Review all drafts internally with activity team.	5d	5/15/95	5/19/95
9	Revise as necessary.	1d	5/15/95	5/15/95
10	Submit to PCT for review and comment.	3d	5/22/95	5/24/95
11	Verify Task list with Process Managers.	7d	5/25/95	6/2/95
12	Submit to HR for grading.	5d	5/25/95	5/31/95
13	Revise as necessary.	2d	6/1/95	6/2/95
14	Submit graded/revised job description for "final" PCT review.	1d	6/5/95	6/5/95
15	**Create job description for LPN.**	**2d**	**6/6/95**	**6/7/95**
16	Write "draft" job description.	1d	6/6/95	6/6/95
17	Review all drafts internally with activity team.	1d	6/7/95	6/7/95

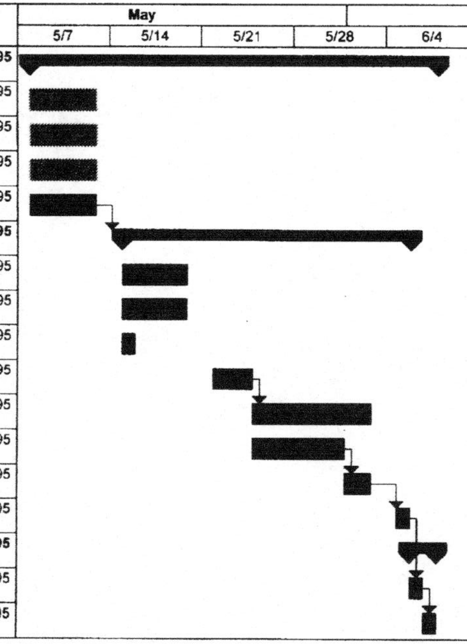

Project: RN SKILL MIX PROJECT
Date: 9/6/96

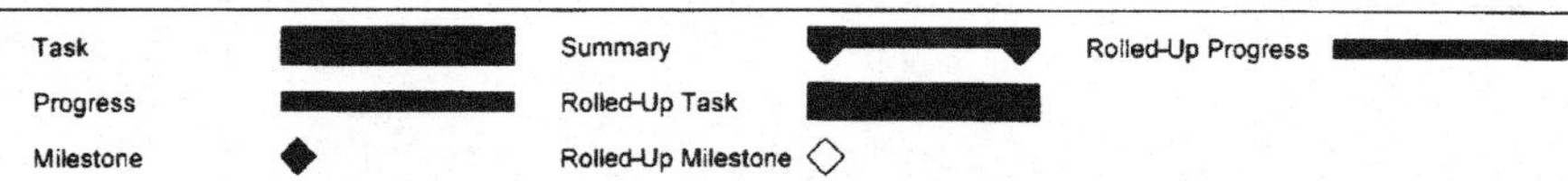

Source: Copyright © 1996, Children's Hospital and Medical Center, Seattle, Washington.

PROJECT STATUS REPORT

Overall Project Status: Green

Teams	*Milestone Description/Progress*	*Completion Date*	*Impacts/Concerns*	*Status*
Role Development (Acute Care, OR/PACU, ICU, ED, Ambulatory)	Acute care—Outstanding issues of LPN role (for example, IV meds) and handoffs to training team regarding 2nd floor LPN role changes PACU—Final draft of LPN/anesthesia tech standards of practice PACU—Draft of competency module for NA D/C IVs PACU—Modify reference binders for LPN role On hold pending heme/onc, ICU, ambulatory care, and IPU decisions on role development	1/17 1/26 1/26 2/1 TBD	The timeline if ICU, IPU, ambulatory, and heme-onc want role development	Yellow pending status of these four groups
Integration	Review blue forms as needed			Green
Training	UPC meeting (ongoing) Wave 6 of training LPN orientation—Finalized content and methodology—Final draft ACFP LPN inservice training materials	1/4, 1/18 1/26 2/7 2/2		Green
Policy and Procedure	P&P activity team—Review policies and procedures for LPN impacts On hold—LPN issues complete	1/18		Green
Service Parameters	RN questionnaires mail out—on hold Follow up on service parameter workshop Review results from surveys Health team questionnaires mail out	1/26 2/96 2/96 2/2	Coordination of future surveys Team project estimated completion date Feb. 29	Green
CAT	FORUM story boards (updated presentation table) Q&As flyer for January	1/17 1/19		Green

Note: UPC = unit project coordinator; PACU = post-anesthesia care unit; DC = discontinue; P&P = policy and procedure; ACFP = acute care float pool; IPU = inpatient psychiatry unit; CAT = communications activity team.

Source: Copyright © 1996, Children's Hospital and Medical Center, Seattle, Washington.

ISSUES TRACKING LOG

Description	*Action or Issue*	*Issue Severity*	*Entry Date*	*Target Date*	*Received From*	*Handoff To*	*Status*	*Status/Action Taken*
LPN student clinical site	Issue	M	10/16/95	10/23/95	Training	PCT	Closed	No clinical sites at this time
Will SCPs be incorporated into RN CPR training?	I	M	11/27/95	12/15/95	3rd flr	TRN	Closed	Incorporated into NSD training
Define distribution of Q&A flyers	A	L	9/29/95	10/13/95	CAT	PCT	Closed	Distribution is the same as for P&P updates
Role of volunteers with SCPs	I	L	9/29/95	10/3/95	CAT	PCT	Closed	Volunteers operate under a different liability umbrella/law.
Matrix of LPNs/NAs comp lists across units	A	L	10/2/92	11/21/95	Training	Role	Closed	Completed
LPN IV certification	A	H	9/6/95	9/13/95	Role	Integration	Closed	Duplicate of LPN IV certification training
New IS report for resource utilization	A	L	10/5/95	11/13/95	SP	SP	Closed	Added to the "plan"
Charge nurse staffing handbook developed	A	L	9/1/95	11/2/95	Manager	Training	Closed	Added to action plan
Will the LPNs give meds?	I	NA	11/10/95	5/5/96	P&P	Role	Closed	See note
Float pool RN training—How do we orient them to differences from unit to unit?	I	M	11/27/95	12/15/96	Manager	Training	Closed	ACFP inservices held Feb. 6 & 20 to orient them to the LPN role
3-month evaluation process for SCPs	A	M	11/27/95	12/8/95	Training	Role	Closed	On OPC mtg. agenda for 11/30. Follow-up work at 12/7 meeting. On PCT 1/9 agenda
Tracking of licensure/registration for LPNs and NAs	I	L	9/1/95		Integration	Human resources	Closed	Genysis system will track.
Will LPNs be epidural certified?	I	NA	11/10/95	12/31/95	P&P	Role	Closed	No
Continuing ed for NAs	I	M	11/06/95		Training	Integration	Closed	Not a state requirement.
NAs floating between floors (?)	I	M	1/4/96	1/16/96	Manager	PCT	Closed	Discussed at PCT. PMs to follow up on in regular PM meeting.

Note: NSD = nursing staff development; PCT = project coordination team.
Source: Copyright © 1996, Children's Hospital and Medical Center, Seattle, Washington.

Building and Managing Effective Teams

The next step was to organize the project participants into a team structure (see the project teams diagram). It was important for the team structure to be organized in a way that supported the achievement of the project plan activities, addressed the individual needs of each of the models, involved a variety of people, and promoted creative thinking. To incorporate these ideals, a team structure was created consisting of six activity teams and one oversight team.

The Activity Team

The six activity teams were based on the categories identified in the project plan. These activity teams were the following: 1) SCP integration, 2) RN/SCP role development, 3) RN/SCP training, 4) SCP orientation, 5) policy and procedures, and 6) communication and service parameters. Each team had defined deliverables or outcomes to achieve. The deliverables or outcomes were either final products (such as

PROJECT TEAMS

Source: Copyright © 1996, Children's Hospital and Medical Center, Seattle, Washington.

a job description) or a component of a product that needed further development by another activity team (for example, a task list validated by the SCP integration activity team that was sent to the RN/SCP role activity team to become the competency/skills assessment). Some of the outcomes were applicable across the units. For example, the SCP integration activity team defined the hiring process for all units. Other outcomes were customized in relation to individual unit models. For example, the RN/SCP role activity team defined specific RN and SCP responsibilities, creating unit standards of practice. The participants on the activity teams developed an understanding of the redesign focus of their team. As a result, they became subject experts and provided consistency in designing products for specific units.

Each activity team was led by a clinical leader and activity facilitator. The clinical leaders were experts in the content area of their particular team. The SCP integration team that was responsible for writing job descriptions and determining staffing policies was co-led by a nurse manager and a human resources generalist. Likewise, the RN/SCP training and SCP orientation activity team, which created the training program, was co-led by the nursing staff development manager and a unit-based clinical nurse specialist. The activity facilitator offered project-management expertise. They provided the structure to keep the team on the project plan timeline, formulated meeting agendas, and updated the weekly status reports. The team was made up of staff representatives from the seven areas implementing a skill. This brought a diverse group together that promoted innovative ideas to be shared among departments.

The Project Coordination Team

The project coordination team (PCT) oversaw the project. The PCT was overall accountable for achieving project goals within the established timeline. Members of the PCT were activity team clinical leaders and activity facilitators as well as other managers of units implementing a skill mix. The team monitored work generated from each activity team, served as a communication link among the teams, discussed and resolved issues, and provided mutual support for each other.

At the weekly 2-hour meetings, the clinical leaders gave progress updates based on the written activity team status reports. The status reports prompted discussions related to expected completion of work and the potential impact on other teams. For example, the training activity team was ready to receive the standards of practice from the RN and SCP role activity team to plan the SCP orientation before the role team was ready. Further delay would have adversely affected the actual implementation target date. The PCT created a plan to complete the standards and keep the start date on target. The PCT meetings also offered a forum to discuss and resolve issues or make decisions that extended beyond the scope of the individual activity team. For example, the service parameters activity team needed approval for funds to hire an agency to conduct satisfaction surveys. The structure of the teams facilitated a coordinated and thorough approach to complete the work of the project plan.

Advice from Experience

At CHMC, a performance improvement project focused on the integration of a skill mix model to increase the efficiency and effectiveness in the delivery of nursing care. Seven different units required redesign support to implement their unique models. A combination of project-management methodologies provided a systematic and thorough structure to address the impacts of the redesign.

Redesigning the process before actual implementation was key. As a result, the units initiated their implementation on time with the necessary personnel and system supports in place. Currently, implementation is still occurring on four of the seven units. However, preliminary reports from staff indicate that the work produced by each of the activity teams such as the unit standards of practice and RN and SCP training programs was invaluable to understanding how to put the concept into practice.

Thanks to the thoughtful planning and inclusion of CHMC staff from all levels of the organization throughout the project, resistance to implementation of the skill mix has been minimal. A follow-up work sampling study and customer satisfaction survey are planned after implementation is complete to further evaluate the success of the skill mix project.

Tips for Success

- Administration is clear and committed to the proposed model changes.
- Administration understands and supports the effort as a project.
- Project-management processes ensure a comprehensive and structured approach to prepare for implementation.
- A centralized approach is an efficient use of resources.
- The leadership of the project has project-management expertise.
- The project is supported with sufficient resources and a reasonable timeline.
- The managers are actively involved in the decision-making process of the project.
- The RNs determined how the models would be actualized.
- Representatives from a cross section of the units promote sharing ideas from a variety of perspectives.
- Most of all, remember that introducing a skill mix is an opportunity to professionalize the role of the RN!

Courtesy of Jaleh Shafii and Mary Chmelik, CHMC.

Section Two References

Beck, J.D.W. & Yeager, N.M. (1994). *The leader's window.* New York: John Wiley & Sons, p 105.

Beckham, D. (1994). The vision thing. *Healthcare Forum Journal, March/April,* 60–67.

Bridges, W. (1991). *Managing transitions: Making the most of change.* Reading, Mass: Addison-Wesley.

Collingwood, H. (1996). How better people management adds to the bottom line. *Working Woman, March,* 18.

Hackman, J.R. (1992). The psychology of self-management in organizations. In *Classic readings in self-managing teamwork* (pp. 144–192). Rollin Glaser, ed. King of Prussia, Pa: Organization Design and Development, Inc.

Hansten, R. & Washburn, M. (1993). *From barriers to bridges: success strategies for high performing teams.* From a workshop co-copyrighted with the Washington Organization of Nurse Executives (currently Northwest Organization of Nurse Executives).

Hansten, R. & Washburn, M. (1994). *The nurse manager's answer book.* Gaithersburg, Md: Aspen Publishers.

Hansten, R. & Washburn, M. (Ed.). (1996). *Successful restructuring newsletter, 1*(2), Gaithersburg, Md: Aspen Publishers.

Hansten, R. & Washburn, M. (Ed.). (1996). *Successful restructuring newsletter, 1*(3), Gaithersburg, Md: Aspen Publishers.

Hansten, R. & Washburn, M. (Ed.). (1996). *Successful Restructuring Newsletter, 1*(4), Gaithersburg, Md: Aspen Publishers.

Hansten, R. & Washburn, M. (Ed.). (1996). *Successful Restructuring Newsletter, 1*(5), Gaithersburg, Md: Aspen Publishers.

Langer, E. (1995). Give choices to add value. *The Pryor Report, 11*(1a), 4.

Lipton, M. (1996). Demystifying the development of an organizational vision. *Sloan Management Review, Summer,* 84, 86.

Minnick, A., Young, W.B., & Roberts, M.J. (1995). 2000 patients relate their hospital experiences. *Nursing Management, 26*(12), 25–31.

Quigley, J.V. (1993). *Vision: How leaders develop it, share it, sustain it.* San Francisco: McGraw Hill, Inc.

Scott, C. & Jaffe, D. (1989). *Managing personal change.* Menlo Park, Calif: Crisp Publications.

Sibbet, D. & O'Hara-Devereaux, M. (1991). The language of teamwork. *Healthcare Forum Journal, May/June,* 29–91.

Wellins, R.S., Byham, W.C., & Wilson, J.M. (1992). *Empowered teams* (pp. 14–15). San Francisco: Jossey-Bass.

Westrope, R.A., Vaughn, L., Bott, M., & Taunton, R.L. (1995). From vision to reality. *Journal of Nursing Administration, 25*(12), 45–54.

Wheatley, M. & Kellner-Rogers, M. (1996). Excerpt from *A simpler way,* quoted in *On achieving excellence, June,* 10.

SECTION THREE

Interventions To Make It All Happen

Worst Case Scenario:
"The Quick Fix"

It was a mid-sized hospital in a large coastal city. The organization had a rich and successful history and enjoyed a solid reputation in the community. Changes were being made, and the administrative staff were committed to quality, wanting to ensure their marketing edge. Layoffs were being planned, and staffing ratios were changed to reflect a new team-based delivery of patient care. With so much going on, we were asked to come in and present four-hour sessions focusing on customer service to the patient care teams. Our instincts told us that although this information was necessary and would certainly be useful, we believed the staff would see other priorities. However, the administrative team disagreed and insisted that the need and the focus should be on customer service and minimizing patient complaints through courteous communication. Despite concerns, we did as told (highly unusual), and the sessions were met with mixed reviews.

Staff were upset and took various opportunities to display their feelings of unhappiness through unwilling attendance, lack of participation, and overt comments such as *"Why do I have to go to this charm school? I find it insulting and time-consuming when we have so many other things to do. If I haven't learned how to be nice to patients and staff by now, your four-hour session isn't going to change me!"*

Quick fixes do not work. We know that and so do you. But it's amazing how often an organization will sacrifice long-term success for a short-term, limited, and ineffective intervenstion. If you believe in the project and the changes you are going to make, you must also be ready to provide the necessary supports to make it happen. And a four-hour session will never be enough.

❸ INTERVENTIONS TO MAKE IT ALL HAPPEN

"We're not talking about the future, but right now. We're not talking about a nice-to-do activity, but a must-do priority. Increased emphasis on work place

learning is affirming the urgent need for more effective training and performance interventions. Those who fail to answer this call will be left behind."

The Chief Training Officer: A New Strategic Leader (Shandler, 1996, p. 79)

DAMAGE CONTROL: AN OVERVIEW OF THE INTERVENTION PROCESS

At some point in the transition process in your organization, you may have felt some hope, some exhilaration. Despite personal reluctance that you may have felt due to the increased job pressures, you may have held secret thoughts about how nice it would be to finally fix, for once and for all, the recurrent problems in your organization. To start fresh, from scratch, leaves the slate clean and ready to be rewritten with better results. The outcomes you wished to achieve have always been admirable: streamlined, cost-effective patient care, as evidenced by improved client and team satisfaction and better clinical outcomes. But at some point during the process, most managers have shared a sense of being disappointed at the progress being made. Some have pronounced a sense of being overwhelmed by problems, being depressed and burdened by the responsibility. Your life as a health care leader or manager may begin to seem like it's fighting fires instead of preventing them, and you sure aren't getting through to your desired outcomes in the process.

Through our consulting with many organizations along the health care continuum going through these changes, we've developed a list of common hurdles often encountered on the road to patient centered care. (If you aren't calling your care remodeling "patient centered," don't let that phrase make you think our discussion doesn't apply.) Any organization that is trying to maintain or improve quality and outcomes while decreasing expenses is shooting for roughly the same goal. In planning effective interventions for supporting your project and ensuring your goals, it's important to recognize some of the common barriers.

Source: Reprinted from R. Hansten and M. Washburn, *Successful Restructuring Newsletter,* Vol. 1, No. 2, © 1996, Aspen Publishers, Inc.

▼

"Most people live, whether physically, intellectually, or morally, in a very restricted circle of their potential being. They make use of a very small portion of their possible consciousness, and of their soul's resources in general, much like a man who, out of his bodily organism, should get into a habit of using and moving only his little finger. Great emergencies and crises show us how much greater our vital resources are than we had supposed." (William James)

▲

In our experiences as "damage control" experts, the four most common stumbling blocks along the road to quality health care can be characterized as the following:

- Staff resistance to change
- Interdisciplinary team functioning

- Existing system glitches
- Excessive expectations (financial and otherwise)

Problem	*Interventions*
Resistance to change	
Unrealistic world view	Educate, involve
Unclear roles	Involve in planning for role development Clarify
Intolerance for ambiguity, lack of flexibility	Clarify preferred vision Determine the "givens"
Lack of knowledge re: new roles, leadership	Educate re: skills, repeatedly
Unclear accountabilities	Standardize terms of agreement
Interdisciplinary team function	
Unclear roles	Involve, clarify
Professional concerns, fear of layoffs, power drain	Openly discuss concerns Determine best communication methods Clarify formal leaders
Professional stereotyping	Educate regarding this: overcome with understanding of roles, clear common goals
Knowledge deficit re: goals, direction, vision, purpose	Work together to determine
Communication difficulties and conflicts	Educate, mentor re: advanced communication skills
Existing system problems	
Recurring systems problems	Adapt course of action to each specific problem
Task orientation to provision of care	Shift focus on outcomes
Excessive expectations	
Staff unrest, complaints	Research results from other organizations and reevaluate

Staff Resistance to Change

Depending on the degree of participation of staff in the remodeling efforts, there is a normal human avoidance of upsetting the status quo, even if the status quo is not entirely desirable. From working with individuals across the country, we find that there are factors that intensify the staff's negative reaction.

Unrealistic Expectations

Many staff members and managers alike retain outmoded and unrealistic expectations of the world and jobs in general. The "entitlement attitude" springs from our history of employment in the United States. Keeping a 9-to-5 job until one is able to retire, complete with a gold watch, is no longer feasible in the jet-paced outsourced casual worker world of today. When the expectation of "job security and lifetime employment" runs dry, then tempers flare. (Remember that anger = unmet expectations.) Health care has been particularly paternalistic/maternalistic, and certainly we have been caring individuals. Understanding the realities of the work world of today and skills for remaining employable will assist in overcoming this barrier, as will understanding the rationale for the proposed changes and being involved in the planning.

Undefined Roles

Staff who are included in role planning frequently have a positive attitude toward role redesign and will act as advocates. Those who express concerns are also committed health care workers, and their concerns must be given credence. Unclear roles with newly "empowered" staff and management and among all disciplines will create unnecessary chaos and conflict as all wonder "Who is supposed to be doing what?" Repeated role clarification creates a bridge over this barrier.

Blurred Organizational Vision

Because we are dealing with such important issues (i.e., life and death) in health care, ambiguity is difficult. We can't be ambiguous about doses of digitalis or where to make an incision. Intolerance of a certain amount of uncertainty about the organization's future is often a marker of staff resistance. This is often due to concern about how each individual fits in (or doesn't) in that future vision. Clarification of the preferred future vision for the organization will relieve the fear about "I don't know what's going to happen or where we are going, so I'll just keep doing what I know best and hope I don't get laid off." Because this transition time is one when we must truly harvest the creative ideas of all the individuals in the organization, clarity on some issues is essential.

Inadequate Training

Lack of knowledge about how to implement professional and leadership roles and supervisory skills compounds the fear that individuals possess regarding being "incompetent" in new situations. Organizations in the midst of cost reductions often believe that they must also delete education as a "nonessential." Many don't understand that an educational offering, on a given date in 1993, for a percentage of the staff, will not suffice. "The board of nursing taught them about their roles... why aren't they giving feedback and supervising the new multiskilled workers?" The real cost of ignoring educational needs can be multiplied by the number of errors, unsuccessful employees, and disgruntled workers.

Unclear Accountabilities

Because decentralized workgroups have been operational in many organizations for years, individual leadership styles are reflected in each work area. Expectations are variable depending on the charismatic leadership or command-control management style of the area's supervisor. Accountabilities are often unclear (interpersonal behavior, communication, information retrieval and responsibility, response to deadlines, timelines, attendance at meetings, being prepared . . . the list can go on and on). The management "team" often reflects the diversity of the individuals, and there is no common understanding of how people should be acting regarding work responsibilities or interpersonal relationships. "Mama or Papa" management styles do not encourage individuals to grow in self-evaluation or accountability. Sharing expectations and hammering out a performance agreement are essential for workers to feel safe, empowered, and respected.

Interdisciplinary Team Function Less Than Optimal

How many organizations, before restructuring, could safely state that inter- or transdisciplinary teams functioned optimally? Many of the root causes of staff resistance flourish in the interdisciplinary arena.

▼

"Another mistake companies make: when they put a group of people in charge of re-engineering, they seldom take the trouble to fuse them into a team. . . . To use a term from physics, trust is the 'strong force' that binds the atoms of the team. . . . Team building is not a one-time event; it begins the first week and must be reinforced throughout the life of the team."

(Hammer and Stanton, 1995)

▲

Tools in this section focus on the following strategies:

- Again, when roles are redesigned, clarification is needed approximately every three months. This discussion gives each group the opportunity to discuss the members' concerns. Who should REALLY answer patient lights? When should a home health aide telephone for assistance, and who should be called? Can an Administrative Partner call a physician?
- During the scramble for direction and keeping financially afloat, many of our team members are experiencing personal struggles with their employability in their profession of choice. Whether a phlebotomist, respiratory therapist, home chore worker, or physician, concern about professional status, financial remuneration in managed care, and their impact on the team may create anxiety that is reflected negatively in power struggles and inappropriate behaviors. Clarifying direction and roles and listening openly to team members' concerns are essential. All employees must have guided experience in assertive communication and conflict resolution.
- Who will lead the interdisciplinary team across the continuum? Will the hospital remain the linchpin of the system? Many states tell us that physicians and hospitals are locked in struggles regarding where patients (now "covered lives") enter the system. In a microcosmic sense, lack of team leadership, direction,

and accountability are common. Openly discussing these issues and determining what will work best, as a transdisciplinary team, for patient outcomes, is fundamental to success of any reengineering venture. Communication routes must be determined.

- Professional stereotyping is an attitude that prevents health care workers from communicating well. We have defined this term as "a fixed and superficial judgment about another profession, diminishing or eliminating the opportunity to appreciate the qualities of each individual within the profession." (Herrick et al., 1993)
- Again, all members of the team will be unprepared for effective teamwork if a knowledge deficit exists regarding goals, direction of the team, purpose for the team, and a vision of the future. The metaphor often used is that of "a rudderless ship."
- Few professionals or entry level health care workers are given courses and guided experience in advanced communication skills. Being unable to clearly identify the outcome they wish to achieve from an interaction and having little experience in assertively communicating to others will prevent the communication essential for teamwork.

Existing Systems Problems

▼

A fairly accurate, if homely, metaphor for restructuring and redesign includes the picture of a gardener, starting a new garden. The old tired sod has been rototilled, and weeds have been thrown into the garbage heap. Then the gardener lifts up a rock that has been there for ages. Insects of all kinds run out as daylight spreads over their lair. But when the gardener, in dismay, tries to put the rock back, trying to swoop the bugs back under it, it's too late. The insects are loose! But they were there before, just as the gardener suspected.

▲

If you are aware of weak departments in your organizational structure or ineffective leaders, those issues must be dealt with. Some may end up on the weed pile. Or there may be those plants that are salvageable and could use some fertilization with education and mentoring. The systems glitches are like the bugs: They are now free, and there must be some intervention for the garden to grow. The intervention will depend on the type of insect or glitch and what kind of outcome(s) you want to achieve.

A prime example of an existing system glitch is task orientation. Although many members of the team may be clear in their minds about what outcomes they want to achieve, they often are reluctant to take the time to share those goals. When articulated, it allows for the time to discuss proposed outcomes with the patients and families and to verify the direction in which they are going. This does wonders for motivation and staff satisfaction.

Excessive Expectations from the Project

When we've been told that the organization expects to realize a huge savings within two or three years after beginning a reengineering process, we question the possibility of achieving success. To make redesign and transition work, many resources must be poured into the individuals who make the changes occur.

▼

"After 30 years as a change agent, I have never seen a company change. It is people who change, one by one, as they make decisions to adopt new strategies and have the courage to reject the status quo." (Halle, 1996)

▲

The alteration of long-held concepts must be realized before behaviors can change. This process does not happen overnight, nor are plans successful if staff are not involved in the planning and implementation, as well as participating in customized repeated educational programs. The gardener may see the bugs but won't have the tools necessary to get rid of them. Frustration reigns throughout all levels of the organization.

Kathleen Andreoli, vice president for Nursing Affairs at Rush University College of Nursing, stated that *"you don't see any cost savings for about five years"* due to extensive retraining costs. (McEachern, 1995)

Despite the fact that hospitals believe they'll have to make huge cuts, 56 percent of them in the past two years have averaged cuts of less than 4 percent. Reengineering without using clinical paths saved less than 10 percent. (Bebiak, 1995)

Successful Strategies

- Return to your knowledge of the four Ps of transition management (see tool #28): Communicate plan, picture, purpose, and part in as many ways as possible. It helps a lot if you are really committed to improving quality instead of just saving money, as necessary to survival as that goal may be. High-quality care is a purpose that people can get behind. It is also helpful if you add to your plan that you will not lay off current employees and will take the time to retrain or decrease the numbers through attrition.
- Clarify roles: The function of the whole and achievement of outcomes depend on the functioning of each individual and the team together. This means that everyday behaviors and choices made by each member of the team, including handling communications effectively, are the foundation of achieving your targets, which brings us to . . .

- Education: We have listed several of the content areas that will need to be addressed and repeatedly clarified in your organization (specifics follow later in this section)
  1. Change management
  2. Professional practice and accountability
  3. Supervisory skills for those who need it: focusing on outcomes
  4. Communication (conflict resolution, giving effective feedback, assertive communication)
- Allocate resources for group development
  1. Establish purpose, vision of future
  2. Spend time hammering out terms of agreement or group norms
  3. Deal with professional stereotyping issues
- Solve systems problems: Individualize your response depending on problem. There is nothing that drags people down more quickly than having to do the jobs of others who are not behaving in an accountable manner.
- Review your goals and whether they are achievable: Create new ways of meeting the goals, but remember to evaluate cuts or streamlining efforts by outcomes.

Source: Reprinted from R. Hansten and M. Washburn, *Successful Restructuring Newsletter,* Vol. 1, No. 2, © 1996, Aspen Publishers, Inc.

For more details regarding ongoing evaluation of these four major problem areas and your interventions, read on to Section Four.

TRAINING: MAKING THE DECISION TO SUPPORT THE CHANGE

▼

"If someone asks what a human being ought to devote the maximum of his time to, I would say training. Train more than you sleep." (Master Masutatsu Oyama, 1979)

▲

You and the rest of your organization seem to be reeling with the speed of change; all bets are off, and the only routine seems to be your morning cup of coffee. Even more unsettling is your realization that the outcomes of your reengineering efforts seem to teeter on the brink of success or failure related to the daily performance and behavior of each employee as she begins to alter her roles. Not only must each be cross-trained, but also she must improve her skill level and ability to communicate in such a way that she is not only understood, but internal and external customers feel respected and important. Now, the employee must truly understand her accountability to include solving problems, resolving team conflict effectively, and redesigning processes while adjusting her specific role. We are talking about skill development, education, and changing a basic mindset about reality. What interventions are necessary to make this happen?

Does Training Help Achieve Outcomes?

The jury is definitely still out on this one. Many organizations are debating the value of their training efforts and often eliminating the education department altogether. The belief that it's the employee's responsibility to get the knowledge that he needs to do the job is rampant in many industries. According to Michael Schrage, noted futurist and research associate at MIT's Media Lab, *"My bet is that the bulk of organizations are going to abandon training as a strategic core value and embrace tactical training as the easiest and best path of least resistance. In other words, it's your job—so it's your responsibility to develop yourself on your own time. We'll try not to get in your way."* (Peters, 1996)

However, Jeff LeFors of Community Hospitals of Central California reflects on their reengineering project, *"Looking back, I'd probably take our estimates regarding staff education and triple it.... If we could have done more, we would have gotten farther, quicker."* (Davis, 1996)

Beyond the anecdotal, American Management Association has found a correlation with training in increased profit margin as well as worker productivity. At the end of one year after restructuring, 70 and 80 percent of organizations that had shored up their training budgets reported an increase in profits and productivity.

Outcomes Related to Training during Restructuring Projects

	Immediately Postrestructure	
Training Budgets	*Profits*	*Worker Productivity*
Increased	68% report increase	44% report increase
Same	42%	29%
Decreased	40%	31%
	One Year Postrestructure	
Training Budgets	*Profits*	*Worker Productivity*
Increased	80%	70%
Same	46%	41%
Decreased	41%	37%

Source: Data from D. Stamps, Corporate Anorexia, *Training,* p. 30, © 1996, American Management Association.

Potential Pitfalls of the Process

From our experience in consulting and training in health care organizations, we've noted that trying to overcome all the restructuring roadblocks with "an inservice" is a common error. Deciding what you would like to accomplish by the training and whether the identified goals are skills or challenges that would be solved by education (didactic or conceptual information sharing), training (including practice of specific skills), team-building and role clarification processes, managerial or leadership actions, or systems repair remains an often overlooked step.

▼

"Sadly, the goal of the program gradually changes from improving the organization to making certain everyone is trained, even if the time frame is in years, not months. In the end, success is measured by how many employees are trained, rather than how they perform after training." (Martin M. Broadwell,1995, President of the Center for Management Services, Inc., Decatur, Georgia)

▲

Common training/education pitfalls include the following:

- Lack of identification of the desired outcomes for the training
- Lack of analysis of what other interventions may be required to overcome the barriers or solve the problems or the *"throw an inservice at it"* plan
- One-shot education process that does not include actual on-site follow-up and mentoring
- Avoidance of "soft issues" discussions and interventions (e.g., staff anger, confusion, concern)
- Missing the manager and leadership group in training or education efforts
- Failure to identify other systems issues that need to be addressed (i.e., if the staff are being told to provide feedback to those they supervise, but the manager does not seem to be continuing the process with appropriate discipline measures when they are called for, staff feedback behavior will soon be extinguished)
- Lack of intermittent reinforcement

▼

"Knowledge isn't power. *Competence is power.* Power is the ability to create a desired effect. And creating desired effects is what we mean by 'performance.' To educate is to increase intellectual awareness of a subject. To train is to make someone proficient at the execution of a given task. . . . *If the student isn't doing it, it isn't training."* (Georges, 1996)

▲

The on-site performance issues are often missed because this one-to-one interaction is difficult to justify in the budget and more difficult to measure than an inservice attendance sheet. Because *reinforcement* is a standard principle for improving adult learning and the actual learning takes place when the knowledge and skills are applied outside of a classroom setting, employees need assistance in the real world of work for concepts to be cemented into the desired behavior. At Children's Hospital Medical Center in Seattle, Washington, **Unit Project Consultants** provide on-site mentoring and assistance in delegation, assignments, role clarification, and conflict management as staff begin to work together. At Wyoming Medical Center in Casper, Wyoming, a similar support role called the **Professional Development Specialist** was developed to provide reinforcement and intermittent skill practice in the work setting on all shifts.

How Much Is Enough?

So, if education and training do make a difference, how much is enough? **Enough is when you achieve the desired results.** Simplistic? Yes, but wisdom and success lie in implementing the following:

- Understand that education of employees must never stop, and support this understanding with the budget
- Each individual must be able to verbalize his or her own accountability for taking control of his or her learning and performance, taking advantage of offered assistance from the organization
- Discern which issues will benefit from an education or training problem
- Act on the part of needed solutions that come from systems or leadership interventions

What Competencies Really Matter?

▼

"Once the company reforms and begins to settle, training builds trust, it builds futures, it builds common dreams. It allows people to accomplish what they have to accomplish and allows the company to do the same."
(Kevin Daley, CEO)

▲

Once sold on the idea of the need for training, the bigger question becomes what kind of training will most effectively assist the staff in achieving the success that you have envisioned. It stands to reason if you're planning on changing the job, the role, or the system in which staff must now interact, their competencies must be assessed and perhaps changed as well. Because the working world seems to be having a love affair with the term *competencies,* we'd better do a little explaining about the term. Webster would describe competency as "having the capacity to function or respond." Thomas Gilbert asserts that *"competence has to do with the accomplishments that certain behaviors enable us to produce."* (Esque and Gilbert, 1995) This wholeness of behaviors should include a specific knowledge base, psychomotor skills, decision-making skills, communication skills, experience, and attitude. Faced with the need to change, to adapt to a newly redesigned system, employees want to know what to do to prepare themselves to succeed. Defining competencies gives them the information to do so.

Donald Shandler, author of *Reengineering the Training Function: How To Align Training with the New Corporate Agenda* (1996), suggests initially assessing three basic competencies:

- knowledge—does the person know what to do?
- skill—does the person have the skill required to complete the job?
- attitude—is the person willing to do what it takes to complete the job?

Deficiencies in any of these three areas will create a barrier to your planned success. Training will need to be planned based on your determination of what will best overcome the identified barrier. We recommend that you consider which of the following actions would be most effective given your assessment of the basic three:

- clarifying performance expectations
- providing performance feedback
- providing better tools (equipment, forms, other resources)
- teaching specific behaviors that will assist the staff member in achieving the desired outcome

Training as a Strategy for Overcoming Resistance

We love to illustrate concepts with the use of stories and believe the following scenario from Gary Hamel best illustrates an important point about change and the development of competencies.

▼

"Imagine that I coax a flatlander to the top of a snow-covered mountain. After strapping two well waxed skis onto the flatlander's feet, I give the nervous and unprepared nonskier a mighty push. He or she goes screaming over a precipice, and I'm booked for murder. One could well understand how the novice might not appreciate the 'change' I sought to engineer. Now imagine that the nonskier takes lessons for a few days. The now fledgling skier may ascend the same mountain and, though full of caution, voluntarily point the skis downhill. What has changed? Even with a bit of training, skiing is not without risks. But in the second scenario, the skier has been given a modicum of control—an ability to influence speed and direction." (Hamel, 1996)

▲

It's easy to see from this example how important it is to consider if your training will increase staff ability to influence and feel in control. Staff "resistance" to change may only be due to a lack of competency regarding the new skill. In this case, training that is clearly focused on helping the staff to achieve the desired outcome will be an excellent strategy for overcoming resistance.

What To Teach vs. What Not To Teach

If teaching specific behaviors is your choice, fundamental to the success of any training effort will be the consideration of the following question:

▼

What is the briefest training that will allow the staff member to overcome the identified barrier and get the job done?

▲

Too often, we have observed the failure of restructuring plans primarily due to ineffective training in which there has been no determination of what NOT to teach. Training programs designed to fill a requisite number of hours (to facilitate scheduling of staff) often include additional unnecessary information that only serves to confuse and frustrate the participant (and is soon forgotten at the expense of many training dollars). *"Another thing we know from considerable research is that the typical adult learner tends to recall no more than about 20 to 25 percent of what he or she is exposed to in a typical training day—and even this retention rate drops by half over time. Sessions should be reality linked, with intervals in between for practice of the knowledge."* (Shaw, 1995) Successful training that supports restructuring will meet the following criteria:

- specific to the desired result—determine first the ultimate product or service to be accomplished
- emphasis placed on accomplishment, not process—instruct in rationale for planned outcome, encouraging staff to develop own methods for achieving results
- continuous, not just a "one shot deal"—allow time for practice that is reality based between formal presentations of information
- supported in practice by on-site mentors or experts—competencies develop over time, through supported and repetitive practice
- validated in employee performance reviews—include new competencies in staff performance evaluations
- supported by management—make sure managers/leaders understand the new system and expected outcomes

Focusing on the Outcome

It's obvious to us, and to you by now, that success in any endeavor begins with determining the desired outcome and moving backward from there to plan actions that will get you the anticipated result. Failure to clarify outcomes, early in the game, only leads to frustration and expense on all levels. Yet, many organizations race to include "training" as a part of the restructuring plan, often with no determination of what will spell success.

If you can answer the question—"What do I want the employee to do that is different from before?"—you can avoid over- or underteaching. For example, if you want your new support associate to transport patients to procedures safely, what do you need to include in the training? Criteria for transport, use of safety restraints, and safe body mechanics will be essential. An overview of all procedures that a patient might be transported for will be unnecessary and forgotten information. However, failure to discuss positioning on a stretcher and practicing the process would be underteaching. Likewise, it is extraneous information to discuss William Harvey's discovery of the circulatory system when the desired outcome is proficiency in performing phlebotomies. Yet, failure to discuss the basic differences between arteries and veins would be insufficient preparation for someone who is going to be drawing blood.

Make sure you've also thought through the implications of a more knowledgeable work force. Frederick Kuri, president of Training Design Associates in Los Angeles, advises, *"What often happens is that a company's supervisors will support the training program, but when it is successful, they aren't prepared to deal with the new work environment. Suddenly you have employees who are talking to each other more and questioning decisions, who aren't passive workers. The employees become participants, but then you often see supervisors get their hackles up. They wonder, Why are we being second-guessed? And then the benefits are lost."* (Maruca, 1996)

Equally important is the validation of new competencies through the employee evaluation. Staff who are newly trained will need assurance that their efforts will be recognized through revised job descriptions and evaluations that reflect the changes in their roles. Likewise, senior staff will want some form of assurance that the newly trained individual is competent in the new area. A "skills checklist" is an essential part of the overall training process. (See Section Four for examples of skills checklists.)

WORKSHOP PRESENTATIONS

Formalized training sessions, workshops, retreats, etc., all need to be organized around a predetermined set of outcomes. Once the outcomes are set, an agenda is an essential tool for keeping the process on track. The samples presented here include overviews of the many aspects of personal and professional development discussed in the remainder of this section.

Tool #25: Sample Agendas

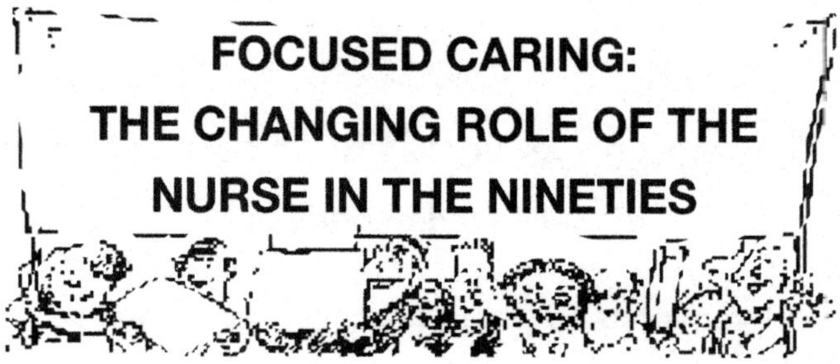

Ruth Hansten, MBA, BSN, and Marilynn Washburn, MA, BSN

FOCUSING

*revisit reasons for becoming a nurse, connecting these personal values with the organization's mission and vision

*determine a workable definition of accountability with the team

THE LAW OF THE LAND

*interpreting your state practice act

*define the legal roles of the RN and the LPN

*implications for working in the newly redesigned care delivery models

CHANGE AND THE TEAM PROCESS

*list the steps in the transition process

*identify behaviors that are commonly experienced

*let go of what is ending for you as you create your new team

ROLE DIFFERENTIATION

*determine team member's expectations of all members of the team

*identify tasks carried out by team members that contribute to the planned patient outcomes

OUTCOMES BASED COMMUNICATION

*practice assertive communication skills

*contrast the costs and benefits of each option for dealing with conflict

*put it all together by applying skills to specific situations

UPDATE: WORKING WITH LPNS

presented by:

Hansten & Washburn

RUTH HANSTEN, RN, MBA, AND MARILYNN WASHBURN, RN, MA

WHAT'S IN IT FOR YOU AS YOU ATTEND THIS 3-HOUR SESSION:

1. Identify the role of the LPN as described in the job description and the skills checklist
2. Delegate appropriately to the LPN according to the law and the role as defined at YOUR facility
3. Clarify the differences in the roles of the CNA, LPN, and the RN
4. Differentiate between assessment and data gathering

Agenda

review of planned outcomes for session

Role Development and Clarification

job descriptions
skills checklist
reference manual
general summary sheet

The Law of the Land

historical perspective
LPN standards of practice
interpretation of delegation and supervision of LPNs

Assessment or Data Gathering: Which Is It?

defining the process
documentation policies
putting it all together

Questions and Answers

"Any discussion relating to LPNs must begin with certain assumptions, i.e., that nursing education, the overall supervision of nursing personnel... and patient care planning are primarily the responsibility of the RN. This does not mean that RNs should not seek, and LPNs should not provide, input and participation in these areas."

Judy Domning, Executive Director, Minnesota LPN Association

FOUR PS OF SUCCESSFUL TEAMWORK

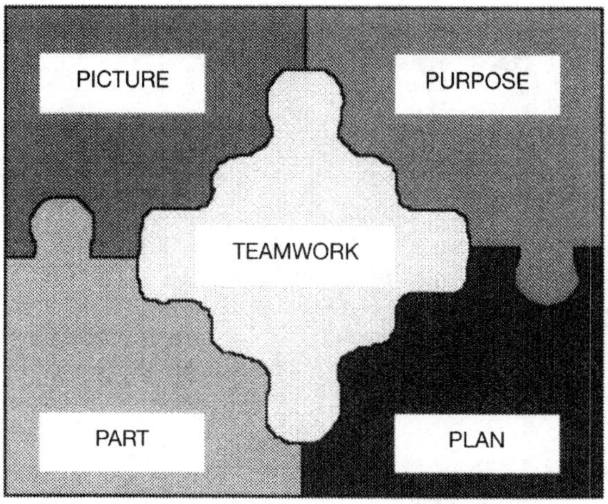

RESULTS-ORIENTED OUTCOMES:

With Application of Skills and Learning

1. Patient care quality and outcomes are maintained (or improved) because the team completes work and coordinates the care of the hematology and oncology patients in an effective and efficient manner, clear on the roles and expectations held by members of the team regarding their work performance and behavior.
2. Conflicts, problems, and mistakes are discussed respectfully, with each member working toward agreed-on outcomes, while involved in improving systems and performance.

PROPOSED OUTCOMES FOR THE DAY:

At the end of this facilitated session, you will be able to

- Describe your team's purpose, those you serve, the members of the team, and the most significant accomplishments you plan to achieve
- Relate the stages of team development and characteristics of effective teams to your own team
- Define professional stereotyping and how the prejudice it engenders can be overcome
- Begin to define the roles of team members
- Choose a method of conflict resolution based on outcomes

"Never doubt that a group of thoughtful, committed people can change the world; indeed it is the only thing that ever has."

Margaret Mead

NO LAND IN SIGHT!

PROFESSIONAL NURSES *SURVIVING* CHANGE

presented by

HANSTEN & WASHBURN

RUTH HANSTEN, RN, MBA, AND MARILYNN WASHBURN, RN, MA

DAY ONE AGENDA: 8:30–3:30 PM

Outcomes for the Workshop

What's Happening at Your Medical Center?

ENDINGS: LEAVING SHORE

Strategies for Navigating the Endings

Let go of behaviors and ideas that will no longer be helpful in the new model of care delivery

NEUTRAL ZONE: DROWN PROOFING

Life-Saving Measures for Handling Change

Apply personal strategies for successful transitions, with emphasis on personal values and the mission of ABC

Increase involvement in transition process through meaningful participation

continues

BEGINNINGS: MAKING THE CHANGE

Navigating Change: Tools for Change Management
Integrate the Four Ps of Success (Purpose, Picture, Part, Plan)
Assess personal strategies for managing change and utilization of tools presented

LUNCH

CLARIFICATION OF ROLES AND JOB DESCRIPTIONS

Clarify the part each person will play in teams at ABC
Professional Stereotyping

WHEN IS MY LICENSE ON THE LINE?

Interpret the nursing laws as they relate to delegation and supervision of team members

KNOWLEDGE AS YOUR SOURCE OF POWER: IDENTIFYING LANDMARKS

Apply the four rights of delegation (person, task, communication, and feedback)
Define accountability
Assess competency of team members

EVALUATION AND SUMMARY OF DAY ONE

PLANNED OUTCOMES FOR DAY ONE AND BEYOND

Long-Term Results

1. Patient outcomes/quality of care will be maintained or improved due to enhanced skills and strategies to improve teamwork and performance of staff.
2. Personal satisfaction will be improved due to an expanded understanding of team member roles and methods by which managers can facilitate employee accountability.
3. Be able to problem solve unit issues effectively.
4. The goals of your unit redesign will be achieved.

*****

Today's Outcomes

- **Let go of behaviors** that will no longer be helpful in the new model of care.
- Apply **personal strategies** for successful transitions, with emphasis on personal values and the mission of ABC.
- Increase involvement in the transition process through **meaningful participation.**
- Integrate the **Four Ps of Success** (Purpose, Picture, Part, Plan).
- Assess personal strategies for **managing change** and utilization of tools presented.
- **Clarify the part** that each person will play in teams at ABC.
- Reduce **Professional Stereotyping.**
- Interpret the **nursing laws** as they relate to delegation and supervision of team members.
- Apply the **four rights of delegation** (person, task, communication, and feedback).
- Define **accountability.**
- Assess **competency** of team members.

"If someone asks what a human being ought to devote the maximum of his time to, I would say training. Train more than you sleep.

Master Masutatsu Oyama (1979)

LAND IN SIGHT!

PROFESSIONAL NURSES
***LEADING* CHANGE**

presented by:

HANSTEN & WASHBURN

RUTH HANSTEN, RN, MBA, AND MARILYNN WASHBURN, RN, MA

DAY TWO AGENDA: 8:30–3:30 PM

Making Professional Practice Effective and Visible: Determining the Destination

Describe importance of the RN role using the PTA Model (Professional, Technical, Amenities)
Plan assignments based on outcomes rather than tasks

Developing Accountability: Charting the Course

Create a climate of positive motivation
Assertively communicate to team members regarding a problem (skill-building session)
Select the appropriate method for resolving conflict based on the cost and benefits
Utilize reciprocal feedback to develop the performance of fellow team members

LUNCH

Staying the Course

Approach problem solving from a positive view and incorporate outcomes based communication and reciprocal feedback (Experiential Exercises)

Workout Session

Identifying solutions for current problems identified by participants

Evaluation and Summary of Day Two

continues

Proposed Outcomes for Day Two

At the end of this workshop, the RN will be able to

- Describe the **importance of the RN role** using the PTA Model (Professional, Technical, Amenities)
- **Plan assignments** based on outcomes rather than tasks
- Create a climate of **positive motivation**
- **Assertively communicate** to team members regarding a problem
- Select the appropriate method for **resolving conflict** based on the cost and benefits of your choice
- Utilize **reciprocal feedback** to develop the performance of fellow team members
- Approach **problem solving** from a positive view and incorporate outcomes based communication and reciprocal feedback
- **Create solutions** for current problems identified by participants

"Let whoever is in charge keep this simple question in her head (NOT, how can I always do this right thing myself, but) how can I provide for this right thing always to be done?"

Florence Nightingale

NO LAND IN SIGHT!

MANAGERS SURVIVING AND THRIVING THROUGH CHANGE

presented by

RUTH HANSTEN, RN, MBA, AND MARILYNN WASHBURN, RN, MA

Your Medical Center

Date

8:30 AM–3:30 PM

GETTING STARTED

Review of Planned Outcomes for Day
Clarifying Expectations
What Works and What Doesn't

LIFE IN THE FAST LANE OF CHANGE

A Process of Change
Assessment Findings to Date
The Wall of Resistance

9:45-10:00 **BREAK**

SURVIVAL TOOLS

The Four Cs, The Four Ps
Role/Expectation Clarifications, Terms of Agreement
Managerial Support for Outcomes and Professional Practice
Performance/Outcomes Agreements for Enhanced Accountability

11:30–12:30: **LUNCH**

LAND IN SIGHT! MANAGERS LEADING CHANGE

Managerial Rounds
Reciprocal Feedback Process
Positive Problem Solving

2:00–2:15 **BREAK**

STAYING THE COURSE

Summary Discussion of Your Issues/Evaluation

"It is a terrible thing to look over your shoulder when trying to lead—and find no one there." Franklin Delano Roosevelt

PLANNED OUTCOMES FOR THE MANAGER WORKSHOP

Long-Term Results

1. Patient outcomes/quality of care will be maintained or improved due to enhanced skills and strategies to improve climate and performance used by managerial staff.
2. Employee and personal satisfaction will be improved due to an expanded understanding of managerial roles and methods by which managers can facilitate employee accountability.
3. The goals of your redesign will be achieved.

Today

1. Clarify expectations of management.
2. Identify the resistance of the staff.
3. Discuss proven tools and strategies for working with change and increasing performance accountability.
4. Apply the concept of managerial rounds in a standardized fashion.

*****

The Picture:

The Purpose:

The Plan:

My Part:

Hansten & Washburn

206-842-1189 or 0912

TRAINING THE TRAINER

8:00–8:45
Overview of the Project and Process
Training Activity Team

8:45–9:00
Discussion of Outcomes for the Day

9:00–9:30
Setting the Stage

9:30–9:45 Break

9:45–12:00
Developing the Relationship
The Learning Cycle
Principles of Clinical Training

12:00 –12:30 Lunch

12:30–1:15
Identified Competencies
Evaluation Process
Training Activity Team

1:15–2:00
Service Parameters
Training Activity Team

2:00–2:15 Break

2:15–4:00
Developing Accountability
Ensuring Success

"In a time of drastic change it is the learners who will inherit the future."
Eric Hoffer

PRECEPTOR TRAINING OUTCOMES

Overarching Outcome

As a result of attending this workshop, the preceptor will be able to

Facilitate the successful orientation and development of team members at ABC Medical Center.

Supporting Outcomes:

- Differentiate between content to be taught and what is extraneous information.
- Follow the three phases of developing a preceptor/orientee relationship.
- Apply principles of adult learning to the process of precepting.
- Describe a working definition of accountability that is mutually acceptable.
- Develop accountability in the orientee through application of reciprocal feedback and reinforcement communication.
- Apply methods of evaluating progress of the orientee to determine completion of orientation.

"The educator must above all understand how to wait;
to reckon all effects in the light of the future, not of the present."

Ellen Key

Timing Is Everything

It's a judgment call as to whether time or money wins out in the battle for balancing resources. When undertaking the support of a major redesign project, the intent is usually to save money. Organizational leaders become very uncomfortable when they see their targeted savings being consumed by the costs of education and training to make the change happen. In an effort to "save money," the decision is often made to shorten training and to "get it done as quickly as possible." One of our most difficult concepts that we convey is the truth we have experienced: A quick approach is more costly in the long run in terms of decreased productivity and increased turnover of personnel.

One approach that we have found to be most successful is that of a two-day session involving the leaders of the team. Typically, these are the RNs of a care delivery team, and often they have not been accustomed to working as leaders of other personnel. Their anxiety is high, and their resistance strong, and a four- to eight-hour session is not going to be enough to overcome these barriers. When two days are devoted to the process (see the "No Land in Sight" agenda for RNs in tool #25), staff have the opportunity to raise concerns and voice criticisms during the first day. Problems are often described from an outsider perspective, and there is little if any ownership in the resolution of identified problems.

With a night to "sleep on it," the participants come back the next day with a different attitude, willing and able to learn and apply the leadership strategies of communication, supervision, feedback, and problem solving. Yesterday's problems now belong to them, and they are active in seeking solutions. Energy is created, and enthusiasm replaces the concern of the day before. There is no doubt that this a large investment in resources, but the dividends are evident when supported by continuous follow-up on the units and within the departments.

Getting Started

To get everything started and to make the expectations understood, it is helpful to clarify the roles of the trainer/educator/facilitator and the participants. Unless this is a very didactic presentation (which seldom works), the expectations of participant involvement should be clearly spelled out. Simply written on a flip chart, we have found the following to be most effective:

As Facilitator

- to clarify: information the participants share that may be misunderstood
- to keep on track: to ensure progress toward the planned outcomes for the session
- to protect: creating a supportive environment in which all opinions can be shared without risk

As Participant

- to be honest: straightforward and direct in sharing thoughts and concerns
- to participate: this will be the only way to increase the personal value of the session on an individual basis
- to have fun: learning and sharing should be a positive experience, not one that has to be endured!

Although these are basic and rather simplistic, they cover the main points and get everyone on the same page of understanding accepted behaviors. Sometimes, organizations go a little further in developing "ground rules" for further expectations of detailed behavior.

Tool #26: Ground Rules: An Illustration MultiCare Medical Center, Tacoma, Washington

After the first year, we found that ground rules were essential to support group process. Setting expectations around group performance was an effective forum for discussion. Groups have normal developmental stages. We used Tuckman's work (refer to the discussion of tool #43 for more information on Tuckman's theory) to describe the roller coaster that the group would experience. The ground rules were used primarily in the storming stage to assist the group in regaining control. The rules were defined by the task force and enforced by each member, but in reality, the project support team enforced the rules.

Ground Rules: An Illustration

Participation	*Leadership*	*Consensus and Decision Making*	*Resetting Priorities*	*Parking Lot and Workload*
Be on time and be present	Take accountability for participation	Record all decisions	Park the "issue of the moment"	Ideas in parking lot will be reviewed before end of task force
Explore and clarify rather than debate or defend	Keep coworkers informed	Present position in logical and unemotional manner	Items not supporting scope of work will be "parked"	Park your personal agendas
Assignments are completed on items	Support the efforts of the group	Agree on recommendations —agreements will not be altered		
Initiate discussion	Provide constructive evaluation of process at regular intervals	Decisions are data-driven and support principles, vision, and scope		
Equal participation from all members—watch "air time"	Accept accountability for team role	Resolve difference creatively		
Deal with disruptions in a constructive manner: seek clarification, listen, provide feedback	Acknowledge movement toward recommendations	"Sell" recommendations to staff, administration, and Ops Team		
Seek clarification as needed	Celebrate successes			
Park the BMW at the door	Manage your personal transition			

Courtesy of MultiCare Medical Center, Tacoma, Washington.

Another hospital we had the opportunity to work with recognized the need to clarify behavior among the managers. The monthly meetings they had been having were not thought to be too effective; in fact, most thought that they were a waste of time with much of the real discussion taking place after the meeting. When the behaviors were named, the causes of these perceptions were clear. Members were not consistently attending, and of those who were, not all were prepared. Some chose to remain silent and voice loud objections outside of the meeting, whereas others were somewhat boisterous and interrupted frequently. As a result, discussion was disorganized and often one-sided. It was clear that some correction was needed.

Working together, the group members drafted a list of desired outcomes for any management meeting and then identified the behaviors that would get them there. Their covenants are included here as an excellent template for your consideration. Although these statements may appear rather basic in nature, until you have named them and obtained the support of all team members, you may find that your team is not as functional as it could be.

Tool #27: Covenants for Conducting Management Council

We agree to treat our team and all its members with respect by

1. Giving the speaker/presenter—whoever has the floor—our undivided attention.
2. Remembering that only one person speaks at a time and that person does so at the recognition of the Chair or person making a presentation.
3. Sharing the responsibility for the management meeting among all members of the group. Every member is responsible for the success of our meetings.
4. Dealing with one another in an honest, straightforward, and direct manner.
5. Not withholding significant input into our team processes of discussion, problem solving, and decision making. It will be our mutual assumption that if we have something significant to say it will be said in our management meeting rather than after our meeting adjourns.
6. Supporting the decisions that are made by the team and supporting one another in the process of making those decisions.
7. Agreeing to disagree with mutual respect.
8. Seeking to be specific in our communication and avoid generalities.
9. Seeking to speak for one's own self rather than others in the group.
10. Dealing with each other with a generous spirit, avoiding unnecessary criticism/sniping. Letting others know when we are offended.
11. By practicing our customer relations standards with each other.

Anonymous.

CHANGE MANAGEMENT

Once again, we learn best from a story, this one from Taoist origin:

▼

It was in the days of the great chariot races. The praying mantis had enjoyed a successful existence, living his own life near the roadside. One day he ventured out onto the dusty road and heard a rumbling in the distance. The ground began to shake, and he could see a cloud of dust in the distance. As the chariot drew near, the praying mantis thought to himself, "How shall I handle this?" He assumed his most fierce position, planting his feet firmly in the dirt and looking angrily at the oncoming chariot. As the chariot ran over him, he had one last thought, "What did I do wrong?"

▲

Three lessons can be learned from the plight of the praying mantis:

1. He waited too long to act.
2. He took the wrong action.
3. He relied more on past experience than current reality.

This simple story sums up the many different aspects of change, from resistance to the ultimate errors made from that behavior. We have discussed assessing that resistance in Section One (see tool #2). It is essential to address the issue of change and to be aware of the impact it will have on any new proposal, no matter how beneficial the outcome might be.

Change as a Process

Adults do very well with models, finding that a visual aid often clarifies a nebulous concept. We have found the work of William Bridges (1991) to be exceptionally useful and have referred to his ideas periodically throughout this book. His approach to change as a three-part process of transition emphasizes the idea that change is not cumulative but requires the ending of something (e.g., behavior, practice, task performance, lifestyle). This is very important to help staff who see their role changes as role enlargement, which will be impossible because "there's no time to do it all."

We remind you to refer to tool #5 in Section One, based on this process.

The Emotional Side of Things

▼

Change is not made without inconvenience, even from worse to better.
Richard Hooker

▲

Bridges's model identifies behaviors and is definitely emotionally based. It is impossible to separate the two, even though we have had a few groups (usually managers) insist that this is feasible. One group raised the argument that there are intellectually based decisions and actions that are separate from emotionally based behavior and wanted to focus on promoting the intellectual side while eliminating the emotional component. This would spark an interesting discussion, one that we believe to be of questionable benefit. If you can find a way to have employees leave their emotions in the parking lot before they enter work, we would submit that the care provided by these individuals would be "heartless" indeed and certainly not desirable. Because we are not of Vulcan descent, our actions do have an emotional connection, and it then becomes necessary to address those feelings in a manner that makes sense. We believe the following three phases of Bridges's model do just that. (Bridges, 1991, pp. 20, 34, 50)

- **Ending:** *All changes, even the most longed for, have their melancholy; for what we leave behind is part of ourselves; we must die to one life before we can enter another.* (Anatole France) Behaviors often seen during this phase include initial suspicion, uncertainty, and resistance. Staff are reluctant to support the change, unsure of "what's in it for them" and how they will be affected. Their approach is from a selfish perspective, and they will need repeated opportunities for direct communication and involvement.
- **Neutral zone**: *It's not so much that we are afraid of change or so in love with the old ways, but it's that place in between that we fear. . . . It's like being between trapezes. It's Linus when his blanket is in the dryer. There's nothing to hold on to.* (Marilyn Ferguson) Behaviors during this time include anxiety, decreasing effectiveness, confusion, frustration, polarization of groups, and creativity. This is a very intense, high-energy time, and the challenge will be to direct that energy into positive actions that are creative and supportive of the project and not to allow confusion and frustration to take the lead in a negative sense.
- **Beginning:** *Beginnings are always messy.* (John Galsworthy) Once people have come through the above two phases, recognizing what is ending for them and the support they have to make it happen, they will be ready to actively participate in integrating the change into the day-to-day activity of the organization. To do this effectively, according to William Bridges, they will need to have the "four Ps" of the change clearly understood. (Bridges, 1991, chapters 1–4)

  1. PURPOSE behind the outcome
  2. PICTURE of how the outcome will look
  3. PLAN how the outcome will be achieved
  4. PART that each person will play

Tool #28: The Four Ps of Successful Change

PURPOSE

WHY is change being planned?
WHAT OUTCOMES do you intend to achieve?

PICTURE

Paint a PICTURE of how the outcome will look, feel, taste, smell, sound. What spells SUCCESS?

PLAN

Develop and lay out a detailed PLAN, step by step, with schedules.

PART

Determine what PART each person will play in the plan, clarifying roles repeatedly.

CLARIFYING ROLES

OK, so you have gone "live" on your first pilot unit or your first restructured department. Freshly written job descriptions are hot off the press, and everyone is ready (sort of) to take on a new life. But all is not as it should be or was planned. Patient complaints are up, morale is down—some of your key staff members are complaining of the overwhelming workload and putting in too much overtime. They have also noted that not everyone is doing his share. What's happening?

▼

In this newly designed world, we have multiskilled and multitasked to the point of ambiguity. To maximize the members of the team, you have "enhanced" roles, often to the point of confusion. If your situation looks like this: *everyone* can do the task, *anybody* should, *somebody* will; how come *nobody* does?

▲

Tim Porter-O'Grady reminds us that *"ambiguity of roles and expectations is the enemy of successful empowerment."* (Porter-O'Grady, 1996) Lack of clarity of who does what often leads to a chaotic and dysfunctional department. It is no different than if you had not restructured; the premise is the same: Clearly defined roles will help to ensure a successfully coordinated work effort that is satisfying for patients and staff alike. Overlap of skills is great and will certainly add to the flexibility and efficiency of the unit but only if everyone is clear about determining who will be primarily responsible for the performance of a given task.

Some Basic Terms in Role Theory (MacLeod and Sella, 1992)

- role: the expected and actual behaviors associated with a position
- role development: when a new position is established
- role socialization: process by which a person becomes accustomed to the position
- role ambiguity: lack of clarity of role expectations
- role stress and strain: results of role ambiguity

In our work, we have found that performance weaknesses generally have four distinct causes:

- The individual does not know what is expected of her.
- The individual has not received any feedback regarding performance.
- The individual needs additional education/information to do the job.
- The individual needs additional supervision to support her performance.

The first cause, unclear expectations, is easily identified but requires continued effort with the entire team to iron out the overlaps and go on line with personal expectations of each other.

▼
The operational definition of anger is unmet expectations.
▲

Think about it. If you expect someone to do something and they don't follow through, you are left feeling angry and frustrated, even if you never shared your expectation in the first place.

When we change the traditional roles of the team, we step away from the norm, but we don't necessarily let go of time-honored expectations. If Sally, the housekeeper, has taken a break at 9 AM for the past 10 years in her role as housekeeper, she will continue to expect that routine structure even though her role is now expanded to that of a service associate who must respond to patients' needs as well as the needs of the unit. She *expects* the system to support a time-honored practice, despite the change in her role, which now demands a more flexible worker who is available at the demanding time of 9 AM for early morning discharges. Meanwhile, Sally's coworkers expect Sally to respond to the needs of the unit and to be flexible, delaying her break (maybe not even taking it!) to meet the demands of the team. Unspoken, and not clarified, both Sally and her team members will be frustrated.

How do you solve this dilemma? Job descriptions and skills checklists are a good place to start. It's amazing how many of us only read our own job description, and then only during the annual evaluation. Every member of the team should review ALL the job descriptions for the entire team and be familiar with the tasks on the skills checklists. Take these papers out, make them available for everyone to review, and then hold staff meetings to discuss them. Comparison lists, outlining who does what, are also helpful visual aids. This will create a baseline understanding of the tasks to be done, and by whom, and offers a useful roadmap for sorting out who does what.

Valley Medical Center, Renton, Washington, has spent a good deal of time creating the most comprehensive scope of practice list that we have seen to date. As they began to implement a "blended" unit based staff, adding care providers such as physical therapists and respiratory therapists to the core staffing plan, clearly delineating roles and responsibilities became a critical task. To provide a reference and a foundation for practice, the Nursing Scope of Practice document was revised to include all direct bedside care providers.

The goals of this project were to

- ensure compliance with existing regulatory standards and laws
- define generic responsibilities
- set maximum practice levels

- define tasks in which additional education and skill demonstration were required
- create an assessable and easily understandable reference for the staff

The Patient Care Services Scope of Practice was developed in draft form by the managers with the skillful facilitation of Sheila Ball, RN, MBA, and then was disseminated to staff members for comment and additions. It continues to evolve as practice issues arise.

Tool #29: Valley Medical Center Patient Care Services Direct Caregiver Scope of Practice

X = Approved   – = Not approved   X with comment = Approved after education and skill demonstration or with exceptions

GENERIC TASKS	RN	LPN	Pharmacist	Physical Therapist	Occupational Therapist	Respiratory Therapist	Dietitian	Social Worker	PTA/COTA	PCA/US	PCA/Phlebot.	Psych Tech	Housekeeper
Answer call light	X	X	X	X	X	X	X	X	X	X	X	X	X
Assist with transfer, ambulation	X	X	X	X	X	X	X	X	X	X	X	X	X
Pass meal trays	X	X	X	X	X	X	X	X	X	X	X	X	X
Answer telephones	X	X	X	X	X	X	X	X	X	X	X	X	X
Initiate CPR	X	X	X	X	X	X	X	X	X	X	X	X	X
Obtain emergency assistance	X	X	X	X	X	X	X	X	X	X	X	X	X
Report significant observations to Team Leader (*See attached list)	X	X	X	X	X	X	X	X	X	X	X	X	X
Transport equipment, patients, specimens	X	X	X	X	X	X	X	X	X	X	X	X	X
Assist with room cleaning, bed making	X	X	X	X	X	X	X	X	X	X	X	X	X
Protect confidentiality and other patient rights	X	X	X	X	X	X	X	X	X	X	X	X	X
Witness consents	X	X	X	X	X	X	X	X	X	X	X	X	X
Access Phamis	X	X	X	X	X	X	X	X	X	X	X	X	X
Assist with measurement of weight, height	X	X	X	X	X	X	X	X	X	X	X	X	X
BSP	X	X	X	X	X	X	X	X	X	X	X	X	X
Postmortem care and transport	X	X	X	X	X	X	X	X	X	X	X	X	X
Determine and record I&O	X	X	X	X	X	X	X	X	X	X	X	X	X

	RN	LPN	Pharmacist	Physical Therapist	Occupational Therapist	Respiratory Therapist	Dietitian	Social Worker	PTA/COTA	PCA/US	PCA/Phlebot.	Psych Tech	Housekeeper
ASSESSMENT													
Admission assessment	X	History only	–	–	–	–	–	–	–	–	–	–	–
Nutritional, functional, suspected abuse screen	X	–	–	–	–	–	–	–	–	–	–	–	–
Shift assessment	X	X	–	–	1B only	–	–	1B only	1B only	–	–	X	–
Response to therapy	X	X	X	X	X	X	X	X	–	–	–	X	–
Functional assessment	–	–	–	X	X	–	–	–	–	–	–	–	–
Nutritional assessment	–	–	–	–	–	–	X	–	–	–	–	–	–
Psychosocial/suspected abuse assessment	1B only	–	–	–	–	–	–	X	–	–	–	X	–
Breath sounds	X	X	–	–	–		–	–	–	–	–	–	–
Heart sounds	X	X	–	–	–	–	–	–	–	–	–	–	–
Bowel sounds	X	X	–	–	–	–	–	–	–	–	–	–	–
Neuro signs	X	X	–	–	–	–	–	–	–	–	–	X	–
Hemodialysis, shunt assessment	X	X	–	–	–	–	–	–	–	–	–	–	–
Neurovascular assessment	X	X	–	X	–	–	–	–	X	X	X	X	–
Vital signs	X	X	X	X	X	X	–	–	X	X	X	X	–
Pronouncing patient's death (MD only)	–	–	–	–	–	–	–	–	–	–	–	–	–
PLANNING													
Initiates problem on Patient Problem List	X	X after conferring with RN	X	X	X	X	X	X	–	–	–	X after conferring with RN	–
Initiates Plan of Care	X	X only after conferring with RN	X	X	X	X	X	X	–	–	–	X after conferring with RN	–

continues

	RN	*LPN*	*Pharmacist*	*Physical Therapist*	*Occupational Therapist*	*Respiratory Therapist*	*Dietitian*	*Social Worker*	*PTA/COTA*	*PCA/US*	*PCA/Phlebot.*	*Psych Tech*	*Housekeeper*
Evaluates progress toward outcomes	X	–	X	X	X	X	X	X	–	–	–	–	–
INTERVENTIONS													
MEDICATIONS:													
Oral	X	X	X	–	–	Resp. drugs only	–	–	–	–	–	–	–
Subcutaneous	X	X	X	–	–	–	–	–	–	–	–	–	–
IM	X	X	X	–	–	–	–	–	–	–	–	–	–
Intradermal	X	X	X	–	–	–	–	–	–	–	–	–	–
Z Track	X	X	X	–	–	–	–	–	–	–	–	–	–
Suppository	X	X	X	–	–	–	–	–	–	–	–	–	–
Epidural	X Certified	–	X Certified	–	–	–	–	–	–	–	–	–	–
Ophthalmic	X	X	X	–	–	–	–	–	–	–	–	–	–
Topical	X	X	X	X	–	–	–	–	–	X	X	–	–
Aerosol	X	–	X	–	–	X	–	–	–	–	–	–	–
Installation of meds into artificial airways	X	–	X	–	–	X	–	–	–	–	–	–	–
Administration of investigatory/experimental drugs	X	May assist RN	X	–	–	–	–	–	–	–	–	–	–
Administration of drugs during code	X	–	X	–	–	–	–	–	–	–	–	–	–
IV solutions	X Chemo-therapy: Certified RN only	X Except chemo & thrombolytics, Iron, dextran, insulin, vitamin K, urokinase, dopamine, dolbutamine	X	–	–	–	–	–	–	–	–	–	–

	RN	LPN	Pharmacist	Physical Therapist	Occupational Therapist	Respiratory Therapist	Dietitian	Social Worker	PTA/COTA	PCA/US	PCA/Phlebot.	Psych Tech	Housekeeper
IV push meds: *LPN Exceptions:* Beta blockers, Pronestyl Verapamil, Epinephrine Magnesium, Atropine Diltiazem, Iron dextran Lidocaine, Chemotherapeutics Bretylium, Digitalis Adenosine, Urokinase	X	X See exceptions	X	–	–	–	–	–	–	–	–	–	–
IV MANAGEMENT													
Insertion of a peripheral IV	X	X	X	–	–	X	–	–	–	–	–	–	–
Discontinuation of peripheral line	X	X	X	X	X	X	–	–	X	X	X	–	–
Discontinuation of central line	X Certified RN only	–	–	–	–	–	–	–	–	–	–	–	–
Discontinuation of epidural	X Certified RN only	–	–	–	–	–	–	–	–	–	–	–	–
Site assessment, tubing changes	X	X	X	–	–	X	–	–	–	–	–	–	–
Central line dressings	X	–	–	–	–	–	–	–	–	–	–	–	–
Declotting of external venous access device	X Certified RN only	–	–	–	–	–	–	–	–	–	–	–	–
Access of internal port	X Certified RN only	–	–	–	–	–	–	–	–	–	–	–	–
Patient controlled analgesics	X	X	X	–	–	–	–	–	–	–	–	–	–
Femoral lines/sheaths	X	CC only											
BLOOD													
Initiation of blood/blood products	X	X	X	–	–	–	–	–	–	–	–	–	–
Monitoring	X	X	X	–	–	–	–	–	–	–	–	–	–

continues

	RN	LPN	Pharmacist	Physical Therapist	Occupational Therapist	Respiratory Therapist	Dietitian	Social Worker	PTA/COTA	PCA/US	PCA/Phlebot.	Psych Tech	Housekeeper
Drawing T&CM sample	X	X	X	–	–	X	–	–	–	X	X	–	–
Verification of Blood Request Form	X	–	X	–	–	–	–	–	–	–	–	–	–
TUBES/DRAINS													
NG/Salem Sump insertion	X	X Certified LPN only	–	–	–	X	–	–	–	–	–	–	–
Manipulation	X	X Certified RN only	–	–	–	X	–	–	–	–	–	–	–
Discontinuation	X	X	–	–	–	X	–	–	–	–	–	–	–
Irrigation	X	X	–	–	–	X	–	–	–	–	–	–	–
Feeding tube insertion (Radiologist only, except in Critical Care where non-stylet-type tube is used)	–	–	–	–	–	–	–	–	–	–	–	–	–
Manipulation	X	–	–	–	–	–	–	–	–	–	–	–	–
Discontinuation	X	X	–	–	–	X	–	–	–	–	–	–	–
Instillation of feeding/pump management	X	X	–	X	X	X	X	–	–	–	–	–	–
Irrigation	X	X	–	X	X	X	–	–	–	–	–	–	–
Gastrostomy tube reinsertion (MD only)	–	–	–	–	–	–	–	–	–	–	–	–	–
Foley/straight catheters													
Insertion	X	X	–	–	–	–	–	–	–	X Certified	–	–	–
Monitoring	X	X	–	–	–	–	–	–	–	X	X	–	–
Discontinuation	X	X	–	X	X	–	–	–	–	X	X	–	–
Irrigation	X	X	–	X	X	–	–	–	–	–	–	–	–
Drains													
Monitoring	X	X	X	X	X	X	–	–	–	X	X	–	–
Removal	X	X	–	–	–	–	–	–	–	–	–	–	–

	RN	LPN	Pharmacist	Physical Therapist	Occupational Therapist	Respiratory Therapist	Dietitian	Social Worker	PTA/COTA	PCA/US	PCA/Phlebot.	Psych Tech	Housekeeper
Chest tubes													
Monitoring	X	X	–	–	–	X	–	–	–	–	–	–	–
Assisting with insertion	X	X	–	–	–	X	–	–	X	X	X	–	–
Insertion/Discontinuation (MD only)	–	–	–	–	–	–	–	–	–	–	–	–	–
CAPD	X Certified	X Certified	–	–	–	–	–	–	–	–	–	–	–
PULMONARY CARE													
Insertion of airways	X	X	–	–	–	X	–	–	–	ED only	–	–	–
Oral suctioning	X	X	–	X	X	X	–	–	–	X	X	–	–
NT suctioning	X	–	–	–	–	X	–	–	–	–	–	–	–
Oxygen monitoring	X	X	–	–	–	X	–	–	–	X	X	–	–
Pulmonary toilet	X	X	–	–	–	X	–	–	–	–	–	–	–
Ventilator management	CC only	–	–	–	–	X	–	–	–	–	–	–	–
Changing/replacing tracheotomy	CC only	–	–	–	–	X	–	–	–	–	–	–	–
Endotracheal intubation	–	–	–	–	–	X	–	–	–	–	–	–	–
Nebulizer treatments	X	X	X	–	–	X	–	–	–	–	–	–	–
Incentive spirometry	X	X	X	–	–	X	–	–	–	X	X	–	–
Oximetry	X	X	–	–	–	X	–	–	–	X	X	–	–
TREATMENTS													
Simple dressing change	X	X	–	X	X	X	–	–	–	X	X	X	–
Complex dressing changes	X	X	–	X	–	–	–	–	–	ED only	–	–	–
Wound irrigations	X	X	–	X	–	–	–	–	–	ED only	–	–	–
Suture/clip removal	X	X (abd. wound after RN assess)	–	–	–	–	–	–	–	ED only	–	–	–
Enemas/colostomy care	X	X	X	X	X	X	–	–	X	X	X	–	–

continues

	RN	*LPN*	*Pharmacist*	*Physical Therapist*	*Occupational Therapist*	*Respiratory Therapist*	*Dietitian*	*Social Worker*	*PTA/COTA*	*PCA/US*	*PCA/Phlebot.*	*Psych Tech*	*Housekeeper*
Sitz baths	X	X	–	–	–	–	–	–	–	X	X	–	–
Packing removal	X	X	–	X	–	–	–	–	X	–	–	–	–
ACTIVITIES OF DAILY LIVING													
Bathing	X	X	X	X	X	X	–	–	X	X	X	X	–
Dressing	X	X	X	X	X	X	–	–	X	X	X	X	–
Feeding	X	X	X	X	X	X	X	–	X	X	X	X	–
Ambulation	X	X	X	X	X	X	–	–	X	X	X	X	–
Oral hygiene	X	X	X	X	X	X	X	–	X	X	X	X	–
Positioning	X	X	X	X	X	X	–	–	X	X	X	X	–
Toileting	X	X	X	X	X	X	X	X	X	X	X	X	–
EQUIPMENT USE													
Bed scale	X	X	–	–	–	–	–	–		X	X	–	–
Telemetry	X	X	–	–	–	X	–	–	–	X Certified	X Certified	–	–
IV pumps	X	X	X	–	–	X	–	–	–	–	–	–	–
Syringe pump	X	X	X	–	–	–	–	–	–	–	–	–	–
Wheelchairs, walkers, canes	X	X	X	X	X	–	–	–	X	X	X	X	(should do)
Crutches	X	X	–	X	X	–	–	–	X	X	X	X	–
Overbed frame	X	X	X	X	X	–	–	–	X	X	X	X	–
Traction, CPM	X	X	X	X	X	X	–	–	X	X	X	–	–
Thermal applications (K-pad, ice bags, etc.)	X	X	X	X	X	X	–	–	X	X	X	X	–
Child equipment: crib, crib bubble, high chair	X	X	–	–	–	X	–	–	–	X	X	–	–
Restraints	X	X	X	X	X	X	–	–	X	X	X	X	–
LABORATORY TESTING													
Specimen collection	X	X	X	X	X	X	–	–	X	X	X	–	–

	RN	LPN	Pharmacist	Physical Therapist	Occupational Therapist	Respiratory Therapist	Dietitian	Social Worker	PTA/COTA	PCA/US	PCA/Phlebot.	Psych Tech	Housekeeper
Chemstrips	X	X	X	–	–	X	–	–	–	X	X	X	–
Guaiac	X	X	X	X	X	X	–	–	X	X	X	X	–
Hemastik	X	X	X	–	–	X	–	–	–	X	X	X	–
ABG	Certified RN only	–	–	–	–	X	–	–	–	–	–	–	–
Venipuncture	X	X	X	–	–	X	–	–	–	Certified only	X	–	–
Urine screens/pregnancy tests	ED only	ED only	–	–	–	–	–	–	–	ED only	–	–	–
Pediatric urine collection with diapers	X	X	–	–	–	–	–	–	–	–	–	–	–
Specific gravity	X	X	–	–	–	–	–	–	–	X	X	–	–
PATIENT EDUCATION													
Standardized instructions	X	X	X	X	X	X	X	X	–	–	–	–	–
Nonstandard instructions	X	–	X	X	X	X	X	X	–	–	–	–	–
Discharge summary	X	X in collab. with RN	–	X	X	–	–	X	–	–	–	X (RN cosign)	–
DOCUMENTS													
Documentation of care provided	X	X	X	X	X	X	X	X	X	X	X	X	X
HIV consents	Certified RN only	–	–	–	–	–	–	Certified only	–	–	–	–	–
Telephone/verbal orders	X	–	X	X	X	X	X	–	–	–	–	–	–
Receiving telephone critical lab reports	X	–	X	–	–	–	–	–	–	–	–	–	–
Assistance with advance directives	–	–	–	–	–	–	–	X	–	–	–	–	–

Courtesy of Valley Medical Center, Renton, Washington.

REPORTABLE OBSERVATIONS

Recognizes and reports the following significant signs and symptoms and reports to Team Leader.

ADULT PATIENT

a. BP: Systolic above 150 or below 100
Diastolic above 90

b. Temperature above 99 degrees or below 97.

c. Pulse above 100 or below 60.

d. Respirations above 24 or below 16.

e. Postural blood pressure change of more than 10 or rise in pulse rate of 20.

f. Any nausea or emesis.

g. Any change in level of consciousness or mobility.

h. Any rash, reddened skin, abrasion, skin tear, decubitus, bruising, swelling in extremities or IV site, or abdominal distention.

i. Any low IV or tube feeding bag (less than 50 cc).

j. Any problem with chewing, swallowing, or poor dietary intake.

k. Any change in skin color, moistness, pallor, cyanosis, diaphoresis.

l. Any change in breathing pattern, shortness of breath, apnea.

m. Any complaint of discomfort or pain.

n. Any wound drainage.

o. Any change in urination: frequency, pain, cloudy, foul-smelling, brownish or red color, amount less than 250 cc in a shift.

p. Any change in stool; diarrhea, constipation, tarry or bloody, results of guaiac testing.

q. Any significant change in patient or family behavior or emotional status.

r. Rings or other jewelry that is fitting too tightly.

s. Jagged toenails—**do not** attempt to trim.

t. Any nose bleed.

u. Any report of dizziness or witnessed patient unsteadiness.

v. Any problem with patient compliance to care.

w. Significant weight gain or loss (2 pounds in 24 hours in an adult, 10% of birth weight in a neonate).

REPORTABLE OBSERVATIONS IN PEDIATRIC PATIENTS

Recognizes and reports the following significant signs and symptoms:

PEDIATRIC PATIENT

Abnormal breathing

a. *Infant/toddler respirations:* less than 25 or greater than 50 per minute
b. *Child respirations:* less than 20 or greater than 40 per minute
c. *Adolescent respirations:* less than 12 or greater than 30 per minute
d. *Abnormal sounds:* rales, rhonchi, wheezing, grunting, stridor (high-pitched sound with breathing), "barky" cough, "whooping" cough, any abnormal cough or breathing sound
e. *Respiratory distress:* nasal flaring, retractions seen at ribs, sternum, stomach, labored breathing, lack of breathing for greater than 15 seconds

Pulse outside the following parameters:

a. Infant (B–1 yr): less than 100, greater than 160 beats per minute
b. Toddler (1–3 yr): less than 100, greater than 120 beats per minute
c. Preschool (3–5 yr): less than 80, greater than 110 beats per minute
d. School age (5–12 yr): less than 70, greater than 110 beats per minute
e. Adolescent (12–16 yr): less than 60, greater than 90 beats per minute

Blood pressure outside the following parameters:

Infant:	Range 60/20 to 90/60
Toddler:	Range 95/50 to 105/65
Preschool:	Range 95/50 to 105/70
School age:	Range 100/60 to 120/75
Adolescent:	Range 112/65 to 130/80

Pulse oximetry less than 93% at rest or play

Decrease in level of activity, lethargy, fatigue, difficulty in awakening or keeping awake, difficulty in concentrating or answering questions, difficulty recognizing parents, family, friends

Unresponsive

Slurring of speech or difficulty with speech

Unexpected irritability or restlessness

Parent concerned about child's behavior or change in behavior

continues

Color change—pale, cyanotic, rash, purple spots (purpura) or tiny red/purple dots (petechiae), mottling

Temperature—greater than 99.5° F (38.0° C) or less than 97.0° F (36.0° C), cool extremities

Bleeding, swelling, redness, drainage at any surgical or wound site

No urine output in four hours

Vomiting

Not eating

Blood in stool or urine

Unusual color urine (i.e., coke color, Kool-Aid color, cloudy)

Diarrhea

Full, bulging, or depressed fontanel

Any weight loss during admission

Unexpected swelling or edema

Feeling by PCA or parent "that something isn't right"

Feel that child in wrong type of bed (should be in crib, not bed)

Child less than five is playing with bed controls and could potentially be harmed

Parent leaving child unattended in potentially harmful situation (crib with rails down, in high chair without seat belt)

Child being served trays not appropriate for age (i.e., hot dog, raisins, peanuts, adult diet to toddler)

Inappropriate interaction between parent/child or visitor/child

Recognize teaching needs of parent (i.e., parenting, toys and play, nutrition, safety issues, coping, support)

NEWBORN INFANTS

Recognizes and reports the following significant signs and symptoms:

Abnormal breathing

continues

Respirations less than 25 or more than 60 per minute

Abnormal sounds—rales, rhonchi, wheezes, grunting, high-pitched cry

Respiratory distress—nasal flaring, retractions, labored breathing

Lack of breathing greater than 15 seconds

Pulse greater than 170 or less than 100. MAP <35

Temperature above 99 or below 97.6. Needing the warmer lights more than twice

Blood pressure—systolic greater than 80 or less than 60; diastolic greater than 50 or less than 36

Decrease in muscle tone, reflexes

Color change—cyanosis, jaundice, pallor, acrocyanosis returning after being gone, mottling, rash

Bleeding, swelling, infection at circumcision site

Jitteriness, weak cry

Lack of voiding

Lack of feeding

Blood in stools

Swelling on head or of fontanels

Uneven movement or arms, legs, or facial muscles

Head circumference less than 32 cm; 4 cm > chest; less than chest circumference

Weight loss of 10% of birth weight

No response to sound

Feeling of "something isn't right"

Courtesy of Valley Medical Center, Renton, Washington.

Once you've reviewed the formalized roles, you must still answer those issues such as when Sally takes a break. We have found a facilitated discussion using the following tool to be most helpful in ironing out those detailed personal expectations. You can take this basic format and apply it to any member of the team, leading a discussion in which everyone responds to the following: "I expect the (nurse, respiratory therapist, pharmacy tech, service associate, etc.) to. . . ." Have everyone agree to the basic human rights issues of being honest, treating each other with respect, etc., so that you can move the discussion into the specifics of who answers the phone, who notifies admitting, who determines the assignments, break schedule, work flow, and so on. Lest you think this trivial work, remember that many a divorce has been caused by failure to put the cap back on the toothpaste!

▼

"Employee's concerns are not 'What can I do to create value?' but 'What do they really want me to do?'" (Stevenson and Moldoveanu, 1995)

▲

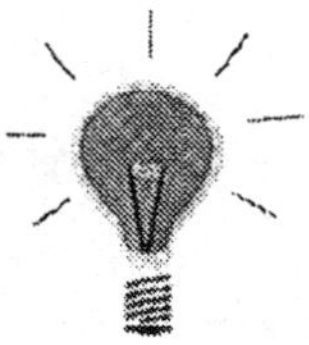

Tool #30: Clarifying the Roles of the Members of the Team

I expect the manager to:

I expect the RN to:

I expect the LPN to:

I expect the assistant to:

I expect the physician to:

I expect the administration to:

Success Story: Structuring Learning Opportunities for New Roles

Huntington Memorial Hospital, Pasadena, California (Hansten and Washburn, 1996)

As we explore how to make restructuring work effectively, we showcase an organization that provides a benchmark for training, a hospital that has not only supported staff with the necessary resources for growth but has also been measuring success and taking steps to continue the training process based on outcomes.

One of the most important challenges presented to an institution as it restructures its work is that of retraining the affected work force in an economical and effective manner. Huntington Hospital restructured four bedside roles:

- Registered Nurse (RN)
- Patient Care Associate (PCA)
- Patient Support Associate (PSA)
- Business Support Associate (BSA)

With the exception of the RN role, the other jobs were opened to candidates with varying backgrounds. This necessitated the development of an education strategy that was flexible enough to build on existing knowledge while ensuring that the person became competent. The structuring of additional needed learning was identified per learner. In this way, we attempted to reduce redundancy and cost and acknowledge prior learning. Each task force that developed the new role's job descriptions also developed a competency validation tool. This tool was used to structure the learning curriculum. Practicing and actual work were designed into the learning environment to assist the learners in application.

Managed Care Education

A unique feature of our education program was the development of a mandatory session for all direct care providers including RNs, RCPs, PTs, OTs, etc. Because more than 90 percent of the dollars we receive are predetermined (managed), it is critical that the caregivers are aware of how they have an effect on the dollars we spend. It is essential that our caregivers understand the managed care environment and the far-reaching changes it requires of the staff.

The importance of and necessity for the program was communicated through the managers. This day-long session "Managed Care for Caregivers" was designed around the following objectives:

Managed Care for Caregivers

- Describe the different methods of payment available: Medicare, MediCal, contracted plans, capitated plans, indemnity plans, and self-pay.
- Explain the difference between per diem rates and case rates and how both affect our operation.
- Define managed care.
- Describe how capitation works and the impact it will have on care delivery and future planning.
- List at least three ways in which we need to restructure our care based on service and price.
- Describe the role of the hospital in the new health care system.
- State ways to look at the hospital from the patient's perspective.
- List at least four ways in which we need to redesign Huntington Memorial Hospital to be successful in the future.
- Explain ways to deliver quality care that is cost-effective and only uses resources important to the patient's outcome.
- Develop at least five ways that you can personally affect the cost and quality of patient care at Huntington.

A combination of lecture and case study guided the staff through the process of understanding the reimbursement systems and the impact the individual can have through communication, participation, development of knowledge and skills, quality improvement, expense reduction, and ambassadorship to the community.

Role Development Education

With this content as a foundation, we began the process of role education. A multidisciplinary group planned the curriculum for all four roles based on job description and role expectations. After the training of the pilot unit, extensive evaluation of the training was done, and appropriate revisions were made.

The RN staff attended three additional sessions to prepare them for role changes under patient-focused care (PFC): PFC Skills, Critical Thinking, and the RN as Team Leader for a total of 32 hours. These were designed to help prepare the RNs to perform to a new and higher level job description as the patient's care coordinator. The topics included understanding the new roles, delegation, team development, communication, preceptoring, patient teaching, utilization review, discharge planning, and concepts of critical thinking.

The PCAs, PSAs, and the BSAs received role-specific training in addition to guest service skills, team development, and communication. The length of the training was both role-dependent and employee-specific. The average time for training was PCA 4 weeks, PSA 3 weeks, and BSA 6 to 8 weeks, which included supervised clinical experience.

Many of the staff initially questioned the need for the length of education, but as PFC was implemented, it became clear that these sessions form only the base knowledge needed for the transition. Worksite follow-up was necessary to help the staff cement the skills and use them daily. Manager follow-up is also essential. Unfortunately, not all our managers attended the sessions, and therefore follow-up was inconsistent. The training would have been more effective if all managers had attended in advance of the staff.

Source: Courtesy of Elaine Goehnor, Joyce Johnson, Huntington Memorial Hospital, Pasadena, California.

Training for All Members of the Team

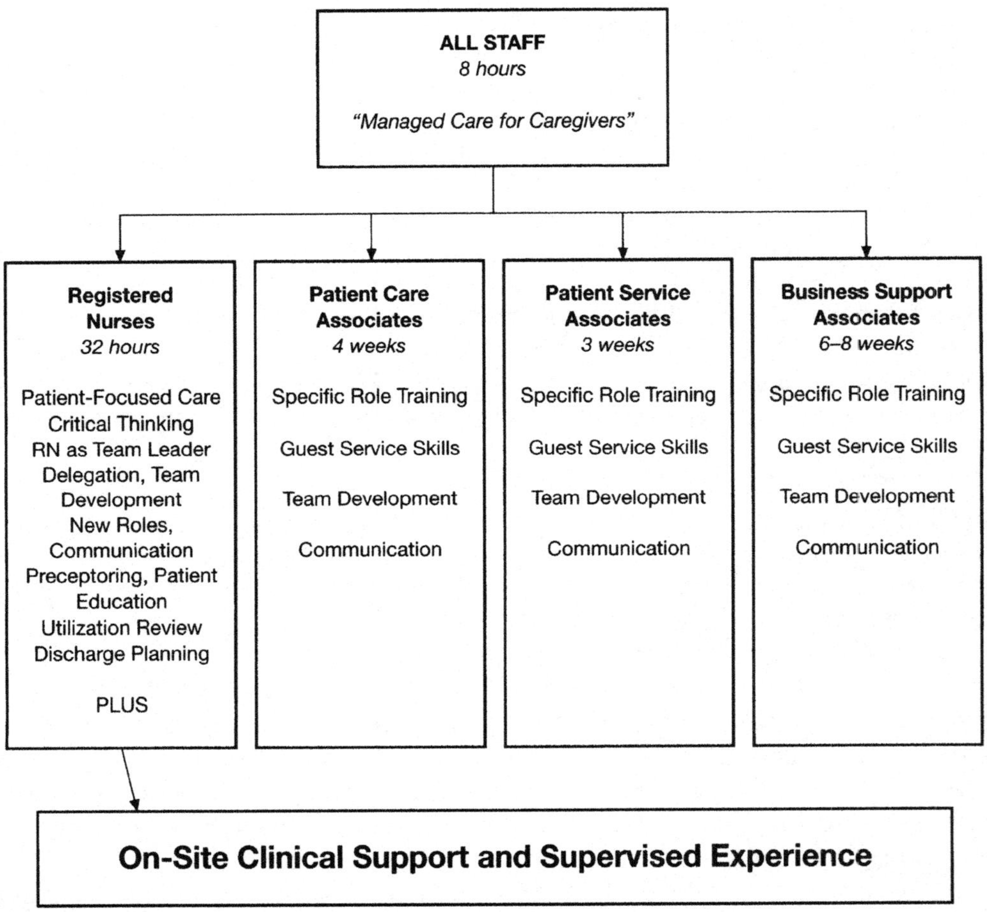

Source: Reprinted from R. Hansten and M. Washburn, *Successful Restructuring Newsletter,* Vol. 1, No. 5, © 1996, Aspen Publishers, Inc.

See Section Four "Lessons Learned" for the rest of the Huntington Memorial Hospital story.

DEVELOPING ACCOUNTABILITY

▼

Accountability: "being answerable for what one has done and standing behind that decision or action." (Hansten and Washburn, 1994)

▲

The most frequently repeated phrase we hear from leadership at all levels is the fervent wish "if only the staff/employees would be more accountable!" This is true in most organizations, whether or not a redesign project is underway. It should be a reasonable expectation that an employee would be actively engaged in doing his own job without continual supervision. Yet, managers and staff alike are surprised when the contrary is quite true, and people race to find ways to shift the accountability of their performance (read blame) on someone else's shoulders. So much for teamwork and the esprit de corp we were hoping for!

Lest you lose hope altogether, there are some very effective tools for developing a sense of personal accountability. And believe it or not, the midst of redesign is a perfect time for moving staff in this direction if they aren't there already. An alteration in the type of personnel within the work unit, whether it's downsizing to simply reduce the numbers or it's a change in the mix of employees, results in a tightening of the ship, so to speak. Where the old system might have allowed some room for carrying the load of individuals who are less than peak performers, your new system will require that everyone do her share. Tolerance for marginal performance will also be minimized among the team members themselves, as they see the workload increasing. There is no better time to support ownership of individual behaviors.

The Four-Part Process

As with any other significant concept, accountability can be best described as a process of connected behaviors. And although it is important to present this idea, you must also discuss what accountability is NOT. In many instances, the reluctance of ownership for behavior comes from a past experience in which quality assurance models were based on a "seek and destroy" mission. Once a trend was identified, it became the imperative to find out "who is accountable for this mess" and to deal with them accordingly. Although today's continuous quality improvement programs strive to focus on the problem and not the person, history has a very strong hold on many, and there are serious doubts in the employee's mind that he will not be punished for a mistake. Therefore, the predominant behavior becomes one of running for cover, of being invisible so as not to be at risk for blame. Unfortunately, this leaves the employee out of the limelight as well, and when positive outcomes are realized, there is little opportunity for ownership and personal recognition, and so the employee does not feel motivated to do more. What a vicious cycle!

▼

"Accountability: An attitude of continually asking, 'What else can I do to rise above my circumstances and achieve the results I desire?' It is the process of 'seeing it, owning it, solving it, and doing it.' It requires a level of ownership that includes making, keeping, and proactively answering for personal commitments." (Flarey, 1994)

▲

1. **Seeing It**
   People "see" problems around them all day long. There is a ready identification when something is not going as it should, when the person on the phone is abrupt and rude, when the lab results aren't available at the agreed-on time, when the meal sent is the wrong one, and so on. The bigger issue becomes what one does when the problem is seen.
2. **Owning It**
   Ownership is the Grand Canyon leap for some folks. It is easy to see and identify a problem situation but equally hard to muster up any ownership that would lead behavior toward a solution. Boundaries are set by those who say that "it's not my patient (unit, shift, job, etc.)." On the other extreme is the view held by some that all problems are a direct result of their behavior, and they are constantly trying to assume responsibility for issues clearly outside of their realm. These self-designated martyrs are often abused by the system, particularly one in which the norm is not to be accountable. This codependent-type behavior can be just as difficult to overcome as the type in which limits are clearly set and you would like to broaden those limits.

   Ownership has much to do with the person's connection to the overall values and mission of the place in which he works. If the department mission is in alignment with the overall mission of the organization and the road is clear, it will create a much stronger sense of ownership on the part of the individual employee who is "seeing" the problem. Such is not always the case, particularly when the mission is no more than a plaque by the elevator that no one talks about or makes real in any sense. We are reminded of the telling example of one individual who shared her story:

   > I know just what you mean about accountability of departments. Since we have redesigned the housekeeping department, the place has gotten dirtier and dirtier. It's the worst I've seen it in many years. Just a few weeks ago, I was taking the back stairway up to my unit, and I noticed a half-eaten bag of potato chips on the stairs. And do you know, that bag was there for two weeks!

3. **Solving It**
   Clearly, in our story above, you see a lack of ownership. Without that connection, there is no movement in the process to the next step, solving it. There

were many options available, and when asked why no action was taken, the reply was that "it's not my job to be the housekeeper." Although she felt embarrassed at the obvious ease in which she could have solved this, there was no sense of seeing the big picture, no recognition that we're all in this together. Without that, the solution, no matter how easy, will not be acted on. When colleagues suggested the employee could have called housekeeping, her response was that "they should be patrolling this area anyway." Shifting ownership (blame) is a common response that we need to address if individual accountability is ever to be realized.

4. Doing It

A willingness to follow through on an identified solution is the final step in full accountability. It is important to emphasize that the action necessary to solve the problem situation may not necessarily be taken by the person who sees the problem but that his role may be in alerting the involved party of the problem and suggesting appropriate steps to remedy the situation. For instance, if our reluctant employee thought that it was not a good use of her time to tidy the stairs, she could have alerted someone in a position to do something about it (i.e., called housekeeping).

Tool #31: Developing Accountability

Accountability Is:

the process of seeing it
owning it
solving it
doing it

This level of ownership includes making, keeping,
and proactively answering for personal commitments

Accountability Is NOT:

being the one to blame
reactive
historical explanations

DEVELOP ACCOUNTABILITY IN THE ORIENTEE BY:

clarifying role expectations
seeking his input first regarding performance
requesting his solution to problems
resisting the urge to "fix it" for the orientee
identifying the cost of accommodation and avoidance

"Ambiguity is the enemy of accountability."
Tim Porter-O'Grady

Legal Boundaries

▼

"Accountability can never be delegated. Each role and the accountability associated with it are essentially connected." (Porter-O'Gracy and Wilson, 1995)

▲

Setting legal limits is done through many avenues. State regulatory agencies, as well as internal policies and procedures, establish parameters within which staff perform their roles. However, this does not mean that the staff are aware of the limits or that they have a working knowledge of regulatory documents. This results in a fairly effective resistive behavior, as staff claim that they are unwilling to participate in the newly redesigned role because of the fear of legal repercussions. For instance, in nursing, the cry is often heard, "I'm not going to put my license on the line to work with these people!" Interestingly enough, these same individuals often do not have any knowledge of the real legal boundaries but are working on assumptions or horror stories told by colleagues.

Overcoming the FEAR factor (*f*alse *e*vidence *a*ppearing *r*eal) is an essential first step in developing accountability. We have found that acquiring copies of the various legal acts (the nurse practice act, nursing assistant regulations, rules for the physical therapists, respiratory therapists, and all members of the multidisciplinary team) and making them available to the staff can be effective. However, the staff are not going to grab these documents and read them from cover to cover with delight (or understanding), so some vehicle for facilitating interpretation will be necessary. We have included a tool that we use frequently for nursing personnel. This true/false quiz fosters many questions and allows for a good review of the law. It is particularly helpful if each individual has his own copy of the appropriate law and is asked to find supporting evidence of his answers. This requires a hands-on involvement that helps the employee to become acquainted with an important aspect of the legal limits of his role. We have adapted this test for many different types of care providers, changing the questions to reflect therapists, assistive personnel, etc., and found its usefulness is not limited to nursing alone.

Tool #32: When Is My License on the Line?

True or False: circle T or F:

T or F 1. Once I delegate a task to a member of the team, I am no longer accountable for what happens.

T or F 2. The state practice act specifically allows me to delegate patient care activities.

T or F 3. The state practice act specifies that I must know the competencies and abilities of the person to whom I delegate.

T or F 4. The state practice act states I may be in violation of the standards of conduct if I delegate tasks to those I have reason to know lack the ability to perform the task.

T or F 5. If I fail to supervise those to whom patient care activities have been delegated, it could mean I could lose my license.

T or F 6. If a delegate makes a mistake performing a task I have delegated, it could mean I could lose my license.

T or F 7. Employer policies relieve me of my responsibility for making judgments about the delegation of patient care activities.

Source: Reprinted from R. Hansten and M. Washburn, *Clinical Delegation Skills,* p. 53, © 1994, Aspen Publishers, Inc.

Another effective method for identifying limits is demonstrated in the following "Scope of Practice Grid" developed by Group Health Cooperative in Puget Sound. As opposed to the "Patient Care Services Scope of Practice" (tool #29), this perspective is limited to nursing services and highlights the regulatory limits of the various ambulatory care team members.

Tool #33: Scope of Practice Grid

	MA	*Patient Care Technician/HHA/CNA*	*Health Care Assistants (HCA)*	*Nursing Technician*
Credential	Certified or eligible for certification as MA (eligibility 1-yr employment full-time or 2-yr part-time as MA)	Registration required in all health care facilities. Certification required in nursing homes only	Certification by Department of Health for specific functions allowed by scope of practice, documented training per category requirements, by qualified trainer	Currently enrolled in state Board of Nursing approved RN program and completed at least one academic term (qtr or semester)
Scope of Practice	• By GHC policy, functions under the supervision and direction of RN • Performs nursing tasks and activities as delegated by RN • Takes direction from ARNP, PA, or MD for provision of medical care • Assists with procedures under direction of MD, RN, PA, ARNP • May phone prescriptions to pharmacy provided written order of prescription is present from MD/PA/ARNP (class 2 controlled substances prohibited) • At direction of MD/RN may review lab results as directed • May perform procedures under direction and supervision of RN/MD/ARNP PA providing skill and competency validated (including but not limited to suture removal, ear washes, simple dressing changes, wart treatment, nebulizer treatment, spirometry)	• Functions under direction and supervision of RN or LPN (WAC 246-841-400 for certified NAs) • Assists, as delegated, in the delivery of nursing and nursing-related activities to patients in health care facility (see WAC competencies)	• Limited authority to administer skin tests and subcutaneous, intradermal, intramuscular, and IV injections and to perform minor invasive procedures to withdraw blood only by delegation from and under the supervision of a licensed practitioner with designated authority (WAC 246-826) See categories for detail • May perform functions listed above only when designated by a licensed MD, osteopathic physician, surgeon, podiatrist, or RN with prescriptive authority • HCA may perform limited functions only when delegator is physically present and immediately available in facility during injections • Delegator must maintain list of specific medications/diagnostic agents and route of administration authorized for injection • Delegator need not be present for blood withdrawal	• Provides opportunity for student nurses to gain work experience within the limits of their education but not limited to scope of functions of nursing assistant-certified • Function only under the supervision of RN—RN retains accountability for total nursing care • May gather information about patients as directed by RN and administer care to patients according to plan of care • May administer medications, but only under direct supervision of RN (RN must be on premises, available, patients have been assessed by RN before delegating medication duties to nursing tech)

	MA	*Patient Care Technician/HHA/CNA*	*Health Care Assistants (HCA)*	*Nursing Technician*
Limitations/ Prohibitions	• By law and GHC policy, may not administer medications, perform venipuncture, phlebotomy, administer blood or blood products • May not practice as RN, LPN, or MD or independently undertake treatment or cure of disease, pain, injury, deformity, or physical conditions • May not insert Foley catheters unless practicing in urology/ obstetrics and verification of training exists • May not phone prescriptions to pharmacy without written order from MD/ PA/ARNP	• May not administer medication or practice as RN or LPN • May not be assigned to provide care until registered NA has demonstrated skills necessary to perform required function • By GHC policy, may not perform procedures that involve piercing skin (e.g., Accu checks) • By GHC policy, may not insert Foleys, perform NT suctioning, D/C IVs	• May not perform any procedures or administer medications not specifically addressed in the HCA rules and regulations	• May not administer chemotherapy, blood or blood products, intravenous medications, or scheduled drugs • May not carry out procedures on central lines • May not function as independent practitioner, team leader, charge nurse, or in supervisory capacity • May not independently perform ongoing assessment, planning, implementation, and evaluation of patient care

Courtesy of Group Health Cooperative, Puget Sound, Washington.

Determining Who Does What

▼

"Too many people are eager to volunteer to carry the piano stool when it's the piano that needs to be moved!" (Anonymous)

▲

The typical redesign involves the shifting of some duties that previously belonged to one department to those of another. For example, when nursing "takes back" some basic respiratory therapy tasks and housekeeping takes on some direct patient care responsibilities, it becomes essential to determine who does what for the most effective use of resources. Often, this necessary coordination of role performance comes from the licensed leadership of the department in the form of assigning or delegating. Assisting leaders in making the best decisions is important if staff are to be used appropriately and your redesign goals achieved. Without this direction and coordination, people either will tend to maintain their old ways or will do what they like the most. Focusing originally on the nursing aspects of delegation, we created the Four Rights of Effective Delegation in our book, *Clinical Delegation Skills.* As our work expanded to all disciplines, we have adapted this simple concept to the Four Rights of Collaborative Teamwork. It's easy to see that without covering these four bases, teamwork can be inefficient and even dysfunctional.

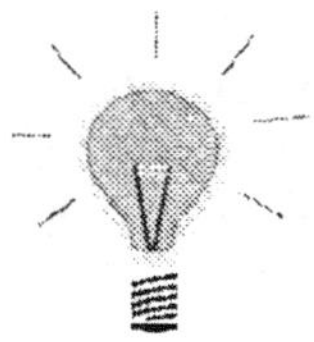

Tool #34: The Four Rights of Collaborative Teamwork

RIGHT TASK

- within the scope of practice
- according to job description
- on the shared task list
- based on desired outcome

RIGHT PERSON

Assess competency by:

- certification/licensure
- job description
- skills checklist
- demonstrated skill

RIGHT COMMUNICATION

- Outcome-Based
- The Four Cs of Initial Direction
    - Clear
    - Concise
    - Correct
    - Complete

RIGHT FEEDBACK: the reciprocal process

- ask for the teammate's input FIRST
- recognize his effort
- get the teammate's solution to the problem

Supervision for Successful Performance

In matching the right person to the right task, based on the desired outcome, supervision must be part of the process. Many staff, unless bearing a formal title of leadership (house supervisor, charge nurse, lead therapist, manager) are reluctant to believe that they have any supervisory obligations at all and are all too willing to let management bear the total responsibility for this aspect of work. However, we stress the point that supervision is an obligation shared by any who delegate a task to another team member. It may not mean that they have the authority to take disciplinary action or to terminate an employee (although some may like to), but they certainly have a responsibility to give clear initial direction and to follow up to see that the task was done and that the outcome achieved was the desired one. Communication, then, is the essential key ingredient, and we shift our attention to tools that assist in making communication more effective.

▼

Supervision at any level should be viewed as a process of giving initial direction, following up periodically to evaluate progress, and having the authority to take corrective action if necessary.

▲

Four Cs of Initial Direction

The first aspect of getting any job done correctly is the direction that is given. We suggest a helpful mnemonic to assist in evaluating whether initial direction covers all the bases and truly does convey the expectations in such a way that the fellow team member stands a chance of satisfying the request.

Initial direction should be

- clear
- concise
- correct
- complete

Clear: Does the person understand what is being asked? For example, if I am asking someone to weigh a patient, is it clearly understood that a body weight is what is being asked? Sometimes, people will think that they are asking by simply stating "the new admit is in the room." This mental short-hand is thought to convey the expectation that the desired action will be for the team member to go into the patient's room and weigh her. Imagine the frustration when this is not done, and instead the team member takes a break or attends to another task! If you are requesting a weight to be done, say so—make your message clear!

Concise: Some people have a very lengthy and colorful style of dialogue, others are abrupt and to the point. Whatever the style, it is helpful if the message is not confused or cluttered with too much detail. Conciseness, which is enough information to do the job and no more, is an art, but one well worth developing. We all feel the urgency of the work and are likely to get distracted if too much extraneous information is given, which will only be ignored. The team member may be thinking, "Just get on with it—I have work to do!"

Correct: Armed with scopes of practice, job descriptions, and policies, you must make certain that the request is one supported by the role. It would not be appropriate to ask a respiratory therapist to insert an indwelling urinary catheter (or would it?). What does your design look like? If roles are clarified (see tool #30), then it will be relatively easy for the team member to refuse, or worse, to accept a task that he is not legally supported to perform.

Complete: Similar to concise, this aspect of initial direction is often lacking. Arguments range from the rationale that "if I have to tell him how to do the job, I might as well do it myself" to "I don't want to insult him by implying he doesn't know his job." Somewhere there lies a midline, in which the benefit of having the other person perform the job is seen and he has enough information to be successful. The best way to find out? Ask the team member if he understands what is being assigned.

▼

Initial direction works best if it is a *dialogue, not an edict from on high.*

▲

To support initial direction, we also offer another tool regarding effective communication. If members of the team have not taken an assertive communication course, we strongly encourage this action. Communication is the backbone of our success, and if people are unable to be direct in their expectations and to convey when things are not right, then once again, the goals that you had hoped for will not happen. This tool outlines a basic format based on assertive communication. It is particularly useful if participants are encouraged to practice, using examples that they identify or some of the generic ones we have included.

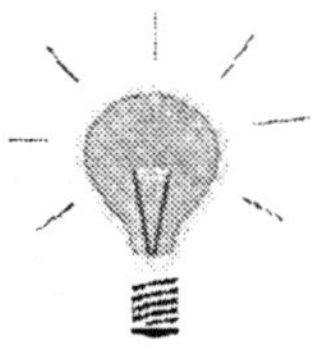

Tool #35: Effective Communication

Step One:

Determine what outcome you want to achieve from this interaction

Step Two:

Proceed with the following assertiveness formula

"When you . . ." or "I noticed that . . ."

- What have you seen, heard, or read
- Focus on actual observable behavior
- Give specific details

"I feel . . ."

- Give your reaction to the behavior
- Focus on your feeling, not the other's motivation

"I want . . ."

- State what you want the other person to do
- Focus on modifiable behavior
- Be realistic

"Ask for what you want, it improves your chances of getting it."

Supervision and the four rights of effective teamwork rely on giving and receiving feedback. In fact, studies show that when feedback is combined with an identification of the desired goals, performance effort increases by 60 percent!

In our earlier discussion regarding performance weaknesses (see Clarifying Roles in this section), not receiving feedback was cited as the second cause of performance weaknesses. But as you might expect, how the feedback is given can go a long way in developing personal accountability. Instead of racing in to say thank you or to offer some well-meaning advice on how to improve the team member's performance, ASK the individual first for his input regarding the situation. Resisting the urge to go first is not easy but well worth the effort. Asking the individual for his assessment encourages self-evaluation of personal performance and is the first step in developing accountability. Once you've heard his side, if you don't agree and have advice to offer or your own observations, make certain that you engage the individual in the solution. Fixing the problem for others lets them off the hook, and leaves them out of the ownership of their own actions once again. Feedback should be a two-way discussion, with both parties sharing observations and potential solutions to the problem.

Unlike the typical one-sided feedback process, however, we recommend a dialogue beginning with the question that gets the other person's side of the story. Too often, we see team members act on information, something they have heard or observed and formed a judgment about, run to the offending party and tell him what he did wrong. This is more likely to happen if they feel in a position of power and authority over the offending party. However, if the other party is an equal, or superior, quite the opposite happens, and they will tend to tell everyone else but the person most involved.

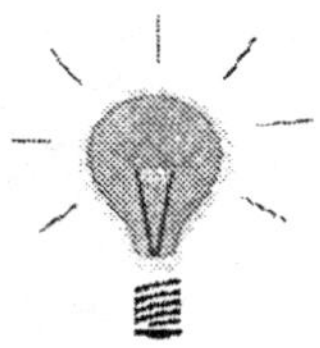

Tool #36: Giving and Receiving Feedback

Ask for the team member's input *(it's not your turn yet!)*

Recognize his/her effort
(remember s/he's working hard!)

Share your perception
(now it's your turn)

Discuss your differences
(you may see things differently)

Agree on a future outcome *(what would you like to happen?)*

Discuss team member's action plan or solution *(HIS plan)*

Set a time to check on progress *(time for follow-up)*

"One man may hit the mark, another blunder; but heed not these distinctions. Only from the alliance of the one, working through and with the other, are great things born."
St. Exupery

▼

Regarding accountability: **This simple act of asking the other person for his or her input first prompts a sense of self-evaluation, and the resulting ownership in one's own performance is further fostered by a genuine interest in what is said. This is reciprocal feedback, once again, a *dialogue and not a soliloquy.***

▲

Making Plans That Work

Training that focuses on a specified set of "correct" actions or behaviors to achieve the desired result will produce rote behaviors and eliminate spontaneous critical thinking, so essential to the flexible work force of the 21st century. Indeed, as Carol Lindeman points out,

▼

"Healthcare systems don't need someone who knows how to do those old routines. And more than that, they don't care how the person does something, as long as it produces the outcome." (Lindeman, 1996)

▲

In evaluating success, we have typically looked at structure, processes, and ultimately, outcomes. Indeed the emphasis has shifted full force to looking at the results of any action rather than the action itself. Although that may be the case in the literature and trade journals, the front lines are still focusing most of their energy in getting tasks done, with very little subsequent thought as to whether the task that is compelling so much time and energy is really contributing to the desired outcome. Armed with assignments in terms of lab tests, X-rays, treatments, data collection, meds, etc., care providers have physical as well as mental "to do" lists in which they cross off the completed task with a feeling of satisfaction. Work is distributed and measured in terms of who has gotten what done (*"I passed 14 trays and did 6 bed baths," "I passed all the meds and did 8 respiratory treatments"*). Indeed, patients become known by the degree of task involvement. One unit that we worked with identified their difficult patients by the number of intravenous medications that were infusing, *"I had a terrible day—I had 14 drips!"*

Somehow, we need to facilitate the critical evaluation of what is being done in terms of the result that is being achieved. This is a fundamental component in the successful reengineering of a work group. Failing to do this will result in different players doing much the same tasks they have always done, despite different titles, with similar results.

▼

It is only when people begin to think in terms of outcomes, i.e., results, that they are able to see the bigger picture of the care being delivered and to transcend the boundaries of their own department.

▲

WORKING IT ALL OUT

When faced with the concept of focusing on outcomes as opposed to tasks, staff will often resist, claiming that "the patients demand that we change their bed daily, give them fresh ice water, and give their meds on time!" Yes, we agree, most of our actions are reasonable expectations. But the public also needs to have a realistic view of the primary purpose of a health care facility.

▼

We advocate for the inclusion of the patient in all planning and recommend that staff be taught to ask the patient from admission on, "What are your expectations of this hospital stay, treatment, visit to the clinic, etc. (whatever the case might be)?"

▲

Plans based on outcomes, on patient expectations, should be shared at the beginning of the work shift, as staff make determinations regarding how the work will be assigned. Sharing based on outcomes helps the staff to develop a sense of the bigger picture and to see the results of their efforts. Instead of drive-through care or an assembly line approach, the care becomes centered on the purpose of what is being done in the first place.

We have found the following exercise to be useful for all members of the patient care team. It is helpful if actual patients are selected as samples, much like a case review, and all the team members discuss what the outcomes might be for a short- and long-term perspective and then plan work based on the desired results. Small groups may do this, working as team members from the same unit, or this could be used during a staff meeting for guided discussion of how work is currently assigned. Reinforcement by management and educational personnel is important for the process to be carried out, for actual discussion and planning based on outcomes to occur on a regular basis and communicated to all members of the team.

Tool #37: Outcome Planning

PATIENT:	STAFF:	
	this shift	long term
PATIENT OUTCOME		
WHAT NEEDS TO BE DONE		
WHO WILL DO IT		

PATIENT:	STAFF:	
	this shift	long term
PATIENT OUTCOME		
WHAT NEEDS TO BE DONE		
WHO WILL DO IT		

Solving the Problems

Not everyone is a skilled problem solver. In fact, many of your team members may not have had any formalized training in the art of analysis and resolution of problems. Typically, a hierarchy has been provided, leaving the front line worker off the hook when it comes to solving problems of any significance. This creates a lack of ownership and often leads to a "learned helplessness"–type behavior that can be more than a little frustrating when trying to develop teams that are self-directed.

▼

Two points are essential here: (1) Individuals need to come up with their own solutions to problems because they will resent and have no ownership in a solution given to them, and (2) individuals will follow a prescribed process of problem solving if coached and supported.

▲

Recall that in our discussion on feedback, we emphasized the need for the individual involved to identify his or her own solution to the issue, rather than relying on an authority figure to tell him or her what to do. Being involved in determining a solution can be very empowering, and staff will believe that they have a say in the way things are being done.

Focus on the Positive

Another key point to emphasize is the strategy of question #2 of the positive problem-solving process. Asking "What is good about this situation?" does not make you a candidate for Pollyanna of the Year but has real significance in solving the problem. When this question is asked, with the expectation that there will be at least two, if not more, responses, it frees up the right brain to be creative and to think more positively about what is going right. The alternative leads to "ain't it awful" defeatist thinking, when one responds to a problem with "Not again! All we have around here are more problems—this is the worst!" and indeed it is, and there will be no solution in sight as the individual continues downward in the spiral of despair. Not a pretty picture, and one that creates a sense of helplessness, a "What's the use? It won't matter anyway" or "Why bother? Nothing can be done to change things around here" attitude.

▼

To free up creative problem solving and empower the staff, ask the question, "what is good about this situation?"

▲

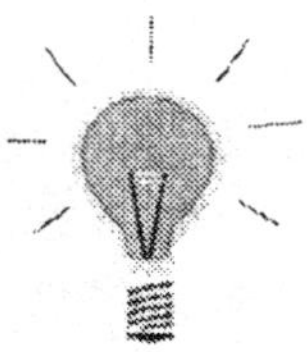

Tool #38: A Positive Approach to Problem Solving

1. What signs tell you that something is wrong here?

2. What is good about this situation?

3. What should be happening instead of what did happen?

4. Do I need to do something about it?
   Does it affect me, my patients, or our team goals?
   What will happen if I don't do something about this?
   What could happen if I do?
   Should I be solving this problem, or do I need someone else?

5. What is the exact nature of the problem, incident, or error?
   What objective criteria will tell me if the problem is solved?

6. What can be done about it?
   Consider possible solutions, and plan steps based on long-term and short-term needs. Establish a timeline for evaluation.

Source: Reprinted from R. Hansten and M. Washburn, *Clinical Delegation Skills,* p. 277, © 1994, Aspen Publishers, Inc.

Resolving Conflict: Making the Right Choice

We have consistently found that unless you provide some support in the area of conflict resolution, the changes that you hope to make within your teams will not be realized. Most people will openly admit that they dislike conflict and would prefer the formal authority members to deal with the difficult issues. This preference is true whether or not you are redesigning, but it is often intensified unless skill development in this area is offered.

There are any number of approaches to the process of conflict resolution, but we have found a review of the five choices outlined by the Thomas-Kilmann Conflict Resolution work to be most effective. (Thomas, 1977) Presenting a sample conflict that represents one that has been observed and then discussing the choices is a successful method of reminding staff that they do have options in any given situation. Following the discussion with practice sessions in small groups, who then report back to the larger group, helps to reinforce and to continue skill development.

Tool #39: Five Choices for Negotiating Conflict among the Team

#1 Avoidance
"There's no problem"
Used as a short-term resolution; to calm down and buy time.
Cost: does not solve the problem
Benefit: allows time for cooling off and thinking

#2 Accommodation
"You win, I lose"
Sacrificing own interests to please the other member of the team. OK if the issue is not important to you, or the resolution is short term, to be problem solved later.
Cost: does not achieve your own interests
Benefit: allows for immediate solution

#3 Completion
"I win, you lose"
For quick, decisive action on vital matters.
Cost: other party might not be satisfied and may be resistive
Benefit: your goals are achieved

#4 Compromise
"I win and lose some, you win and lose some too"
Temporary solutions to complex problems, with resolution by mutual consent.
Cost: takes time, you may have to give up optimum goal
Benefit: both parties feel successful and part of solution

#5 Collaboration
"I win, you win"
Process that evolves over time, working through feelings that have interfered with the relationship, and finding an integrative solution.
Cost: takes strong commitment of both parties
Benefit: long-lasting solution with mutual satisfaction

Sample Story 1: Preferential Treatment

Stan is a worker from a temporary staffing agency who has been assigned to work on one of the units today. He presents himself to the person in charge, explaining how excited he is to have the opportunity to work in this particular organization today. In fact, he implies that he is looking for a permanent position and would like to work weekends, holidays, and the night shift if that's what it would take for him to get a position. However, Stan has just one request, and he states it with every expectation that it will be honored.

"I am pretty excited about getting to work here, and I would certainly like to be part of the team. There's just one thing you should know. I won't take care of any patients who are HIV positive."

This represents a potential conflict for the manager who is in need of someone this shift but who also knows that preferential treatment is against policy. Review each of the five options for resolving this conflict, for both the short term (today) and the longer term (if Stan were to apply for a position).

Sample Story 2: Chronically Late

Martha frequently arrives late to work. In fact, she is about 20 minutes late the majority of the time. Her fellow team members have noticed this with increasing annoyance in the past month. Discuss the five options facing Martha's teammates. Which would be the best choice and why?

MULTISKILLING AND PATIENT FOCUSED CARE

Often, the changes you propose will involve the addition of skills as you expand the roles of some care providers and delete others. The creation of new roles is not an easy task and requires careful planning and input from several areas. We have developed a list of reminders, included in the following tool, that we have found to be a useful guide as you begin this process. Role development plans can make or break the patient focused or job redesign efforts. Optimal results come from a flexible attitude toward continual redesign.

We offer here a focus on two areas in which changes are most often centered: the laboratory and respiratory therapy. Both of these stories were highlighted in *Successful Restructuring.*

Tool #40: Process of Role Development

- Review the state practice acts regarding who is allowed to do what tasks and processes.

- Encourage a high degree of staff involvement (respiratory therapists, physical therapists, RNs, dietitians, phlebotomists, and other support partners—whoever is affected by the change) in creating the role and jobs. Find out what people are willing to give up and what others are willing to take on.

- Be certain that physicians who will be affected are involved in the process and informed along the way as job descriptions are developed.

- Talk with other organizations that have practice with expanded roles and get their input.

- Maintain alliances and connections with local colleges, universities, and technical schools, so that students and instructors are aware of, and can plan for, the possible role changes within hiring institutions.

- Plan the education and orientation program.

- Discuss the planned roles with surveyors from the state health department as well as with state professional boards, clarifying such issues as what kind of certification is needed to pierce the skin, for example.

Success Story: Decentralizing the Lab: Who Does the Phlebotomies?

One of the more popular new roles in an acute care redesign is that of the "technical team member." Wanting this role to be more advanced than the typical nursing assistant of days gone by, the planning team will usually look for more technical skills that can be added to the role to maximize effectiveness. Decentralizing lab services and placing the responsibility of obtaining blood specimens with the members of the team on the unit require considerable planning and training for success.

When planning to change roles for any reason, Sandie McCreary of Marin General Hospital in California advises that you *"determine your philosophy for doing this in the first place."* At Marin, the goal was to combine services to minimize the number of contacts with the patient, as well as to create a role that was more challenging and satisfying than the current limited role of the assistant.

Role expansion begins with planning, based on a clear idea of what is to be gained in the first place. The process usually includes these basic steps:

- determine overall objective (i.e., downsize lab, reduce number of staff, decrease number of people who are in contact with the patient)
- analyze various state practice acts for analysis of legal restrictions and requirements of certification/licensure for various functions
- create list of routine/special skills
- determine who can do what
- create new role
- plan training
- create checkpoints for progress and evaluation

At University of Iowa Hospitals and Clinics, nursing assistants and lab phlebotomists have been drawing blood for years. In the acute care setting of these teaching hospitals, however, resident physicians had been drawing the blood and starting the IVs. Jean Barry Walker, Clinical Director of Inpatient and Outpatient Medical and Psychiatric areas, provided RNs as the IV/phlebotomy team for acute care. With budget cuts, the staff decided to change the plan for this important task. Now, nursing assistants, LPNs, or RNs draw blood. The RN decides who should complete the task, depending on the patient's assessment. One rule stands for all:

After two sticks, get someone else to attempt phlebotomy. In the clinics, people with minimal training (phlebotomists) had been drawing blood without incident for years, *"but it took some time for the inpatient staff to recognize that their veins didn't change when the patients entered the hospital doors."*

Training Is the Key

After nine months of study of the roles of the phlebotomist, the ECG tech, the respiratory tech, and the physical therapy tech, the design team at Holy Family Hospital determined several functions that could be combined into a new role of "Certified Care Associate." One of the major new skills contained in the role was that of phlebotomy—obtaining the blood samples necessary for lab testing.

▼

"Looking back, we seriously underestimated the initial training time."
(Cathy Simchuk, Associate Administrator for Patient Care Services at Holy Family Hospital)

▲

The training at Holy Family included a skills lab and the performance of 10 practice sticks before the new worker could take on this function on "real patients." Patient complaints, and then physician complaints, increased, as multiple sticks were the result. No surprise here, as patient studies rank the skill and courtesy of the technician who draws the blood in the top 15 criteria for determining a satisfactory hospital stay. (*Top fifteen factors,* 1992) Increased sticks, coupled with bruising and pain, do not spell success. Lab workers become upset, as well as the rest of the staff members, who are then reluctant to delegate this task. How do we ensure success in this new role?

The team at Holy Family went back to the drawing board and made some decisions regarding commitment to the original role development. Despite initial increases in complaints, it was still believed that in the long term, this would be a successful strategy. A skills competency check was developed, lab personnel observed the draws performed by the new workers, and RNs assess whether the draw will be routine or complex (lab personnel will then perform).

At Marin General, the initial training was more extensive. Lab personnel wanted a lengthy training, and there was much debate around the issue of how many sticks were enough to demonstrate proficiency. The final training plan included 16 hours of classroom and two weeks of practice sticks, or a total of 50 sticks. *"It's important to really look at the training as what is brand new and then do what you need to do to support it."* McCreary tells us that the current policy allows for two sticks and then you must get someone else. In the middle of a quality monitor now, they are beginning to measure success. Unlike Holy Family's experience, there was not the initial increase in patient complaints, probably due to the differences in training.

Recommendations for training for skill in phlebotomy

- involve the lab personnel
- develop a policy restricting complex draws to experienced personnel
- limit number of attempts made by each tech
- provide 8 to 16 hours of classroom
- provide opportunity for 40 to 60 practice sticks
- use a preceptor to provide support for initial six weeks

Problems and Benefits

Despite renewed training efforts at Holy Family, there were still problems. Accuracy and completion of lab slips were issues that were resolved by the creation of sample picture boards of complex lab slips with detailed information for the new techs to follow. Physicians continued to doubt the wisdom of the project and required considerable proof of success to support the idea. In addition, some shifts do not provide sufficient opportunity for the tech to remain proficient in the new skill. After careful consideration, the techs on these shifts are no longer required to perform the occasional draw, and lab is summoned.

After nine months, the positives are starting to outweigh the beginning difficulties. Some actual proof of success at Holy Family: *"When I was a patient here before, someone woke me up at 4 AM for my blood pressure, at 5 AM somebody came and drew my blood, and at 6 AM somebody else came and weighed me. This time one person came in at 5 AM and did it all, and then I could go back to sleep. That's much better—thanks!"*

And from a satisfied physician: *"What have you done with the lab? Now my lab results are ready when I make rounds at 7:30 and I don't have to wait!"*

Parting Comments

Reviewing the process at Holy Family, Cathy Simchuk, CNE, offers some good advice if she had to do it all over again.

- Realize the impact of the "take-aways" (laboratory personnel will not be happy with the change in their role).
- Consider a pilot project on one unit before rolling out the entire facility.
- Cultivate a "physician champion," one who will support your project objectives.

Our thanks to Cathy Simchuk, Associate Administrator Patient Care Services, Holy Family Hospital, Spokane, Washington, Sandie McCreary, Director of Quality and Management at Marin General Hospital in Marin, California, and Jean Barry Walker, Clinical Director, University of Iowa Hospitals and Clinics, for their candid comments. (Hansten and Washburn, 1996)

Tool #41: Expanded Role of the Clinical Assistant To Include Phlebotomy

Although this enhanced role includes the additions of several skills not normally included in the role of a nursing assistant, we are focusing on the addition of the skill of phlebotomy in the accompanying success story. We include this job description from Holy Family Hospital to assist you in determining the scope of this technical provider.

Holy Family Hospital
Spokane, WA
Certified Care Associate

Statement of Purpose: The certified care associate assists nursing, laboratory, physical therapy, and respiratory therapy personnel in the delivery of patient care and services to deliver supportive bedside care to patients, as directed by an RN care manager. Treatment will be provided in accordance with the established methods and procedures of Holy Family Hospital.

Qualifications:

1. High school graduate, ability to read, write, and comprehend medical terminology
2. Required certifications
    a. current certified nursing assistant
    b. ability to complete the requirements for HCA (health care assistant) category A annually. Fee paid by hospital
3. Able to work under pressure and relate to patients, hospital staff, and visitors

Reporting Relationship: This position will report to the RN care manager.

Environmental Factors

1. Work in conditions involving possible physical/mechanical hazards common to hospital environment (e.g., blood-borne pathogens, infectious and contagious diseases)
2. Moving objects/persons in excess of 100 pounds with frequent lifting and/or carrying items weighing 50 pounds or more.

Job Responsibility/Performance Standards

Job Responsibility 1: Gathers and communicates patient data (wt 15 percent)

1.1 Gathers and records vital signs, height, weight (and other measurements as applicable) in an accurate manner.
1.2 Identifies variations from normal in data collection (e.g., vital signs, appearance, pain, skin condition, gait) and reports significant findings to RN care manager.
1.3 Performs CSM check with/without Doppler.
1.4 Measures and monitors patient fluids.
1.5 Documents all data collected on the appropriate hospital forms.

continues

1.6 Gathers admission data and documents. Does not include patient assessment.
1.7 Regularly reports changes in patient status. Communicates relevant patient information.

Job Responsibility 2: Performs general care activities (wt 15 percent)

2.1 Nutritional support: prepares patient for meals, assists with feeding and documents these activities.
2.2 Isolation: performs general care activities for patients in isolation according to policy.
2.3 Mobility: assists out of bed to chair, assists to ambulate, turn, dangle, and position.
2.4 Elimination: assists patient to bedpan or commode or bathroom.
2.5 Weighs patient using scales, bedscale, or chair scale.
2.6 Hygiene: completes mouth care, bathing (bed bath, therapeutic sitz bath, shower).
2.7 Assists with admission/discharge activities.

Job Responsibility 3: Performs special procedures (wt 15 percent)

3.1 Completes glucose monitoring, documents and reports findings to RN care manager.
3.2 Performs Foley catheterization. Certified in either male or female catheterization.
3.3 Performs cast/traction care.
3.4 Assists with or performs treatment procedures such as enemas (Fleets, soap suds, tap water enema), surgical skin preps, application of ice packs, application of K-pads.
3.5 Completes specimen collections as directed (e.g., urine, stool).
3.6 Performs simple dressing changes, replaces Band-Aid dressings, and covers surgical wounds for shower.
3.7 Provides specified ostomal therapy treatments under guidance of ostomy nurse or RN care manager.
3.8 Performs routine and procedural teaching to patients and families.
3.9 Assists with postmortem care.

Job Responsibility 4: Maintains intravenous infusion (wt 15 percent)

4.1 Observes and reports changes in IV site (peripheral, epidural, and central).
4.2 Assists with insertion of IV.
4.3 Monitors IV rate, patient controlled analgesic pump, blood.
4.4 Performs dressing change on peripheral IV site.
4.5 Documents IV activities on Parenteral Fluid Sheet.

Job Responsibility 5: Delivers simple respiratory therapy treatments/activities (wt 15 percent)

5.1 Performs suctions with Yankhauer suction.
5.2 Assists patient to cough, deep breathe, and use inspirometer.
5.3 Monitors set-up of simple oxygen.
5.4 Performs pulse oximetry (set-up, measure O_2 sat, communicate data and document).
5.5 Performs 12-lead ECGs (set-up and documentation).

Job Responsibility 6: Assists/performs therapy activities (wt 15 percent)

6.1 Assists with/performs simple patient transfers.

continues

6.2 Applies CPM machine under guidance of RN care manager.
6.3 Assists physical therapists.
6.4 Assists with occupational therapy/speech therapy activities.
6.5 Uses equipment safely and appropriately.
6.6 Performs passive range of motion (PROM).

Job Responsibility 7: Performs phlebotomy (wt 15 percent)
7.1 Performs phlebotomy correctly and safely and documents.
7.2 Chooses correct tubes for lab tests.
7.3 Performs venous draws, antecubital, butterflies, hand veins.

Job Responsibility 8: Responsibility for team effectiveness (wt 10 percent)
8.1 Customer orientation: demonstrates knowledge of his or her main customers and tries to meet or exceed their needs.
8.2 Problem-solving skills: responds to stressful situations in a calm and rational manner.
8.3 Motivation/initiator skills: demonstrates a willingness to improve his or her own work.
8.4 Conflict management skills: demonstrates the ability to look at an issue objectively and find acceptable compromises.
8.5 Communication skills: expresses him- or herself verbally and in written form at a level equal to his or her own responsibilities.
8.6 Integrity: demonstrates truthfulness and discretion and conducts him- or herself in a professional manner, making proper use of organizational resources.
8.7 Confidentiality: discusses confidential matters only in an appropriate manner and setting.
8.8 Referrals: requests consultation with staff nurses, social services, pastoral services, and nutrition services to assist in problem solving or facilitation of care.

Job Responsibility 9: Demonstrates responsibility for mission and values and organizational stewardship (wt 10 percent)
9.1 Attendance/punctuality: follows hospital policy and procedure related to notification of absence from work.
9.2 Time management: demonstrates effective time management to ensure that duties are performed in a timely and cost-effective manner.
9.3 Resource management: uses equipment, services, and supplies in a nonwasteful manner.
9.4 Financial management: demonstrates support of the departmental effort in complying with budgetary standards.
9.5 Follows hospital policy and procedure related to notification of tardiness.
9.6 Complies with established dress code.
9.7 Compassion: displays sensitivity to the needs of the patient as his or her priority.
9.8 Attends more than 50 percent of unit meetings annually.
9.9 Maintains OSHA and HFH safety standards.
9.10 Participates in QA activities.

Courtesy of Holy Family Hospital, Spokane, Washington.

Success Story: Redesigning the Role of Respiratory Therapy

Keeping a focus on serving the patient's needs, rather than staff and organizational needs, organizations have restructured the therapist's role in such a way as to improve quality measures, increase patient and employee job satisfaction, and shore up the bottom line. Multiskilling of therapists has been completed in many facilities with excellent results. In many of the current programs, multiskilled therapists work in the acute care ICUs, step down units, and medical areas, where the volume of respiratory care treatments would encourage full productivity.

A core of therapists for the general acute care, long-term, and subacute units has been maintained to do some of the more complex respiratory care, such as

- CPAP (continuous positive airway pressure)
- chest percussion
- assisting with bronchoscopy
- drawing of arterial blood gases, or other high-risk, low-volume procedures

RNs are now completing small-volume nebulizer treatments, incentive spirometry, deep nasotracheal suctioning, tracheostomy suctioning, and oximetry. In ambulatory care, therapists have been cross-trained to medical assistant jobs so that their expertise can be used to draw and interpret arterial blood gases and to educate patients about the use of their nebulizers or home airway maintenance.

Tasks Therapists Now Complete

- Continue to perform respiratory treatments, ventilator management, and traditional respiratory therapy skills
- Assist with mobility and toileting needs
- Assist with feeding and passing trays
- Perform such skills as phlebotomy, ECGs, and simple lab tests
- Bathe patients and change linens
- Take vital signs, data collection
- Assist with line placement (arterial, central)

Training Needs

People need to know how to work as a team. How to delegate and how to receive delegation and communicate clearly are as essential as understanding how to perform the skills and tasks. Be certain to clearly delineate legal aspects of the new roles, because staff often focus their legitimate fears on their licensure or certification boundaries. Consider using in-house or community nursing assistant training programs for the nursing assistant certification education of the therapists.

- How to work as a team, delegation, receiving direction, and communication skills are as essential as legal accountabilities.
- Consider certification programs for the therapists in nursing assistant expanded roles.
- Plan for orientation and professional development after the initial system is in place.

The Challenges

Several challenges face organizations undertaking this kind of role expansion. Often, the organization will assign therapists specifically to the units and retain a "core" group to float where needed. Deciding who is really their boss then becomes an issue. If respiratory therapists are totally decentralized and the central department no longer exists, then integration on respective units is a little easier. But if a core group is retained, along with a central department, then therapists may do their work on the assigned unit and return to a "home base" in the central department and never be fully realized as part of the team on their specific unit. They will then identify with the respiratory lead and may not see the unit manager as their leader.

Some areas (medical and respiratory patients) might also have two therapists at a time, but volumes of specific treatments may vary. Now, therapists help move patients, pass trays, and do some of the nursing assistant work. Not all therapists welcome the change in identity when role expansion is first introduced.

Staff Responses

Managers have told us that not everyone was thrilled with the idea to begin with, but many were spurred on by understanding the positive employability aspects of being multiskilled. *"Since trust was already there, the adult ICU day shift therapists and nurses fit it together like puzzle pieces right away. It took almost a year for those who had reservations to really become a part of the team and prefer the current system to the past one,"* observed Jolie Knudtson, RN, MBA, Clinical Director of Adult Critical Care at MultiCare Medical Center, Tacoma, Washington. Some stated that they were concerned about losing their identity as therapists as well. Some RNs were not happy to give up any of their task work, such as bed baths. Two years after role redesign, nearly all now enjoy the teamwork and assistance when they work together to care for patients.

Outcomes

"Improved extubation times for post coronary artery bypass graft patients could not have been so successful without the therapist's new role being in place," asserts Knudtson.

Cost savings are difficult to measure due to the complexity of the system, but there are great financial advantages to the deletion of phlebotomy and ECG departments while moving the personnel to other positions as needed throughout the system. Leveraging the RN's ability to provide professional care management while delegating to and working with assistive staff has been a cost saving as well.

Although many organizations stated the actual savings figures were hard to define due to the changing methods of budgeting (from departments to central in a constantly changing, managed care environment), logic would dictate that keeping all individuals productive throughout the day, working as a team, would improve the financial picture. *"The respiratory therapy staff wouldn't go back to the old way now, after two years,"* Knudtson confirmed.

The budget challenge, in terms of looking at the whole picture financially, is also important. Because most therapy departments are used to being revenue centers and billing for treatments, being a part of a capitated managed care system must be reflected in budget performance evaluation as well as service costing and measurement of productivity. Budgeting responsibility and cost allocation have to change to reflect that.

Future of Respiratory Care Practitioners

Some multiskilled respiratory therapists have asked us, *"Will we ever go back to the 'good old days' when we had a distinct, more narrow role?"* Although all roles in the restructured health care system are bound to continue to evolve, the success of the "technical partner" or cross-trained respiratory therapist in achieving positive patient outcomes, improved quality indicators, and staff and patient satisfaction would indicate that a return to the past is improbable. Respiratory care practitioners have adapted well to the changing health care system by combining their highly specialized respiratory skills with additional competencies, thus adding value in any setting across the continuum. Flexibility and a willingness to learn are key to survival. And if a sense of professional purity is lost but the care to the patients in a team process improves, benefits outweigh the potential challenges. (Hansten and Washburn, 1996).

Tool #42: Respiratory Therapists in an Expanded Role

The following excerpts are from the job descriptions and competency checklists for a "technical partner" in the acute care, patient-focused setting at MultiCare Medical Center, Tacoma, Washington. Although the job description was made generic so that respiratory therapists, licensed practical nurses, or emergency medical technicians were able to interview for the jobs and fill the roles, we have focused on the specific skills in the expanded role of the respiratory care practitioner.

MultiCare Medical Center
Nursing Service
Tacoma General Hospital
Mary Bridge Children's Health Care Center

Technical Partner

General Description

The Technical Partner is a team member working under the direction of a Registered Nurse to provide quality care that is focused on the comfort and well-being of the patient and family.

Reporting Relationship

The Technical Partner reports to the Clinical Director or designee. Input or performance will be received from the Care Team, patients, and other customers.

Distinguishing Features

This position requires a service-oriented individual with strong interpersonal skills for the purpose of delivering care and services to patients from diverse ethnic and social groups. Independent decision making is expected in the execution of daily routine duties. Decisions regarding patient care or services require the review and approval of the Clinical Partner.

Principal Accountabilities

- Performs direct patient care activities under the direction of the care team, such as basic care activities (excerpted from Critical Care RT/TP Skill Assessment)
- Verbalizes/demonstrates correct hand washing technique/frequency
- Demonstrates and verbalizes complete understanding of isolation technique in handling of equipment and supplies
- Identifies the patient and explains the procedure

continues

- Observes universal precautions as indicated
- Performs/charts vital signs (BP, body temperature, HR, urine output, and RR)
- Identifies abnormal vital sign readings and notifies RN
- Performs bed bath in a systematic fashion
- Reports any abnormal findings to RN (i.e., skin, tol. of procedure, etc.)
- Performs oral care
- Demonstrates ability to straight cath patient bladder and change drainage bag
- Accurately identifies and reports sites of impaired skin integrity
- Identifies proper diet for the patient (regular, soft, etc.)
- Identifies patients who will need assistance with feeding
- Positions patient for feeding to prevent aspiration and/or choking
- Documents intake and output
- Verbalizes the concepts of body mechanics
- Demonstrates the technique for moving a client up in bed using a sheet
- Demonstrates the technique for assisting client to ambulate with assist, with a walker, using a cane, braces
- Performs postmortem care
- Maintains a clean, comfortable, and safe environment in assigned patient rooms
- Assists the Clinical Partner in providing patient care as needed
- Performs required documentation ensuring that it is reflective of patient needs, actions taken, and patient response
- Assembles and disassembles specialty equipment
- Responds promptly and with caring actions to the patient's requests, notifying the Clinical Partner of the situation/request when appropriate
- Respects the rights and dignity of all patients
- Provides for and maintains privacy
- Maintains confidentiality of all patient and employee documents and privileged information
- Establishes and maintains professional relationships with patient care providers, management, and physicians
- Offers and acts on constructive feedback
- Conducts self in a calm, purposeful, and professional manner
- Contributes to cohesive group relationship
- Resolves issues in a manner that maintains self-esteem of all parties
- Maintains clinical competency
- Maintains current knowledge of procedures and practices specific to assigned clinical areas (e.g., a partial list excerpted from the Multicare Critical Care RT/TP Skill Assessment)

Cardiovascular:

- Prepares the skin before electrode placement
- Places leads correctly
- Obtains a 12-lead ECG when indicated per MD or hospital protocol
- Recognizes lethal dysrythmia
- Distinguishes artifact and 60-cycle interference from patient's own rhythm

Chest Tubes:

- Identifies the presence of and function of chest tube
- Identifies problems related to chest tube malfunction and trouble shoot prn

continues

- Sets up/assists with chest tube insertion
- Recognizes air leak in patient chest tube system
- Demonstrates how to measure drainage from chest tube

Phlebotomy:

- Demonstrates the ability to perform phlebotomy procedures following accepted standards and procedures

Respiratory Care:

- Demonstrates ability to perform procedure (including set-up/change of equipment, patient delivery, and charting)
- Verbalizes knowledge of written procedure, patient charges, and risk of complications of the following respiratory procedures:
  - Airway protection
  - Extubation
  - Intubation (assist)
  - Suction NT
  - Suction ET
  - Sputum sample
  - ET tube care
  - Trach care
  - Trach tube change
  - Trach change assist
  - Vent set-up
  - Vent equipment change
  - Vent—hours
  - Vent check (patient restraints, control panel, patient monitor, setting alarms, charting)
  - O_2 delivery and charting
  - Pulse oximetry
  - $ETCO_2$
  - Hyperinflation
  - Metered dose inhaler
  - Small-volume nebulizers
  - Cardioversion
  - CPAP
  - BIPAP
  - Incentive spirometry
  - Aerosol
  - USN
  - CPPD
  - Transport
  - Code 4
  - Bronchoscopy (set-up, MD assist, RT assist)
  - Pulmonary function testing
  - Blood gas machine
  - RT medications
- Participates in orientation and ongoing educational activities, attends staff meetings

continues

- Identifies and works with clinical director or designee to ensure that personal educational needs are met
- Maintains current licensure and required certification or registration
- Communicates effectively regarding patient care needs
- Complies with departmental and organizational policies and procedures
- Performs other related work as needed or directed

Minimum Qualifications

Knowledge, Skills, and Abilities:

- Basic knowledge and ability to perform specific tasks
- Concept of medical and surgical asepsis and the disease process
- Knowledge of medical terminology
- Knowledge of communication skills with ability to listen actively and respond to fellow employees/customers in a timely, competent manner both verbally and nonverbally
- Skill in interpersonal relationships with emphasis on reaching out, being friendly, and showing courtesy
- Skill in time management
- Skill in problem solving
- Skill in interpersonal communication
- Ability to be sensitive and show positive regard for fellow employees, patients, families
- Ability to work independently and take initiative
- Ability to willingly accept responsibility
- Ability to set priorities and use good judgment
- Ability to meet organization and department appearance standards on the job
- License to pass medications may be required

Education and Experience:

- High school graduation or equivalent
- Graduate from an approved LPN, respiratory therapy (RT), or emergency medical technician (EMT) training program
- Current state license as an LPN, RT, or EMT
- Previous experience as an LPN, RT, or EMT
- Willingness or ability to gain competency in the areas outlined in patient care procedure guide
- Case-by-case exceptions will be considered

Courtesy of MultiCare Medical Center, Tacoma, Washington.

TEAM BUILDING

"We trained hard—but it seemed that every time we were beginning to form up into teams, we would be reorganized. I was to learn later in life that we tend to meet any new situation by reorganizing . . . and a wonderful method it can be for creating the illusion of progress, while producing confusion, inefficiency, and demoralization." (Petronius, 60 AD)

What a Difference a Team Makes

If we heed the words of Petronius, confusion, inefficiency, and demoralization are the byproducts of reorganizing. This certainly does not describe a productive, harmonious work force! Changing roles, and the players involved, redirecting the focus and increasing the expectations of all in terms of accountability wil need specific support in developing teamwork.

However, "team building" is an overused phrase that we have found often causes many decision makers' eyes to glaze over as they think, "Oh no, not this again! We've been there, and done that, and it's just a consultant/trainer way of drumming up business to make more money." To this resistance, we offer the following observations.

> *"Indeed, nothing replaces the staff education that must occur before, during and after operational improvement programs of this scope. Not only is it important that employees know the realities their institutions face, but they must be given the resources and tools to help them implement the changes that reflect those realities."* (Lumsdon, 1994)

According to a survey by Dale Carnegie Training of Garden City, New York, building and maintaining personal relationships are the most critical skills for career success. *"The most technologically advanced workplace will find it difficult to compete effectively if employees cannot work together,"* says Stuart Levine, CEO of Dale Carnegie. *"It's an area of training that must be addressed by America's corporations in order to succeed."* (*Gets along well,* August 1996)

The need for additional education and/or supervision is often underestimated or overlooked when restructuring roles. Some leaders have the fervent hope that on-the-job training will suffice, thereby saving expensive training costs. According to the American Management's 1995 Survey of Corporate Downsizing, *"Companies that expanded their training budgets following work force reductions* [were] *nearly twice as likely to show increased profits as firms that maintained or cut training expenses."* (*Axman,* January 1996). Training and support are essential in developing a functional work team. Shortcuts in this area, as in any other, will only lead to *UN*successful restructuring.

Strategies for Improving Team Performance

- **clarify roles**
  review job descriptions and skills lists
  have staff meetings in which everyone states expectations
- **develop accountability through feedback**
  ask for the other person's assessment first
  ask the team member to participate in the solution
- **offer adequate training and supervision to support the new roles**
  one-shot sessions are not enough, enforce on the job and review quarterly

Sometimes, it's a good idea to get people on their feet and to have them participate in a game that highlights some of the existing team dynamics. There is an abundance of resources in the form of games, ranging from the most simple to the more refined, including those with video support. One that we have used for years tends more toward the simplistic side, requiring very little in terms of set-up but offering a multitude of opportunities for interpretation. We have used our version of what we call the "Domino Game" with a variety of participants, in numerous settings from executive teams to interdisciplinary staff. We have also taken this out of the health care arena, using the tool with graduate students in management.

Tool #43: The Domino Game

You will need: a box of dominoes (20 to 30)
red, white, and blue poker chips, about 30 of each color
flip chart, markers, tape
two bowls to hold the dominoes in one and the chips in the other

Basically, the game has two rules. Post these on a flip chart for the group to see. Do not give detailed explanation but clearly state the rules and limit questions to the interpretation of the rules themselves.

Rules

1. one red + one blue + one white chip = one domino + one chip of any color
2. three dominoes = seven chips of any color

These equations are not reversible.

Set-up

This game works best for a group of 7 to 10 players. If you have more than that, appoint the remaining members as roving anthropologists who will observe the process and report back to you.

The Play

Have each participant choose two chips. They may select any color. Once they have done so, review the rules and state the object of the game: "The object of the game, using the two rules, is to have a domino in your possession when time is up." Tell the players that they may begin. Allow 60 seconds for play, providing support as participants come to you to exchange their chips for dominoes. When time is up, have the play stopped. Tally how many have dominoes, "the winners," and how many do not. Record the session number and the totals on the flip chart. Ask for observations regarding what happened, what worked, and what did not. Focus also on the group dynamics and how people felt about the exchange. Were they excited, frustrated, confused, etc.? Make notes on the flip chart.

Repeat the process by taking away all the dominoes and giving the players two chips to start again. Keep sessions timed at one minute and analyze after each session as described above. Continue until everyone gets a domino by the end of one minute or until the group says they have had enough.

Findings

This game generates a lot of enthusiasm and usually an accurate portrayal of the existing state of team performance within the organization. Skilled facilitation and caution are necessary, however, as you must avoid making sweeping conclusions if they are not supported by the group. Usually, the participants will freely share their observations and feelings, many having an "aha!" experience as play imitates what's really happening within their respective workgroups in real life.

Tuckman's theory of four phases of team development (Sampson and Marthas, 1990) is often evident in the process of the game. In the first round, the group will be **forming:** focusing on the purpose and goal of the group. There may be much confusion and unwillingness to work together at this point if the team in reality has difficulty trusting each other. If they lack organized direction, often this will be displayed as they look to you for answers, "Can we share our chips? What are we supposed to do?" This is a very telling time, as players will demonstrate their natural behaviors.

As progress continues, the group may move into the **storming** phase: Natural leaders may try to organize the play, and there may be disagreements if there is more than one strong personality. Those in a follower role may voice anger or frustration if they donate their chips to the cause and are left with none at the end of the round.

Moving past disagreement and beginning to organize, the group progresses to **norming:** focusing on reaching consensus and developing cooperative working relationships. A leader/organizer may emerge, and the process of exchanging chips for dominoes may become very orderly.

The final phase of **performing:** As a functioning group with high energy, success is realized.

Facilitator Hints

- The group usually does not take any time to plan, nor have they discussed the definition of the goal. It is usually assumed that 100 percent attainment of dominoes is the goal. You may want to point this out during discussion after two to three rounds. Has anyone discussed the criteria for success?
- The group may also be restricted by the rules and not see that they have any options. It is a healthy, functional team that will ask for planning time before the next round officially begins. This is not stated in the rules, but most participants will not believe that they have the power to ask for any time between rounds.
- By round three or four, some individuals will often question whether this game will work mathematically. Someone will usually sit down with paper and pencil and try to calculate whether, by using the exchange according to the rules, all members of the group can actually get a domino. The answer is yes, but play

must be monitored. If people get excited or in a hurry, they will often forget the second part of rule one, taking a domino, but forgetting to take a chip of any color as well. This will throw off the exchange.

- Rule 2 is not necessary for success. In fact, it is a derailer of sorts, taking people off track. Trading in three dominoes for seven chips will set back the exchange considerably, and time will be lost as this is figured out. It is there to remind people that not all rules must be put into play to be successful.
- People will identify you as the leader and look to you for the answers and for direction. Clarify your role as exchange agent only; this is their game. Often, the group may elect to take over the exchange process, seeing you as the source of the problem, being too slow in the exchange.
- Room set-up may be a benefit or a barrier. If people are seated when they take their chips and play is begun, do not tell them to stand. Instead, watch them to see if they identify the physical restrictions and actually get up and move from their seats! (It's amazing how many people do not until the third round or so.)

Recall the discussion of William Bridges's work in Change Management earlier in this section. Tool #28, The Four Ps, may also be applied here as an interpretation. Lacking a clear *picture,* a sense of the *purpose,* a *plan,* and the *part* for everyone, the team will not function well enough to achieve its goal.

Above all, this is a game, not a psychiatric intervention. Have fun and don't take it too seriously! Most learning takes place in a relaxed atmosphere. Offer encouragement and support, and let the players do the rest.

More Rules of the Road

Remember our discussion of clarifying roles with tool #30? Ground rules and covenants were also shared as formalized products of clarifying expectations. We will add one final tool to this box, completing the set of role clarification from a team perspective.

▼

The continual message is clear: Do all that you can to clarify expectations and to establish "a code that you can live by."

▲

Over time, and through a series of meetings with representatives or the entire department, use this tool to direct discussion regarding the major issues of interpersonal relationships. Many of the organizations we have worked with have used this process to create a handbook of sorts, one that is very useful in sharing with new employees as they get to know the culture and in resolving conflicts as they arise among the staff.

It is a good idea to have each team member complete the worksheet individually and then to share as a group. Keep track of the responses by appointing a "scribe"

Tool #44: Terms of Agreement

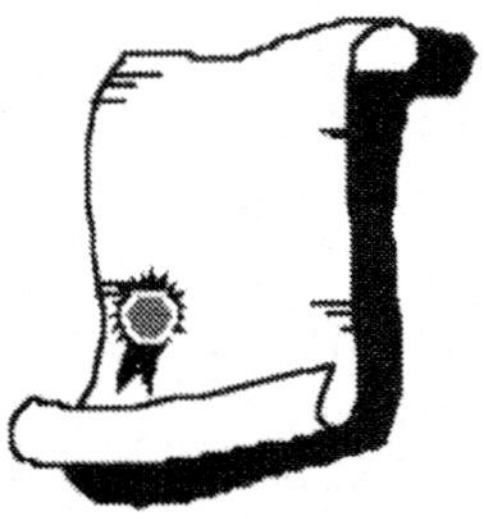

1. Communication (HOW, WHEN?)
   with Administration . . .
   Other Staff . . .
   and Each Other . . .
2. Workload Issues ("Equality": HOW?)
3. Resolving Staff Conflicts (WHO? HOW?)
4. Performance Issues (WHO, HOW, WHEN?)
5. Proposing/Initiating Change (HOW, WHO?)
6. Dealing with Mistakes (HOW?)

Sample Completed Terms of Agreement

Unit Purpose: to provide comprehensive quality care to our patients and their families

Communication							
With Administration	*With Each Other*	*With Other Depts*	*Workload Issues*	*Resolving Staff Conflicts*	*Performance Issues*	*Initiating Change*	*Dealing with Mistakes*
How: Written (grapevine) e-mail	Leave note on time card	Call when there is a problem; if not resolved, pass on to Charge RN	Tell the person working with you first, being specific	Go to the person first	Go to the person first	Talk with other staff for ideas	Tell the person
Meetings: Staff meetings: what percentage attendance	Mailboxes		If not resolved, ask the Charge RN for assistance	If not resolved, go to the Charge RN	Some issues need follow-up with mgr. or Charge RN (clarify which)	Leave a note	Person(s) responsible to come up with ways of avoiding in future
Verbal: Forums			If not resolved, call the supervisor				QA memo as needed (clarify)

from the group to write answers on a flip chart and then to transfer to a more manageable document when consensus is achieved. An example of this "more manageable document" format follows the worksheet.

▼

"We are what we repeatedly do. Excellence, then, is not an act, but a habit." (Aristotle)

▲

References for Section Three

Axman, spare that trainer. 1996. *Training 33* (January):12.

Bebiak, J. 1995. Process design and discipline are critical to cost-reduction success: Three case studies. *Strategies for Healthcare Excellence* (July):8–11.

Bridges, W. 1991. *Managing transitions: Making the most of change.* Reading, Mass: Addison Wesley, chaps 1–4.

Broadwell, M. 1995. Why command and control won't go away. *Training 32* (September):67.

Davis, S. 1996. Adapting to the accelerated health care revolution. *Reengineering the Hospital 3,* no. 1:4.

Domning, J. 1994. LPNs and the ethics of healthcare reform. *Creative Nursing* (November/December): 9–10.

Esque, T., and T. Gilbert. 1995. Making competencies pay off. *Training 32* (January):44–50.

Flarey, D. 1994. The OZ principle. *JONA 24,* no. 12:12–13.

Georges, J.C. 1996. The myth of soft-skills training. *Training 33* (January):49.

Gets along well with others. 1996. *Training 33* (August):17–18.

Halle, S., as quoted by J. Lapp. 1996. *The Change Letter 5,* no. 4:2.

Hamel, G. 1996. Strategy as revolution. *Harvard Business Review 33* (July–August):69–82.

Hammer, M., and S. Stanton. 1995. quoted in *Fortune,* May 15, 1995, 108 (from *The reengineering revolution.* 1995. [Harper Business].

Hansten, R., and M. Washburn. 1994. *Clinical delegation skills.* Gaithersburg, MD: Aspen Publishers, Inc.

Hansten, R., and M. Washburn. 1996. Redesigning the role of respiratory therapy. *Successful Restructuring 1,* no. 1:6–7.

Hansten, R., and M. Washburn. 1996. Damage control during re-engineering. *Successful Restructuring 1,* no. 2:1–4.

Hansten, R., and M. Washburn. 1996. Decentralizing the lab: Who does the phlebotomies? *Successful Restructuring 1,* no. 2:1, 6.

Hansten, R., and M. Washburn. 1996. Structuring learning opportunities for new roles: What worked, what didn't. *Successful Restructuring 1,* no. 5:1, 3–5.

Herrick, K., R. Hansten, and M. Washburn. 1993. From barriers to bridges: Success strategies for high performing teams. A portable workshop with the Northwest Organization of Nurse Executives. Contact Karen Herrick, 206/285-0102.

Lindeman, C. 1996. A vision for nursing education. *Creative Nursing* no. 1:8.

Lumsdon, K. 1994. Want to save millions? *Hospitals and Health Networks 68* (November 5):24–32.

MacLeod, J.A., and S. Sella. 1992. One year later: Using role theory to evaluate a new delivery system. *Nursing Forum 27,* no. 2:20–28. [Citing Hardy, M. 1978. Role stress and strain. In *Role theory: Per-*

spectives for the health professional, eds. M. Hardy and M. Conway, 73–109. New York: Appleton-Century-Crofts.]

Maruca, R. 1996. Looking for better productivity? *Harvard Business Review* (July–August):9–10.

McEachern, S. 1995. Nurses resist change, need CEO's attention. *Health Care Strategic Management 13,* no. 5:1, 19–23.

Peters, T. 1996. Employee training: Panacea or placebo? *Fast Forward* (October):8–9.

Porter-O'Grady, T. 1996. Seven basic rules for successful redesign. *JONA 126,* no. 1:46–54.

Porter-O'Grady, T., and C.K. Wilson. 1995. *The leadership revolution.* Gaithersburg, MD: Aspen Publishers, Inc.

Sampson, E., and M. Marthas. 1990. *Group process for the health professions.* Berkeley, CA: Delmar Publishers.

Shandler, D. 1996. *Reengineering the training function.* Delray Beach, FL: St. Lucie Press.

Shaw, E. 1995. The training waste conspiracy. *Training 33* (April).

Stevenson, H.H., and M.C. Moldoveanu. 1995. The power of predictability. *Harvard Business Review 73* (July–August):140–144.

Thomas, K.W. 1977. Toward multi-dimensional values in teaching: The examples of conflict behaviors. *Academy of Management Review 2*:487.

Top fifteen factors determining patient satisfaction. 1992. *Modern Healthcare* (June):44.

SECTION FOUR

Evaluating Our Progress and Celebrating Success

Worst Case Scenario:

"Don't Confuse Us with the Facts"

In one highly acute department at a regional medical center, a new model of care delivery (now patient focused) was adopted. The entire department had decided to adopt an RN/nursing assistant partnership for direct care while multiskilling other roles in the support of these pairs. The decision was made to use nursing assistants, because the budget required it. An additional factor in the determination process was that nurses who were designing new jobs felt unsure of their own roles and were challenged by the possibility of working with assistive personnel with additional skills, such as LPNs. One group of nurses, those working in the intensive care area, expressed continued concern about the abilities of the CNAs to assist them in that particular area. As the project rolled out, the CNAs were not finding enough work to keep them busy. At first, managers and charge nurses believed this was due to the nurses' inability to delegate. During this time period, discussions with the State Board of Nursing revealed that some of the tasks originally planned for the CNAs to do were no longer approved. Despite continued evaluation, with new information being provided, one year later no decision had been made to change the care delivery system. Staff continued to feel overwhelmed and angry. Nursing assistant turnover was accelerated by the negative feelings and anger misplaced on them by their coworkers. Appropriately, staff were heard questioning, *"Why bother to evaluate what we've done if they have no intention of changing it if it doesn't work?"* and *"We have learned how to be specific in our feedback and recommendations for improvement, but it falls on deaf ears!"*

However, in "best case scenarios" we hear statements such as *"This is a much better way to work!"* and *"I feel excited to get up and come to work in the morning!"* in other organizations. Why do some seem to be able to produce outcomes that are worthy of admiration and replication, but others seemed destined for failure? Besides the need to adequately and accurately assess the organization's needs, plan an organized participative interdisciplinary process for the change, and deftly implement the plan, there remains one continuous part of the process: **evaluation**. And evaluation by itself is not enough; the very performance of evaluation processes must guarantee that the data received will be translated into information and responses. These responses may be reinforcement and celebration or may consist of activities varying from slight course correction to revamping of the system. Health care professionals' training in biology tells us that the system that does not continue to change and evolve in response to environmental conditions will die. Translated into a health care organization, the organism's death would be a parallel for detrimental patient care, closing facilities due to financial ill health, loss of jobs for health care workers, and loss of health care access to communities.

❹ EVALUATING OUR PROGRESS AND CELEBRATING SUCCESS

One never notices what has been done—one can only see what remains to be done.

Marie Curie

In this section, we discuss

- measuring success from an organization-wide, unit-based, or individual perspective
- use of shared governance councils or management–labor groups to guide the process and evaluate progress
- evaluation of training outcomes
- tools to support the ongoing nature of evaluation

EVALUATION: WHAT'S HAPPENING?

To get started, here's a quick tool that can be used to determine how your organization is faring during the chaos of restructuring, reengineering, or whatever quality improvement process is ongoing at your facility.

Tool #45: Evaluating an Organization for Successful Restructuring

Yes No

____ ____ 1. Decision-making task forces or teams are interdisciplinary in membership, including personnel from all areas of the continuum of care, with each discipline making contributions respected by all team members.

____ ____ 2. Staff (from chief executive throughout organization) demonstrate personal accountability for their roles in achieving our organizational mission through individual actions with all our publics.

____ ____ 3. Members of each discipline can clearly state the mission, the values of the organization, the vision for the restructuring effort, and how these relate.

____ ____ 4. Our management team is unified in its presentation of restructuring plans or processes.

____ ____ 5. Our quality of service and clinical outcomes are being measured and continuously improve.

____ ____ 6. Members of our organization are handling the stress of change effectively, with many expressing hope and enthusiasm for the future.

____ ____ 7. Empowerment of all personnel is welcomed with eagerness.

____ ____ 8. Problems are identified in terms of solvability, without blame.

____ ____ 9. Employees are comfortable taking risks with open communication, expressing unpopular opinions, and sharing creative ideas.

____ ____ 10. Follow-through on action plans made by groups or individuals is supported and sustained.

Source: Adapted from R. Hansten and M. Washburn, *Successful Restructuring,* Vol. 1, No. 1, p. 3, © 1996, Aspen Publishers, Inc.

If you answered yes to all these questions, we'd like you to contact us with your story so that we can share it with others! If you answered:

7 to 10 Nos: Sorry! There's some work to be done, but identification of problems is the first step! You may have been focusing primarily on the reengineering tasks rather than responding to the problems that have surfaced as a result of your efforts. Don't despair, redesign is an ongoing process.

3 to 6 Nos: There's a lot to be done, but it sounds as if you are keeping in touch with the "real life" of your organization.

1 to 2 Nos: Wow! You are well on your way to creating an organization that brings excellence in health care to your publics, as well as caring for the precious human resources who deliver it. Best wishes for continuing on your current path!

MEASURES FOR SUCCESS

Living in a nation abuzz with questioning new methods of health care finance, discussing ideas of ethical delivery of illness care (is health care a right or a privilege?), ensures that many groups are beginning to determine how health care should be measured. Health care is in the balance: How do we define quality, and how can we continue to measure the value of the care that we receive? Does everyone have a right to the same care or just to basic care? Is rationing the only way that we can deliver basic care to all? The change from fee-for-service medicine to managed care has demanded that monitoring of quality is essential.

Outcomes: What's Possible?

The Bad News

At the beginning of each section, we've given the reader an example of a "worst case scenario" from a change process that has not achieved the desired outcome. As we read the newspapers and weekly news magazines, listen to broadcast media, and review the most recent articles and books published in the scientific or popular press, we've noted that the public has expressed a fear of reengineering of the health care system. Nurses have gone to the media to express their outrage at staffing cuts and replacement of RNs with poorly trained assistive personnel. To many, managed care has come to mean financial management (read: cheap care) rather than high-quality, coordinated clinical care that delights the consumers and providers. Mistakes that have been made in prestigious institutions have become the topics of talk shows and news events, and in many cases, care delivery redesign has been incriminated in the fray. Health care administrators, along with the public, have come forth with concerns about cost cutting in the face of pending Medicare fund deficits.

From our perspective as consultants who see the worst and the best, it is terribly unfortunate that we, as health care providers, have often moved ahead too quickly in change efforts in our attempts to cut costs and ensure organizational viability. Survival of our missions has also been at stake, and rarely, if ever, have leaders or followers made changes in care delivery systems or processes with malicious intent. Well-meaning people have made decisions that were the most logical, at the time, given the information they possessed. But once evaluation occurs, the better part of leadership is to admit that blunders were made and then to continue the perpetual process of improving the system.

All of us in health care would agree that health care systems have needed changing and will likely continue to need to adapt and improve in the coming years! We have labored, for decades, with frustration at systems' problems such as supplies not being available and at patients not receiving the care we know they should have in the best of worlds, and yet it has taken financial imperatives to move us from inertia to experimentation. The message of the worst case scenarios is this: Evaluation must occur as an ongoing process in every organization to minimize the potential negative effects of the ensuing chaos of transition.

▼

Negative outcomes can and do occur from the chaos of transition; therefore taking the time necessary for assessment and planning, careful oversight of the reengineering process and interventions, and continual evaluation throughout are necessary to protect the public trust in health care providers.

▲

The Good News

Good news abounds in the literature, and we have talked with individuals in different organizations who state that they "love their jobs," that "this is working much better than before for our patients and the staff." There are many examples of improved consumer satisfaction, of better clinical outcomes including better functional status at home, better patient management of their own conditions. Systems that support patient care throughout the continuum are working in ways that show true interdisciplinary communication and teamwork. We mention these positive outcomes as a jump-start for those who are exhausted from their restructuring efforts and to provide hope for the faint-hearted as they continue their own processes at home organizations. You'll see specific examples of positive outcomes in this section as we discuss some familiar organizations and the tools that will help with the evaluation process.

Measuring Success: Overall System Measures

A positive side effect of our scrutiny of health care delivery systems and the need for better financial management of health care has been the trend to develop better, standardized quality measures. The National Council for Quality Assurance (NCQA) has developed performance measurements for objective evaluation of care provided in the managed care setting. The Health Plan Employer Data and Information Set (HEDIS) standards look to five areas of performance: quality of care (includes data such as birth weights, immunization, and screening rates), access, patient satisfaction, membership and utilization, and finance and descriptive information. (Towers, 1996)

The American Nurses Association (ANA) has developed a Nursing Care Report Card for Acute Care, including seven core indicators: skill mix (RN/LPNs/LVNs/assistive personnel); hours of care per patient day; nursing staff satisfaction; outcome indicators such as nosocomial infection rate; maintenance of skin integrity; patient injury rate; and patient satisfaction with nursing care, pain management, and education information. (Stanley and Foer, 1996)

Although each health care provider is interested in outcomes for every specific patient he or she cares for, the most helpful research from a redesign perspective would provide some evidence that certain interventions by an interdisciplinary team, within a specific type of care delivery system, would produce the most positive patient outcomes from an individual and collective viewpoint. Patient outcomes research is on a growth curve but has not revealed all that we would like to know as we prepare for best practices in reengineering. Some nursing leaders suggest that a combination of the elements of Werley and Lang's Nursing Minimum Data Set with the Uniform Hospital Discharge Data Set could allow for evaluation of the relationship of nursing management processes and patient outcomes, although these focus more on errors, morbidity, and mortality than on clinical outcomes. (Mark and Burleson, 1995) Because standardization of measurement and tracking has not occurred, it is difficult at this time to correlate practices across organizations and draw a causative relationship for patient outcomes based on patient care delivery systems. We have encouraged those who are engaged in the planning stages of redesign to do a comprehensive journal search and review the elements of care delivery redesign that would indicate improved outcomes for patients, nursing staff, and other disciplines. For use of assistive personnel in hospital settings, we recommend an article that evaluates 24 different studies of models of care delivery systems by Greta Krapohl and Elaine Larson (1996), "The Impact of Unlicensed Assistive Personnel on Nursing Care Delivery."

In the planning section, we discussed the necessity of defining success measures when planning the vision and the purpose for the project. Measures for success of the project may include

1. Patient satisfaction measures
   - wait time
   - numbers of faces seen during a hospital or clinic visit
   - patients' perception of their treatment
   - whether they believed they were given the knowledge and tools necessary to care for themselves, or be cared for, during their next phase of treatment
   - patients' ease of access to care

- patients' perception of the degree of participation in care decisions
- whether the health care professionals seemed to collaborate and have a clear idea of what direction they are planning with the patient
- loyalty (or return business intent)

2. Staff satisfaction measures
   - staff perception of their autonomy, level of respect, and the impact of teamwork
   - intent to stay in their job
   - intent to leave
   - whether they or their family would use the facility for health care
3. Other stakeholders' satisfaction
   - physician
   - ancillary departments
   - home health or other areas within the continuum of care
4. Clinical outcomes
   - quantity of (or absence of) untoward incidents (i.e., falls, accidents, stasis ulcers, treatment or medication errors, emergency department [ED] visits due to improper medication usage)
   - recidivism and readmission to intensive care units (ICUs) when transferred
   - ability of patient/family to maintain self based on home or clinic support, appropriate adherence to physician direction
   - variances along clinical pathways
   - hospital-acquired infection
   - discharge or transfer time
   - functional status of the individual (improvement or maintenance)
5. Financial measures
   - budget variances
   - patient census or number of procedures (linked to positive public image) per reporting period
   - productivity measures
   - cost of care per covered life
   - patient care hours per patient day (acute or long-term care)
   - recidivism of patients in a capitated system (e.g., return to the ED after discharge from acute care)
   - use of overtime or agency workers

Overall success of reengineering projects is generally measured on a facility-wide or departmental basis but may not be communicated effectively to those at the front lines. Often, we find that although a few individuals may be aware of successful outcomes of a project, most staff are laboring in new systems, feeling awkward and ineffective, deep in the self-absorption common during transition. Pointing out the actual progress that has been made, supported by statistics, may infuse individuals with the necessary energy to continue.

The knowledge of results, in conjunction with understanding of the purpose, creates an environment that encourages individuals to self-organize. As Margaret Wheatley (1992) discusses in *Leadership and the New Science, "Information is an organization's primary source of nourishment."* (p. 107) *"We create order when we invite conflicts and contradictions to rise to the surface, when we search them out, highlight them, even allowing them to grow large and worrisome. We need to support people in the hunt for unsettling or disconfirming information, and provide them with the resources of time, colleagues, and opportunities for processing the information. . . . Through constant exchanges, new information is spawned, and the organization grows in effectiveness."* (p. 116)

▼

Establish a person or group who is accountable for collecting overall measurement data and communicating results in as many ways as possible, written, verbal, graphic and colorful, repeatedly.

▲

EVALUATION OF OVERALL SUCCESS AND QUALITY INITIATIVES

We invite you to review two examples of successful outcomes from a project perspective, along with some tools used to support the process of evaluation: MultiCare Medical Center in Tacoma, Washington, and Legacy Health Systems in Portland, Oregon. You have seen examples of their work in previous sections of this book. First, we will celebrate MultiCare's successful outcomes.

Success Story: Evaluating Results at MultiCare Medical Center, Tacoma, Washington

1995 Service quality results are revealed in the following table:

REENGINEERING RESULTS
MULTICARE MEDICAL CENTER
TACOMA, WASHINGTON

- 65% of team's time is allocated to direct care
- 12 minute turnaround time for EKG
- 18 minute turnaround time for lab whole blood analysis in Emergency Department
- Lab turnaround time reduced from 60 minutes in February of 1995 for Chem 7 to 18 minutes
- Number of faces seen by patients decreased to less than 20 for a 3-day stay
- Overall cleanliness score was 87%
- Cumulative Cost Savings: $32 million

Courtesy of MultiCare Medical Center, Tacoma, Washington.

How did this success story unfold? We have discussed MultiCare's strategies throughout the previous sections. Staff attribute their success to the following advice:

- Establish monitoring indicators before you begin and get firm baselines.
- Use teams, targets, and timelines to get results.
- Don't do pilots—use the Nike philosophy: "Just Do It!"
- Adjust budgets as units go live to ensure compliance to new models.
- Learn as you go and make changes based on your learning.

(Advice contributed by Diane Cecchettini and Mary Ellen Swatta.)

Evaluation of Success from a Unit or Department Perspective

In addition to measuring and broadcasting results from the organizational viewpoint, the success of a redesign is created from the departmental outcomes, and clearly these contributing components must be evaluated as well. Unit-based staff are interested in "our success" on a personal basis. The impact of pride in the department's and the organization's success on individual performance and loyalty is difficult to quantify but certainly creates a positive work environment. In the following examples, Legacy Health Systems, Portland, Oregon, shares the methods it has used to measure success on a unit or departmental basis. Later, we view more tools that can be used by managerial or supervisory staff to evaluate the performance of the unit and the individuals who work there.

The Patient Care Councils at Legacy have begun to evaluate their progress with the implementation of the new system. The measures of success they are using to evaluate the system are listed below, and a tool used to document measurement follows.

Tool #46: Measures of Success

Outcomes Unit/Department Accountable For:

Patient/Family, Team, MD Satisfaction

- Improve staff/patient & physician satisfaction
- Reliable communication system, connectedness

Quality Outcomes

- More consistent practice/care for patients; improved patient outcomes—QI indicators
- Clinical quality is improved

Financial Viability

- Decrease cost of supplies
- Decrease cost of agency and overtime
- Meeting unit budget for both labor, supplies and equipment
- Resource utilization is efficient

Individual Staff Accountability for Team Performance & Communication

- Ability to engage in problem solving on multiple levels: interpersonal, practice, and interdepartmental
- Faster response to change as you progress

"Ownership" of Processes and Outcomes and "Partnership" To Get to Where We Want To Go

- Streamlined work processes and decreased duplication
- Increased participation of customers
- Increased understanding of health care, interdepartmental, and organizational issues

Courtesy of Legacy Health Systems, Portland, Oregon.

MEASURING PROGRESS USING SHARED GOVERNANCE TEAMS AND LABOR-MANAGEMENT GROUPS

When working with organizations in the latter phases of redesign, we often hear the frustration of staff who believe that parts of the system aren't working the way that they were designed, but they aren't certain who to talk with to "get things fixed." When shared governance councils are working effectively, supportive issue resolution is an ongoing process. Staff begin to trust that they can have an impact on their work lives and the quality of care rendered to the patients. Often, a redesign project is a perfect time to begin to develop leadership skills of staff and encourage them to begin to take the reins of the department. As "project teams" or "design task forces" learn to use quality management tools and systems thinking processes and develop an empowered attitude, these teams can often begin to function as the "navigation" group or transform themselves into governance councils.

As an example of this, we continue to review Legacy's monitoring process. The development of the shared governance councils was discussed in our Planning section. To use the shared governance councils to supervise progress, Legacy used the following areas of focus and identified resources necessary to make it happen.

Tool #47: Unit Evaluation

PATIENT-FOCUSED CARE UNIT EVALUATION

UNIT ____________________

DATE ____________________

MANAGER ________________

PATIENT-FOCUSED CARE SUPPORT

MONITOR	RESULTS	FURTHER ACTION
Overall Patient Satisfaction Average score on patient relations/patient satisfaction surveys (monthly)		
Staff Satisfaction Survey indicator ratings on unit-based employee surveys (biannual)		
Physician Satisfaction Survey indicator ratings on unit-based physician surveys (biannual)		
Supply Cost Containment Supply expense per patient-day from operating reports (monthly)		
Environmental Cleanliness Daily housekeeping service score on patient relations/ patient satisfaction surveys (monthly)		

Courtesy of Legacy Health Systems, Portland, Oregon.

Tool #48: Areas of Focus/Resources Required

LPH Patient Care Services
Patient Care Council Development
Areas of Focus

Focus Areas	*Skill Sets*	*Education*
LEVEL 1 **EFFECTIVE USE OF RESOURCES:** • Managing supplies and equipment on the unit • Unit quality planning • Review and streamline work processes **INITIATIVE:** • Clinical education and professional development • Standards of practice • Implementation and monitoring clinical paths/outcome planning **TEAMWORK:** • Staff satisfaction • Develop/define staff roles and responsibilities • Patient/family involvement in care **RESPECT AND CARING:** • Patient satisfaction • Facilitate full team involvement • Facilitate understanding of other practices	• Decision-making techniques • Problem-solving process • Basic CQI tools (e.g., flowcharting, run charts, brainstorming) • Project management (plan, implement, evaluation, follow-up) • Data-gathering techniques • Data analysis techniques • Effective communication skills • Understanding group dynamics/ stages • How to be an effective group participant • Delegation and collaboration • Meeting effectiveness • Understanding current health care environment	• CQI tools and techniques • Giving and receiving feedback • Conflict resolution • Delegation module • Outcome planning module • RN role in a changing health care environment module • Facilitation skills • Change and transition management • Planning module • Customer service modules • Videos: CQI tools Team development issues Feedback
LEVEL 2 **EFFECTIVE USE OF RESOURCES:** • Operational issues (staffing, scheduling) • Role in cost management (e.g., budgeting) **INITIATIVE:** • Identify and facilitate needed changes to improve patient care • Ownership of unit performance **TEAMWORK:** • Develop unit norms and behavioral expectations • Peer-to-peer accountability and review • System collaboration **RESPECT AND CARING:** • Articulation of patient/family point of view • Communicating a positive professional image • Value each team member's contribution	• Continue to practice and develop skill sets identified in Level 1 • Raising difficult issues within the team • Advanced facilitation skills • Idealized work redesign ("Thinking outside the box") • Creative problem solving • Business literacy • Win–win negotiation • Consensus building • Self-assessment for performance effectiveness • Advanced feedback skills • Advanced group dynamics	• Attend conferences • Writing and presenting papers • Advanced facilitation • Styles inventory (e.g., LIFO, MBTI) • Innovation class • Advocacy class • Win–win negotiation class • Understanding and working within the budget process • Business of health care • Managed care monopoly

Courtesy of Legacy Health Systems, Portland, Oregon.

This sample agenda from one of the first meetings of the council at Legacy can be a guide to the issues that would be necessary to discuss in the development of effective meetings and optimal results. Tools for improving meeting effectiveness are discussed later in this section.

Tool #49: Sample Agenda

Patient Care Council (PCC) Task Force

Aug. 17, 1996

Agenda

1. Discuss perceptions of shared governance

2. Review PCC summary examples of other council structures

3. Review unit task force's role
   Identify unit PCC structure
   Communicate and get feedback from all staff
   Recruit members
   Assist in member selection

4. Identify unit goals . . . Whatever we do must . . .

5. Identify current committees, unit/staff needs, manager responsibilities . . . (ideas on post-its and affinity diagram into groups)

6. Identify grouped issues/needs; build council(s) structure

7. Address structure issues
   How many councils and types
   Examples of issues addressed by each council
   How many members on each council—types of members
   How long will members serve—rotation pattern
   How often will they meet, for how long
   How will members be selected
   Decision-making structure (PCC-core councils relationship)
   Participation and commitment (?required)

8. Next steps
   Communicate recommendations to all staff
   Regroup and review staff feedback, make any revisions
   Communicate any revisions to all staff
   Recruit members and assist in selection and notification

Courtesy of Legacy Health Systems, Portland, Oregon.

Evaluation of Progress in a Union Environment: Labor–Management Teams

Because unionized environments produce special issues for staff involvement in redesign committees, we thought it would be helpful to include information about how it is possible to make this kind of partnership not only viable, but optimal. We'll share a success story and some advice from an organization we've discussed before.

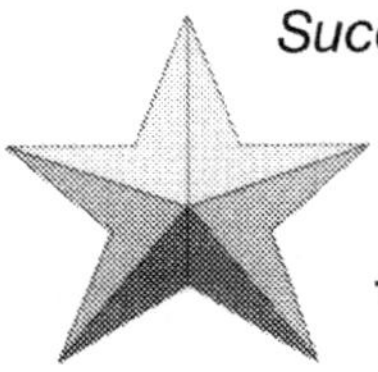

Success Story: Allina Health Labor–Management Teams

We return to Allina Health Systems, consisting of 17 nonprofit hospitals in Minnesota and Wisconsin. Previously, we discussed their labor–management vision during the section on planning. Their outcomes, putting this vision into action have de-escalated a potential powder keg situation into highly successful teams involved in care redesign efforts. A bit of history: Certainly, the past situation in the Twin Cities was a recipe for union unrest: a nurses' strike in 1984 had closed hospitals for weeks, distrust was rampant, and some managers had never met a union representative during 20 years of tenure. Yet, in 1991 teams were functioning so well that when economics necessitated closure of one 800-bed hospital, affecting 1,800 employees, a jointly managed placement process resulted in placing all but 100 employees, with a cost savings of more than $9,000,000. The public and employee trust generated by this effort was phenomenal, decreasing fear of layoff and improving of employee involvement, as well as quality of worklife.

Other significant outcomes of the 150+ labor–management teams include

- Establishment of joint decision making on contracting-in/contracting-out work, which resulted in improved quality measures and savings in excess of $500,000
- Realized cost improvements in excess of $10,000,000 through work redesign
- Reports of key indicators used to measure clinical and community health improvement, customer satisfaction/loyalty, and financial health show improvement throughout the system (Bushick, 1996)

Jack Dobier, Labor Management Coordinator at Allina Health Systems, Minneapolis, Minnesota, gives us some advice to deal effectively with union–management teamwork.

- Be sure of your commitment to the process: For management this is a business decision; for unions this is an organizational decision.
- Recognize that the development of positive relationships takes time, based on trust and good faith. They require a significant investment of time, resources, training, and risk taking.

- Clearly define separate and shared interests and goals for the cooperative process, and be willing to share, learn, and change.
- Invest in development of organizational values, employee relations principles, staff support, budget, training, and education. Each group must pay attention to process, structures, ownership, control, and implementation.
- Involve unions early in developing employee involvement processes.
- Middle management input in developing and managing joint processes is critical: They are stakeholders and will resist if not involved.
- As relationships develop, the decision-making process needs to move away from information sharing and consulting and toward collaboration and consensus.
- Invoking a "no surprises" principle will significantly improve the labor–management relationship.
- Communicate—communicate—communicate!

TOOLS FOR MEASURING SUCCESS FROM A MANAGERIAL PERSPECTIVE

Keeping in Touch by Using Managerial Rounds for Evaluation

Reports by Abraham Lincoln's secretaries document that he spent over 75 percent of his time meeting with people. He would circulate among the people and among the troops, and relieved General John C. Fremont of his command in Missouri in September 1861 for the following reasons: *"His cardinal mistake is that he isolates himself, and allows nobody to see him, and by which he does not know what is going on in the very matter he is dealing with."* (Phillips, 1992) If getting out among the troops, observing, talking, and asking questions, helped put our country together during the War between the States, it certainly would be helpful for those who are in leadership positions during care delivery reengineering.

As we discussed in detail in our section on assessment, we refer again to the benefits of managerial rounds for multiple purposes. Unfortunately, when we discuss this with managers in the midst of a care delivery redesign process, we hear similar responses from managers, administrators, and clinical specialists and educators. "I don't have time." Our response is clear. You don't have time **NOT** to. Reflect on what your personal outcomes must be: If delivery of a predetermined quality of care is bottom line accountability in your role, then seeing what is happening in your department is essential. For those of you who are feeling overwhelmed and still resistive, please agree to add managerial rounds to your daily or weekly calendar, at least for three weeks. We can nearly guarantee that you'll find such positive results from this practice, including saving time and headaches, that you'll include this as a routine fundamental management technique.

Those readers who have been expert clinicians will find that there are many similarities with managerial rounds and the clinical observations you have been making on a frequent basis. In many instances, whether in acute, home, long-term, or ambulatory care, clinical rounds by an expert clinician (whether a manager, educator, or clinical specialist) remain an excellent method by which to evaluate the performance of care providers, the outcomes patients or clients are experiencing, and the need for further education or training. We recommend a clinical or managerial emphasis on a general basis, but with specific focus when indicated, such as on "off" shifts, and in areas where a preponderance of newer employees work, or when errors have occurred. That overall picture of "how we are doing" will become clear through on-site observation.

Individual Performance Measurement

One aspect of restructuring that often becomes an Achilles heel for an organization is a lack of accountability on the part of staff, managers, and the executive group to deal effectively with performance issues. When redesign has taken place, there are no surplus resources available to "take up the slack" and cover for the performance of a marginal employee. And because a team is only as strong as the weakest link, an organization that has allowed substandard performance to be tolerated will find that success is hard to achieve. This means at all levels. If we expect each staff member to develop the skills to give feedback effectively to his or her colleagues, peers, and subordinates, but the board does not deal honestly with the suboptimal performance of an executive, the staff won't either. Common wisdom tells us that accountability flows downhill, and experience teaches us that those organizations that have practiced enabling, nonconfronting behaviors in the spirit of a well-intended (but dysfunctional) "family atmosphere" are not successful in reengineering projects.

In the section on planning, we discussed two examples of performance outcomes agreements, one as a method of group or task force planning and tracking and one for staff performance. In this example (tool #50), we'll use a performance counseling session from an executive to a department manager viewpoint. In this scenario, the department manager has been doing very well with his budget, but the supplies have not been delivered, or available in-house, to the patient care units. Before meeting with the manager, the executive has determined her expectations and the overall goal. During the meeting, the manager will determine the steps that he will take to achieve the goals independently, with the assistance of the executive only if absolutely necessary. The discussion includes how far the manager may flex the departmental budget, and what the repercussions may be if the outcomes are not met. Necessary resources and support will be negotiated as well, and coaching can occur if the manager is new or needs further assistance in developing problem-solving skills.

Role Clarification/Job Priorities

You have probably noted that redesign is on ongoing process; an organization will never achieve total perfection, nor are groups ever "finished" with reengineering. One of the most commonly changed aspects of care delivery redesign is that of roles or job descriptions. Modifications may be necessary as a consequence of the changing needs of the population being served, legislation altering tasks or processes that are condoned by state codes or rules, or the work force in the area is lacking in the number of prepared individuals that could function in a newly designed role. Just as frequently, during managerial rounds a manager may hear from staff that "this role just doesn't work" or "there's too much (or not enough) for these roles to do," and further follow-up will then be required. The following tool can be used to evaluate the effectiveness of roles in a newly designed system of care delivery, determining whether it is the role itself or the manner in which it has been implemented.

Tool #50 Performance/Outcomes Agreement

Employee/Group Name: Department Manager, Central Supply   Date: 4/9/97

Goal/Purpose: Purpose of Role: To ensure that adequate supplies are present where needed in a timely fashion
Goal of discussion: Develop a plan by which nursing units will have the correct number and type of supplies available on a daily basis (including weekends)

Expectations:
1. Plan to be completed and in process within one week
2. Nursing units will have less than one complaint per week regarding supplies (not including new supplies)
3. Plan includes reasonable budget impact (to be discussed)

Steps to Achieving the Goal:
1.
2.
3.

Leadership Style/Resources:

Resources Needed:
Support Needed: High -- Low
Direction Needed: High -- Low

Critical checkpoints: Date:
1. Review plan 4/12/97 10 AM
2. Review results and complaint log 4/18/97
3. Review progress 5/3/97

In a redesign project that added LPNs to the skill mix with RNs in what had been an "RN only" patient care delivery system, managers and some RNs complained that the LPNs had too much to do; they were not doing their charting. As this tool (#51) was used to discuss these issues, the charting issue was discussed. The example shows the LPNs' answers to the questions. This tool assisted the manager and clinical nurse specialists to begin to clarify the real problems: that some RNs were not willing to let go of the charting and that some LPNs were not clear on expectations of what should be charted. Subsequently, the roles of both groups were defined in staff meetings, and the clinical nurse specialist began to observe charting on a daily basis to evaluate the success of their interventions.

Tool #51: Role Acceptance and Role Behavior

Role Expectations: What others think I am responsible for and how I should do it	*An RN told us not to chart at all; "Keep away from my charts," she said.*
Role Conception: What I think my job is and how I have been taught to do it	*I was taught to chart whatever I do on the narrative, and to record vital signs on the graphic form, during orientation, but I am not sure what to say.*
Role Acceptance: What I am willing to do	*I am not willing to chart if an RN will yell at me; but if I am supposed to, I will.*
Role Behavior: What I actually do	*I do not chart at all right now, but it is not because I am too busy.*

Job Descriptions and Peer Evaluation

Job descriptions and peer evaluation are two additional tools that can be used for individual performance measurement. In all cases, the underlying motive with performance measurement is to create a space for individuals to reflect on their purpose and value within the organization, their strengths and their weaknesses, and to open up to the feedback necessary for growth. Keep in mind that when an individual is not performing up to standard, that person is often aware of the mismatch and often needs to become clear on whether the job is the best role for his or her particular talents. Sharing performance success (an easy task!) will inspire the individual and the team to go on with energy. It is just as true that avoiding discussion of poor performance (a more difficult task) in the guise of kindness is not only inhuman to the employee, not allowing him or her a chance to improve or find a better job experience, but also deprives the team of success and denies high-quality care to those served.

Success Story: Job Description Revision

The following narrative, job description, and performance standards demonstrate the process used for improving accountability and role clarity during the redesign process at Legacy Health Systems, Portland, Oregon. The process of revising job descriptions, common to many redesign projects, is itself therapy for role clarity and if many individuals are included in the process, will provide for positive team norms.

A fundamental support to the achievement of performance expectations for any organization is the job description. The Legacy Health Systems (LHS) job description defines four core accountabilities for each job. These performance standards (teamwork, respect and caring, effective use of resources, and initiative) are expected of each employee. Additionally, each job description articulates "job-specific" accountabilities. The current LHS RN job description defines job-specific accountabilities in five categories (patient care, planning and coordination of care, patient/family education, competency, professional development). These performance standards are so specific that they clearly contribute to and perpetuate an orientation to task rather than outcome emphasis on nursing practice and patient care delivery. Desired outcomes for the RN practice at LHS are (1) patient focused caring behaviors demonstrated by the RN in the delivery of patient care; and (2) clinical leadership development that operationalizes the RN Scope of Practice.

Recognizing the need to move the collective orientation to nursing practice from task toward a practice grounded in patient outcome identification and delivery of care predicated on the prioritization of patient needs, the LHS Patient Care Executive Council commissioned a group within nursing leadership of the four Legacy hospitals and the Legacy Visiting Nurses Association to revise the Legacy staff RN job description. The charge in this revision is to reflect the language of the Oregon Nurse Practice Act incorporated into performance expectation.

In the revision, there was only one job-specific accountability defined, Nursing Practice. The Nursing Practice accountability outlines performance expectations for professional responsibility and the nursing process. The language of the new job description is written within the broader context of the Oregon Nurse Practice Act and will be applicable in the many settings in which patients are cared for by RNs at LHS. Although broad in language, the concepts of the RN as the manager, planner, coordinator, implementor, and evaluator of a patient's care are clearly defined. The authority to delegate care is also outlined. An added benefit to prescribing the staff RNs' performance expectations within the context of the law is a defined invitation to the RNs to join in shaping the delivery of patient care in the working environment through active involvement in assessing, planning, and evaluating decisions affecting patient care. (See Job Description, tool #52.)

Peer Review

An important component of the professional RN's performance evaluation is the peer review process. Each RN is encouraged to create value for patient care and professional practice through performance. Competency is determined by the RN's ability to achieve desired outcomes (effectiveness) through effective resource utilization (efficiency). One of the best measures of the "value added" by the individual RN's performance comes from those with whom the RN works and those whom the RN serves.

Peer review is in various stages of maturity within the patient care areas of LHS. It is encouraged concurrently on a shift-by-shift basis as the RN and care team members debrief on what worked and what did not. In addition, there is increased emphasis and structured education ongoing for team building and conflict resolution skills. Annually, there is a peer review component incorporated in the performance evaluation process. This is a formal structure where the RN and the manager each select three peers to provide input into the analysis of the RN's effectiveness and efficiency as a manager of patient care and health care team leader. These data have proven a powerful indicator in the evaluation of the consistency and compatibility of the RN behaviors needed to support and promote the achievement of desired patient care and organizational outcomes. (See tool #53.)

Tool #52: Job Description Draft for Staff RN

LEGACY HEALTH SYSTEMS POSITION DESCRIPTION

TITLE: Staff RN

REPORTS TO:

DEPARTMENT:

DATE LAST REVIEWED:

JOB SUMMARY:

Responsible for patient care within an assigned department/unit and participates as a member of the health care team in cooperation with and under the direction of the clinical manager or designee as defined by the Standards and Scope of Practice for the Registered Nurse {(OAR.851-45-000) Nurse Practice Act (5/94)}. The Staff RN assesses, analyzes, plans, implements, and evaluates patient care following established patient care standards for Legacy Health Systems.

QUALIFICATIONS:

Education/Background:

1. Must be a graduate from an accredited school of nursing and currently licensed by the Oregon State Board of Nursing.
2. Clinical experience requirements are dependent on the specific position.

CORE ACCOUNTABILITIES:

1. *TEAMWORK:* Cooperation, adaptability, flexibility, communication, dependability, supports team goals.
   a. Functions as a member of the health team collaborating and consulting with other members to provide optimum client care.
   b. Assigns or delegates to others those nursing measures that that person is prepared to perform and qualified to perform and are within that person's scope of practice/scope of duties.
   c. Supervises persons to whom nursing tasks have been assigned.
   d. Demonstrates flexibility in response to changes in work volume, emergencies, staffing, and scheduling.
   e. Notifies the appropriate supervisory personnel and confirms that nursing assignment responsibilities will be met when leaving any nursing assignment, including supervisory assignment.
   f. Communicates information to the health care team regarding the client's status in an ongoing and timely manner including maintenance of client records that accurately reflect management of client care.

continues

2. *RESPECT AND CARING:* Compassion, customer relations, professional behavior, confidentiality, valuing diversity.
   a. Respects the dignity and the right of the client/family regardless of social or economic status, race, relation, national origin, sex, sexual preference, nature of health problems, or disability.
   b. Communicates and obtains information regarding the client's status, respecting the rights of privacy, confidentiality of information, or knowledge concerning the client unless disclosure is required by law or by obtaining proper authority.
   c. Acts as an advocate for the client within the team structure.
   d. Uses interpersonal skills to give constructive feedback/criticism in a nonjudgmental, positive, and confidential manner.
   e. Demonstrates commitment to understanding and valuing individual differences and fosters an environment of acceptance, fairness, and mutual respect.
3. *EFFECTIVE USE OF RESOURCES:* Effective use of time, people, supplies, safe and attentive work practices.
   a. Promotes cost-effectiveness through identification and implementation of cost savings measures while maintaining quality.
   b. Delegates, in settings where a registered nurse is not regularly scheduled (e.g., home health, subacute, and ancillary departments), specific tasks of nursing care to an unlicensed person only as described in the board's delegation rules (division 47).
   c. Retains professional accountability for nursing care when assigning or delegating nursing interventions.
   d. Teaches health care practices to patient/families and other health care providers.
   e. Takes action to preserve or promote the client's safety based on nursing assessment and judgment.
   f. Obtains instruction and supervision as necessary when implementing nursing techniques or practices.
   g. Maintains clean, safe work environment and reports unsafe nursing practices and unsafe practice conditions through the appropriate channels.
   h. Prevents client neglect. The definition of neglect includes but is not limited to carelessly allowing a client to be in physical discomfort or be injured.
4. *INITIATIVE:* Self-motivation, takes on projects willingly, acts on opportunities to improve, contributes new ideas.
   a. Supports innovations and improvements in the workplace.
   b. Responds proactively in patient care and interpersonal relationships.
   c. Contributes to the formulation, interpretation, implementation, and evaluation of the objectives and policies related to nursing practice within the employment setting.
   d. Accepts responsibility for individual nursing actions and maintains competency in one's area of practice.
   e. Demonstrates awareness and supports Legacy Health Systems department and operating unit goals through participation in continuous quality improvement and department activities.
   f. Promotes professional development and contributes to the professional growth of others.

GENERAL ACCOUNTABILITIES AND ESSENTIAL FUNCTIONS:

1. *NURSING PRACTICE:* Professional responsibilities and nursing process.
   a. Demonstrates knowledge of the statutes and regulations governing nursing and functions within the legal boundaries of registered nurse practice.

continues

b. Achieves and maintains clinical competency by
   1) Performing acts within the authorized scope of practice for which the individual is licensed.
   2) Conforming to the essential standards of acceptable and prevailing nursing practice.
   3) Assuming duties and responsibilities within the practice of nursing for developmental age-appropriate client care, supervisory, managerial, or consulting roles with documented preparation for those duties and responsibilities, provided competency has been established and maintained.
   4) Performing new nursing techniques or procedures after presenting written documented education and/or a clinical experience.

c. Applies the nursing process by
   1) Conducting and documenting health status assessments of individuals or groups that include but are not limited to
      a) Biopsychosocial status, subtle and overt findings, and evaluation of patient/family participation/learning readiness
      b) Economic, environmental, cultural, community, and spiritual factors affecting health
      c) Risk factors including falls, skin breakdown, aspiration, ETOH withdrawal
      d) Reassessment occurring at a frequency indicated by condition and therapeutic interventions
   2) Developing and modifying the plan of care based on assessment and coordination with other health care team members. This includes
      a) Identifying priorities in the plan of care
      b) Setting realistic and measurable goals to implement the plan of care
      c) Identifying nursing intervention(s) based on the nursing assessment
      d) Prescribing nursing orders
      e) Identifying measures to maintain comfort, to support human functions and responses, to maintain an environment conducive to well-being, and to provide health teaching and health counseling
   3) Implementing the plan of care by
      a) Initiating nursing interventions through
         1) giving direct care
         2) assisting with care
         3) following nursing orders
         4) assigning, delegating, and supervising care
         5) teaching clients, family members, or significant others
         6) referring to appropriate resources
      b) Providing an environment conducive to safety and health
      c) Communicating and documenting nursing interventions and responses to care to other members of the health care team
      d) Promoting continuity of care across the health care settings
      e) Providing client advocacy by defending the client's right to receive care based on the plan of care, which includes receiving complete and accurate information and ensuring that patient autonomy is protected
   4) Evaluating the responses of individuals or groups to nursing interventions. Evaluations should involve the client, family, significant others, and health team members.
      a) Documents and communicates evaluation data to the appropriate members of the health care team
      b) Uses evaluation data as a basis for reassessing the client's status, revising the plan of care, prescribing changes in nursing interventions, and issuing nursing orders

continues

The above accountabilities represent work performed by this position and are not all-inclusive. The omission of a specific accountability will not preclude it from the position if the work is similar, related, or a logical extension of the position.

PHYSICAL FUNCTIONS OF JOB

JOB: ________________ **DEPT:** ________________

Indicate which of the following categories applies to relevant physical functions. Answer any additional questions, fill in appropriate blanks, and add additional comments as needed to help understand the physical movement.

Check if essential function	Activity	Frequency				
		Continually Hourly +	Frequently Daily	Occasional Weekly	Rarely Monthly+	Comments
	POSITION—MOVEMENT					
	Standing					
	Sitting—up to 1/2 hour					
	Moving about work area					
	Bending forward					
	Stoop position—1 min					
	Climbing stairs—1 floor					
	Crawling—hands and knees					
	Reaching overhead					
	LIFTING STRENGTHS					Indicate number of lbs.
	Lifting					
	Patient lifting					
	Lifting/pushing overhead					
	Moving carts, etc.					
	Carry items:					Wt.: Size: Distance:
	DEXTERITY—COORDINATION					Comments (below)
	Keyboard operation					
	Rapid mental/hand/eye coord					
	Operation of motor vehicle					
	SPEECH AND HEARING	Activity Required				
	Correctable vision	To read: (size print) Other:				
	Distinguish colors	Yes: No:				
	Distinguish shades					
	Depth perception	Describe:				
	Ability to hear	Normal speech level: Whispered level:				

continues

Check if essential function	Activity	Frequency				
		Continually Hourly +	Frequently Daily	Occasional Weekly	Rarely Monthly+	Comments
	Other specific hearing req	Describe:				

ENVIRONMENTAL FACTORS (EXPOSURE TO)

Exposure	Item	Frequency	Exposure	Item	Frequency	Exposure	Item	Frequency
	Heat			Dust			Uneven area	
	Cold			Smoke			Ladder/Scaf	
	Humidity			Vibration			Radiation	
	Wet area			Chemical sol				
	Noise			Slippery area				

OSHA Blood/Body fluid (BBF) exposure category:
(Indicate appropriate level)

1 = High risk probability of exposure BBF
2 = Possible risk of exposure BBF
3 = No risk of exposure BBF

Other comments:

AGE-RELATED COMPETENCIES

AGE-SPECIFIC CARE CRITERIA (may be used as addendum to Position Description)

Position Title: ____________________

In addition to demonstrating the competency to perform the required functions listed on the position description for this job, employees must also demonstrate and maintain current knowledge and skills necessary to provide care/services appropriate to the age of the patients served by this position and in this department. Employees must demonstrate knowledge of principles of growth and development over the life span of the patient and possess the ability to assess the data and interpret appropriate information needed to identify each patient's requirements relative to his or her age-specific needs. Employees must also provide the care/services needed as described in the department's policies and procedures. These requirements apply to the following age groups (check all that apply):

Neonatal (<1 month) ____________
Infant (1 month–1 year) ____________
Pediatric (1 year–12 years) ____________
Adolescent (13 years–17 years) ____________
Adult (18 years–64 years) ____________
Elderly/Geriatric (65+ years) ____________

Competence in the applicable areas indicated above must be demonstrated at a satisfactory level to continue employment.

Courtesy of Legacy Health Systems, Portland, Oregon.

Tool #53: Coworker/Customer Performance Feedback

I am preparing to do a performance appraisal for ______________________________.

Our workgroup recognizes the value of gathering input from coworkers and internal customers to increase the accuracy and objectivity of the appraisal. Your input will help me verify specific strengths and/or identify needed development for this employee. I would appreciate your contribution to this process by completing as many of the following items as you can and returning this form to me by ______________.

Your comments will be used only in a general way, summarized with others' input, and your name will be confidential unless you authorize me to share your comments specifically. Thank you for any assistance/input you are willing to provide.

1. What do you consider to be the strengths of this individual?

2. Have you observed her or him demonstrating the following core accountabilities in her or his work?

   Teamwork

   Respect and caring

   Effective use of resources

   Initiative

3. Any general comments you would like to make about this person's work or performance?

Thank you! Please return this to ______________________________________.

My signature authorizes you to identify the above comments as mine.

Courtesy of Legacy Health Systems, Portland, Oregon.

Competency Checklists

Competency checklists are often a part of a job description, or at least a portion of an orientation program. We heartily recommend the use of these kinds of checklists and have discovered the most positive effects when those who will be supervising or precepting the new worker are those who perform the skills assessment and verify competency. The existence and use of these checklists are an essential part of the process of allaying the fears of other professionals that team members have been "checked off," and therefore a beginning level of trust in a coworker's competency can be established, thus initiating the possibility of supportive interdisciplinary relationships. First review Legacy's generic medical surgical nursing competency checklist. (See tool #54.)

Generic Medical Surgical Nursing Competency Checklist

Here is an example of an orientation and job performance evaluation checklist for ambulatory care medical assistants. We thank Barbara Trehearne, Director of Nursing Resources at Group Health Cooperative of Puget Sound, for contributing this document. (See tool #55.)

Tool #54: Generic Medical Surgical Nursing Competency Checklist

LHS Staff RN
Generic Medical Surgical Competency Checklist (1/97)

Name: ______________________ **Hire Date:**__________ **Clinical Area** ________

Preceptor(s) Signature: ______________________________________

____

The competency areas in this checklist are organized under the framework of patient focused functions of care:

Patient Rights   Assessment of Patients   Care of Patients

Education   Continuum of Care

Areas marked with a * have a self-learning module available. Some resources may vary depending on facility.

Please check the appropriate boxes below to describe verbalized or demonstrated competence level using the following key:

0 = No experience/not performed
1 = Minimal—needs review and supervision
2 = Comfortable with resource available, does infrequently
3 = Competent to perform independently and safely
4 = Expert, able to act as resource to others

	Competency Level								
	Self-Eval					Preceptor Eval			
Competency Areas and Statements	0	1	2	3	4	Eval Code	Date & Initials	Reeval	NA
Patient Rights: Treats each person with consideration, dignity, and respect at all times.									
Communicates and obtains information while respecting the rights of privacy and confidentiality of information.									
Involves and respects the patients in their role in determining the nature of the care to be provided including advance directive.									
Complies with nursing staff responsibility included in the hospital policy related to organ donation.									

continues

Competency Areas and Statements	Competency Level								
	Self-Eval					Preceptor Eval			
	0	1	2	3	4	Eval Code	Date & Initials	Reeval	N A
Identifies and meets patient needs regarding communication, including interpreter service.									
Provides accurate information to patient and family to obtain informed consent.									
Assessment of Patients: Performs and documents biopsychosocial assessments according to patient age and condition.									
Cardiovascular									
Pulmonary									
Neurologic									
Renal									
GU									
GI									
Skin									
Musculoskeletal									
Endocrine									
Hematologic									
Immune									
Psychosocial									
Identifies safety needs based on the patient's physical environment, developmental stage, and patient physical/mental/treatment status.									
Reassesses relevant physical, psychosocial, and educational needs and documents according to standard.									
Care of Patients: Formulates and implements a plan of care for each patient that includes intervention, evaluation of response to intervention, and documentation as appropriate to condition and age.									
Clearly communicates plan of care, patient responses, and outcomes in the patient record according to standard.									
Assigns or delegates to another those nursing measures for which that person is prepared and qualified to perform.									

continues

	Competency Level								
	Self-Eval					Preceptor Eval			
Competency Areas and Statements	0	1	2	3	4	Eval Code	Date & Initials	Reeval	N A
Interventions may include:									
Medication Administration									
Pain and Comfort Management									
PCA and Epidural Protocols*									
IV Therapy (access, maint., and specimen collection)*									
Blood and Blood Products Administration*									
Antiembolic Devices									
Airway Management (suctioning, IS, trach, endotracheal care)									
Chest Tube Management									
Oxygen Administration									
Conscious Sedation*									
Seizure Precautions									
Spinal Precautions									
Autonomic Dysreflexia Protocol*									
Restraint Management*									
Urinary Catheterization									
Irrigations (bladder and colonic)									
Dysphagia Management (aspiration precautions)*									
Enteral Feeding Management									
TPN Protocols									
Colostomy/Ileostomy Care									
Skin Care Protocol/Management									
Wound Care									
Traction/Trapeze Management									
Point of Care Testing (specimen collection, results interpretation, quality control)									

continues

Competency Areas and Statements	Competency Level								
	Self-Eval					Preceptor Eval			
	0	1	2	3	4	Eval Code	Date & Initials	Reeval	NA
Education: Identifies patient/client education needs, assesses readiness for or barriers to learning designs and/or obtains instructional materials, and evaluates effectiveness of education.									
Provides education to patients related to medical condition, self-care, health care habits.									
Uses teaching plans and resource tools effectively, incorporating adult learning principles into education strategies.									
Continuum of Care: Anticipates and communicates transfer/discharge needs. Coordinates the provision of internal and community resources for patients and their families.									
Follows Standards of Care for transition planning.									
Communicates discharge needs and arrangements for support through appropriate documentation.									
Coordinates the multidisciplinary plan of care and initiates interdisciplinary referral for identified complex patient needs.									

Courtesy of Legacy Health Systems, Portland, Oregon.

Tool #55: MA Competencies Evaluation Checklist 1996

Group Health Cooperative
Division of Nursing Services
MEDICAL ASSISTANT COMPETENCIES

NAME: ____________________ DATE: ____________________

SELF-EVALUATION KEY N/A = not applicable to unit 1 = unable to perform 2 = performs with supervision or assistance 3 = performs independently but needs additional practice 4 = performs independently and proficiently PRECEPTOR'S KEY ÷ = meets standards * = does not meet standards	Self-Evaluation	Date of Self-Evaluation	Preceptor's Rating #1	Data/Preceptor's Initials	Preceptor's Rating #2	Date/Preceptor's Initials
I. PATIENT VISIT						
A. PREPARATION						
1. Medical Records						
a. Prepares medical record according to standard to include visit forms, progress notes, problem list, logs, reports, test results, anticipatory forms, referrals, order forms, injection/immunization, tobacco use forms, patient education materials. Ensures that all appropriate paper work and forms are available for on-the-job injury cases						
2. Documentation						
a. Patient name, medical history number, date on each chart form						
b. Immunization logs updated; any other logs updated						
c. Telephone Consultation Form (TCF)						
d. Treatment Request Form (TRF)						
B. PATIENT ADMISSION						
1. Orients new consumer to clinic, station, access to care, etc.						
2. Introduces self; using name and job title/Greets patient and makes comfortable						
3. Demonstrates sensitivity to cultural needs of patients						
4. Escorts to examination room						

continues

SELF-EVALUATION KEY N/A = not applicable to unit 1 = unable to perform 2 = performs with supervision or assistance 3 = performs independently but needs additional practice 4 = performs independently and proficiently PRECEPTOR'S KEY ÷ = meets standards * = does not meet standards	Self-Evaluation	Date of Self-Evaluation	Preceptor's Rating #1	Data/Preceptor's Initials	Preceptor's Rating #2	Date/Preceptor's Initials
5. Performs appropriate screening tests						
a. Vision						
b. Hearing						
c. Urine dip						
6. Asks reason for this visit						
7. Takes and records appropriate vital signs						
8. Prepares patient appropriately (dressed/undressed/draped/ensures privacy/etc.)						
9. Explains when the provider will be in						
10. Directs the patient to seek assistance if the provider does not appear within 10 minutes or if the patient needs assistance before that						
11. Asks patient if there is anything he or she needs before leaving						
12. Notifies the RN or other provider if this is a "shared" visit or the patient has additional needs						
C. DOCUMENT IN THE MEDICAL RECORD						
1. Reason for the visit as stated by the patient						
2. Vital signs per standard						
3. Current medications						
4. Allergies						
5. Updates problem list						
a. Tobacco status stickers						
b. Food status stickers						
6. Any procedure initiated/completed						
7. Signature and job title						
D. EXAMINATION ROOM PREPARATION						
1. Appropriate equipment/supplies out and ready to use						
2. Patient undressed and draped appropriately (remove shoes and socks for diabetic visit)						

continues

SELF-EVALUATION KEY N/A = not applicable to unit 1 = unable to perform 2 = performs with supervision or assistance 3 = performs independently but needs additional practice 4 = performs independently and proficiently PRECEPTOR'S KEY + = meets standards * = does not meet standards	Self-Evaluation	Date of Self-Evaluation	Preceptor's Rating #1	Data/Preceptor's Initials	Preceptor's Rating #2	Date/Preceptor's Initials
3. Expected forms available (lab, referral, consent, etc.)						
4. Expected patient education material available						
E. PHYSICIAN						
1. Makes medical record available in appropriate place						
2. Notifies of anything unusual (unexpected patient needs, etc.)						
3. Notifies of time constraints (patient or MD late, add-on, etc.)						
F. PATIENT DISCHARGE						
1. Assists patient in examination room, if necessary, with clean up, dressings, etc.						
2. Makes arrangements for hospital admit when necessary						
3. Ensures completion of all forms, including consents, needed for referrals, labs, radiographs, etc. while the patient is still in the clinic						
4. Gives patient information, instruction, supplies, directions, routine educational material, as needed						
5. Ensures that patient understands the discharge plan and directs to next destination when necessary						
6. Provides preventive care instruction using the Healthwise Handbook						
7. Makes follow-up appointment as required. Confirms with patient or directs patient to PCR						
8. Returns Group Health Cooperative card to patient						
G. FOLLOW-UP						
1. Completes all necessary documentation in the medical record including any procedure that the medical assistant provided for the patient						
2. Checks, labels, and bags all specimens accurately and places in pick-up area						
3. Logs in any specimen as per unit standards (PAP, etc.)						
4. E-mails provider-generated referrals within the hour						
5. Sends all documents, films, etc. back to appropriate department						
6. Sends all forms to appropriate departments						

continues

SELF-EVALUATION KEY N/A = not applicable to unit 1 = unable to perform 2 = performs with supervision or assistance 3 = performs independently but needs additional practice 4 = performs independently and proficiently PRECEPTOR'S KEY + = meets standards * = does not meet standards	Self-Evaluation	Date of Self-Evaluation	Preceptor's Rating #1	Data/Preceptor's Initials	Preceptor's Rating #2	Date/Preceptor's Initials
7. Sends Medical Record back to Medical Records department						
8. Prepares examination or procedure room for next patient						
II. CLINIC FLOW/OFFICE MANAGEMENT						
A. COMPUTER SKILLS						
1. Computer literate (appointment scheduling, data access, e-mail)						
B. PATIENT FLOW						
1. Admits patients in timely manner						
2. Informs patients of delays or other possible problems						
3. Informs providers of delays, patient problems, add-on appointments, other pertinent issues						
4. Manages drop-in patients and additions to schedule appropriately						
5. Orders medical records/radiographs appropriately						
C. TELEPHONE MANAGEMENT						
1. Screens telephone calls appropriately						
2. Completes telephone consultation form according to standard						
3. Telephones referral to appropriate person on team (RN, MD, etc.)						
4. Appropriately refers urgent/emergent calls						
D. PATIENT CONFIDENTIALITY						
1. Demonstrates knowledge of protocols for release of information/legal release/attorney visit						
2. Demonstrates knowledge about GHC confidentiality policies						
3. Demonstrates knowledge of copying and faxing patient information						
4. Maintains patient confidentiality						
E. DIAGNOSTIC TESTS						
1. Completes requests with all required information and attachments when required						

continues

SELF-EVALUATION KEY N/A = not applicable to unit 1 = unable to perform 2 = performs with supervision or assistance 3 = performs independently but needs additional practice 4 = performs independently and proficiently PRECEPTOR'S KEY ÷ = meets standards * = does not meet standards	Self-Evaluation	Date of Self-Evaluation	Preceptor's Rating #1	Data/Preceptor's Initials	Preceptor's Rating #2	Date/Preceptor's Initials
2. Includes all demographics including current daytime telephone number						
3. Provides physician name and number (including "copy to" when needed)						
4. Marks requested test; notes exact source; notes specific time when needed						
5. Names antibiotics, if patient is taking, for culture request						
F. NORMAL TEST RESULTS						
1. Provides normal test results to patients as delegated/directed						
G. PROVIDER "OUT BOX"						
1. Manages provider "out box" timely and appropriately						
2. Processes paper, referrals, orders appropriately						
3. Sends appropriate referrals/information to RN timely						
H. DAILY EXAM/PROCEDURE ROOM PREPARATION						
1. Supplies ordered as per standard						
2. Rooms stocked as per standard and par levels						
3. Public areas stocked as per standard and par levels includes patient education material						
I. SAFETY AND UNIVERSAL PRECAUTIONS						
1. Uses approved disinfectants in appropriate cases/areas						
2. Personal protective devices, supplies, kits available and used appropriately						
3. Changes needleboxes when three-quarters full						
4. Handles biohazardous waste appropriately						
5. Knows location and use of MSDS manual						
6. Cleans and prepares instruments per standard						
7. Disinfects instruments per standard						
8. Uses universal precautions when needed						

continues

SELF-EVALUATION KEY N/A = not applicable to unit 1 = unable to perform 2 = performs with supervision or assistance 3 = performs independently but needs additional practice 4 = performs independently and proficiently PRECEPTOR'S KEY + = meets standards * = does not meet standards	Self-Evaluation	Date of Self-Evaluation	Preceptor's Rating #1	Data/Preceptor's Initials	Preceptor's Rating #2	Date/Preceptor's Initials
III. MANAGEMENT OF URGENT AND EMERGENT SITUATIONS						
A. RECOGNIZES AND RESPONDS APPROPRIATELY TO URGENT/ EMERGENT NEEDS						
1. Knows location of emergency equipment and supplies						
2. Code conditions (cardiac or respiratory arrest)						
3. Chest pain						
4. Breathing difficulties						
5. Bleeding						
6. Hypoglycemia						
7. Hypertensive crisis						
8. Fainting						
9. Seizures						
10. Eye injuries						
11. Burns						
12. Psychosocial crises						
a. Suicidal						
b. Combative						
c. Acute anxiety						
d. Substance abuse						
B. SET UP/ASSIST WITH MEDICAL EMERGENCY MANAGEMENT						
1. Crash cart supplies and equipment						
2. Airway placement						
3. Oxygen: mask, nasal prongs, cannula, rebreather						
4. Suction						
5. 3-Lead cardiac monitor electrodes						
6. IV placement						
7. Eye wash equipment including Morgan lens						
IV. PATIENT CARE						

continues

SELF-EVALUATION KEY N/A = not applicable to unit 1 = unable to perform 2 = performs with supervision or assistance 3 = performs independently but needs additional practice 4 = performs independently and proficiently PRECEPTOR'S KEY + = meets standards * = does not meet standards	Self-Evaluation	Date of Self-Evaluation	Preceptor's Rating #1	Data/Preceptor's Initials	Preceptor's Rating #2	Date/Preceptor's Initials
A. CARDIOVASCULAR SYSTEM						
1. Cardiac monitoring; 3-lead placement						
2. Postural vital signs						
3. Apical pulse						
4. Electrocardiogram test						
5. Application of 12-lead electrodes						
6. Oxygen administration						
B. RESPIRATORY SYSTEM						
1. Airway insertion						
2. Oxygen administration						
3. Pulse oximetry						
4. Suction set-up						
5. Peak flows						
6. Nebulizer set-up						
C. RENAL SYSTEM						
1. Urinary drainage systems						
a. Indwelling/straight catheter						
1) Male						
2) Female						
2. External urinary drainage (condom)						
3. Sets up/assists with procedures						
4. Provides pre- and postprocedure instructions to patients						
a. Vasectomy						
b. Prostate examination						
c. Circumcision						
D. NEUROLOGIC SYSTEM						
1. Documents and refers to appropriate provider						
a. Headache						

continues

SELF-EVALUATION KEY N/A = not applicable to unit 1 = unable to perform 2 = performs with supervision or assistance 3 = performs independently but needs additional practice 4 = performs independently and proficiently PRECEPTOR'S KEY + = meets standards * = does not meet standards	Self-Evaluation	Date of Self-Evaluation	Preceptor's Rating #1	Data/Preceptor's Initials	Preceptor's Rating #2	Date/Preceptor's Initials
b. Dizziness						
c. Sensory/motor loss						
d. Ringing in the ears (tinnitus)						
e. Difficulty in swallowing						
2. Sets up/assists with LP						
3. Provides pre- and postprocedure instructions to patients						
E. GASTROINTESTINAL SYSTEM						
1. Provides pre- and postprocedure instructions to patients						
2. Sets up/assists with procedures/cleans equipment						
a. rectal examinations, anoscopes						
b. sigmoidoscopies						
c. hemocult slides						
3. Administers enemas						
F. MUSCULOSKELETAL SYSTEM						
1. Measures for and instructs for use of crutches, canes, walkers						
2. Measures for and applies						
a. Slings						
b. Ace wraps						
c. Cervical collar						
d. Rib belt						
e. Knee splint/brace						
f. Arm/wrist/finger splints						
3. Cast care and removal						
a. Recognizes cast problems: tightness, rubbing, weakness, etc.						
4. Provides pre- and postprocedure instructions to patients						
5. Sets up and assists with procedures						
a. Joint injections						
b. Joint aspirations						

continues

SELF-EVALUATION KEY N/A = not applicable to unit 1 = unable to perform 2 = performs with supervision or assistance 3 = performs independently but needs additional practice 4 = performs independently and proficiently PRECEPTOR'S KEY + = meets standards * = does not meet standards	Self-Evaluation	Date of Self-Evaluation	Preceptor's Rating #1	Data/Preceptor's Initials	Preceptor's Rating #2	Date/Preceptor's Initials
c. Cast/splint application or removal						
G. ENDOCRINE SYSTEM						
1. Assists in management of patient with hypoglycemia crisis						
2. Performs urine dip for sugar/ketones						
H. INTEGUMENTARY SYSTEM						
1. Removes and applies simple wound/burn dressings using aseptic technique (dry sterile, wet sterile, pressure)						
2. Cleans/irrigates simple wounds						
3. Applies ice packs						
4. Removes simple sutures and staples						
5. Applies UNA boot						
6. Provides pre- and postprocedure instructions to patients						
7. Sets up and assists with						
a. Incision and drainage						
b. Wart treatments						
c. Laceration						
d. Mole removal						
e. Shave biopsy						
f. Skin tag removal						
g. Punch biopsy						
I. FEMALE REPRODUCTIVE SYSTEM						
1. Provides pre- and postprocedure instructions to patients						
2. Sets up/assists/processes specimens						
a. Pelvic examination						
b. PAP smears						
c. Wet prep						
d. Cultures including chlamydia, GC, viral, etc.						

continues

SELF-EVALUATION KEY N/A = not applicable to unit 1 = unable to perform 2 = performs with supervision or assistance 3 = performs independently but needs additional practice 4 = performs independently and proficiently PRECEPTOR'S KEY ÷ = meets standards * = does not meet standards	Self-Evaluation	Date of Self-Evaluation	Preceptor's Rating #1	Data/Preceptor's Initials	Preceptor's Rating #2	Date/Preceptor's Initials
e. Vaginal warts						
f. Diaphragm fitting						
g. Cervical cap fitting						
h. Endometrial biopsy						
i. Colposcopy						
3. Obstetrics in Primary Care						
a. Obtains or assists with monitoring and documenting fetal heart tones using Doppler						
b. Performs urine dip test						
c. Prepares the OB chart						
d. Ensures that prenatal education and preventive care issues have been addressed						
J. OPHTHALMOLOGY/OTOLARYNGOLOGY SYSTEM						
1. Documents and reports						
a. Dizziness						
b. Headache						
c. Maxillary or tooth pain						
d. Difficulty swallowing						
e. Changes in vocalization						
f. Change or disturbances in vision						
g. Ringing in ears (tinnitus)						
2. Performs ear irrigation for wax removal						
3. Performs vision screening test						
4. Performs tritone test when appropriate						
K. PEDIATRICS IN PRIMARY CARE CLINICS						
1. Measures and records						
a. Head circumference						
b. Length/height						
c. Weight on infant scale or standing scale						

continues

SELF-EVALUATION KEY N/A = not applicable to unit 1 = unable to perform 2 = performs with supervision or assistance 3 = performs independently but needs additional practice 4 = performs independently and proficiently PRECEPTOR'S KEY + = meets standards * = does not meet standards	Self-Evaluation	Date of Self-Evaluation	Preceptor's Rating #1	Data/Preceptor's Initials	Preceptor's Rating #2	Date/Preceptor's Initials
2. Plots progress on growth grid accurately						
3. Provides consent forms and patient instructions for immunizations						
a. Updates immunization log						
4. Documents ADD prefill requirements						
L. OTHER PROCEDURES						
1. Positioning techniques						
a. Recovery position						
b. Supine						
c. Trendelenberg/reverse Trendelenberg						
d. Sims						
e. Lithotomy						
f. Fowlers/semifowlers						
g. Log roll (3W)						
2. Weights, standing/chair scale						
M. MISCELLANEOUS SPECIMEN COLLECTION						
1. Urine						
a. Voided/midstream						
b. Culture						
c. Straight catheter						
d. From indwelling catheter						
e. Dip stick						
f. Straining urine and providing patient instruction for use						
g. 24-hour collection and providing patient instruction for use						
h. Bagged urine						
2. Stool						
a. Hemocult test and providing patient instruction for use						
b. Culture/ova and parasites and providing patient instruction for use						
3. Sputum—expectorated						

continues

SELF-EVALUATION KEY N/A = not applicable to unit 1 = unable to perform 2 = performs with supervision or assistance 3 = performs independently but needs additional practice 4 = performs independently and proficiently PRECEPTOR'S KEY + = meets standards * = does not meet standards	Self-Evaluation	Date of Self-Evaluation	Preceptor's Rating #1	Data/Preceptor's Initials	Preceptor's Rating #2	Date/Preceptor's Initials
a. Culture						
b. Cytology						
4. Throat culture						
5. Wound culture						
6. Gram stain						
N. OTHER DIAGNOSTIC TESTS						
1. Provides instruction, information, and directions to patients						
a. Amniocentesis						
b. Arthrogram						
c. Audiology						
d. Bone scan						
e. Chorionic villa sampling						
f. CT scan						
g. Doppler studies						
h. EMG						
i. MRI						
j. Mammography						
k. NCS						
l. PFTs						
m. Stress test						
n. Ultrasound						
o. X-rays						

ORIENTATION

Initials Preceptors Date

______ ______________________________ ________________________

______ ______________________________ ________________________

______ ______________________________ ________________________

Courtesy of Group Health Cooperative of Puget Sound, Seattle, Washington.

Annual Review Checklist

The agenda for annual review is a tool that is also used at Legacy Health Systems in Portland, Oregon, for completing the employee's annual review process. This assists the supervisor to focus on what needs to be completed to meet regulations and stresses an action plan that emphasizes individual accountability, and managerial support, to enhance employee growth. The information from peer review (or the coworker/customer performance feedback form) can be incorporated into the discussion.

Tool #56: Annual Review Checklist

LEGACY HEALTH SYSTEMS
AGENDA FOR ANNUAL REVIEW

Check One . . . ❑ Introductory Period ❑ Annual ❑ Other: ____________________

NAME: ____________________ TITLE: ____________________

DEPT.: ____________________ REVIEW PERIOD: ______ TO ______

This agenda documents that the following items have been discussed with the employee. Check off as completed during discussion. Brief notes on this form are optional. Document specific action plans on the reverse. Incorporate comments from customer/coworkers where applicable.

1. Review and discuss job description ❑
2. Review Joint Commission on Accreditation of Healthcare Organizations (Joint Commission) competency assessment ❑ Met ❑ Not Met
3. Current performance expectations ❑ Met ❑ Not Met
   Future performance expectations—Changes:
4. Accomplishments and contributions to Legacy and strategic pathways—support of Legacy's goals ❑
5. Demonstration of core accountabilities ❑
6. Discuss barriers to effective work and job satisfaction ❑
7. Needs from supervisor/other team members ❑
8. The future—discuss opportunities/goals for development ❑

General Comments/Summary of Discussion:

(May also attach additional relevant documentation and/or comments. Include customer/coworker comments as applicable.)

continues

Action Plan Developed by Team Member and Leader

(Include education, training, performance)

What: When:

Action Plan items from last review addressed: Yes ❑ No ❑
If no, address status in above plan.

Joint Commission/Mandatory education requirements met: Yes ❑ No ❑
(Plan to address requirements not met should be included above)

Annual TB testing completed as required: Yes ❑ No ❑

Information on this agenda has been reviewed by:

Employee: ____________________

Leader(s): ____________________

Date: ____________________

Courtesy of Legacy Health Systems, Portland, Oregon.

MEETING EVALUATION AND RATINGS

Frustration often mounts to a fever pitch when an organization is in the midst of a reengineering project and meetings have not been an engine for redesign planning and evaluation but are instead boring, fruitless, and expensive activities. Group discussions and interdisciplinary involvement are crucial to redesign, and yet entire projects can flounder because of ineffective meeting management. Two tools that have been effectively used in meeting management are featured below.

Meeting Evaluation

In this tool, individual accountability for the success of the meeting is evident. It helps establish the meeting norms (e.g., that it is no longer acceptable to be a passive member of the group or to do paper work during the meeting). Each individual must rate the meeting at the close, discuss his rating with the group, and give a rationale for his decision. After the first experience of this procedure, participants begin to think about how the meeting is going during the group interaction and what they should do to make the meeting successful. From our experience working with groups that are evolving into teams, we've noted that asking for active participation of all members during the evaluation process encourages all to focus on the intended outcomes. Each individual must concentrate on making certain that his efforts contribute to meeting his (or the department's) objectives as well as the group's mission.

Organizations often begin using this tool in the beginning of the redesign effort. Scores are totaled, and groups often compete with each other for the highest ratings. We've heard good-natured discussions such as *"It's ratings week! Our meetings are averaging a 4.5 rating! I'll bet the communications team can't beat that!"* The scores are often totaled, averaged, and kept with the meeting minutes so that redesign task force members can be proud of their team's progress and can celebrate the success of their efforts.

Tool #57: Meeting Evaluation

Rate the Meeting

Using the following scale, rate today's session:

Bad news		OK		Very productive
1	2	3	4	5

List the reasons why you rated the session this way.

-
-
-
-
-
-

Be ready to discuss your rationale at the end of the meeting.

Tool #58: Meeting Evaluation

The following tool has been useful in educating staff to meeting management. It encourages clear discussion of meeting purpose and the intended outcomes.

Question	True (most of the time) 10 points	Sometimes 5 points	Rarely true 0 points
1. The purpose of this meeting has been clearly determined			
2. Intended outcomes of each meeting are discussed at the outset			
3. Agendas are received by all individuals before the meeting			
4. People are clear on the tasks they must do before the next meeting			
5. Participants come prepared			
6. We review our progress during the meeting itself			
7. We consistently end on time or before the projected end time			
8. We allocate time to each issue depending on its importance to the outcomes			
9. We turf individual (not group-related) issues to another forum			
10. Participants keep their attention on the matters at hand			
11. All the meetings we hold are productive and essential to achievement of our goals			
12. Group members attend all meetings or send a substitute			

EVALUATION OF TRAINING

Development of staff is a hallmark of successful reengineering. Employees must learn new roles, new skills and processes, how to interact in different ways, and how to lead meetings and teams. Evaluation of training and cost-benefit ratios is too often overlooked throughout redesign efforts. Skills training can be evaluated by skill performance checklists, concepts can be tested by posttest questions, and problem solving can be evaluated by scenario discussion and role playing. Actual performance and integration of newly acquired knowledge and skills are often measured by results in terms of patient outcomes.

To evaluate the effectiveness of the training itself, we would suggest Donald Kirkpatrick's classic evaluation model from the 1960s. (Pine and Tingley, 1996) Using his model, we can begin to measure the success of training at four different levels.

Level 1: participants' reaction to training at the time (postcourse survey)
Level 2: participants' learning of the content (comparison pre- and posttests)
Level 3: participants' use of skills and knowledge back on the job
Level 4: organization's return on the training investment

Level 4, return on the training investment, has been proven by studies done outside of health care. (See Intervention section.) Evaluation of levels 1 to 3 can be measured by the following tools.

Postcourse Surveys

Postcourse surveys are done routinely as participants are questioned about their reaction to the training session on their participant evaluation forms. These may or may not reflect the true feelings or thoughts of the individual, depending on whether the person is feeling very challenged by the concepts discussed and whether the participant is angry at the change itself. We often asked people to make comments and also to sign their names, because we are often in the process of teaching and discussing accountability and the processes of giving effective feedback. Although some still omit their signatures, it causes others to be thoughtful and take some ownership in their responses.

Tool #59: Evaluation of the Four Ps of Successful Teamwork

Memorial Medical Center

Facilitated by Hansten and Washburn

Date__________________________

NAME ____

1. The outcomes stated at the beginning of the day were achieved.
   yes no somewhat

2. The speakers were knowledgeable about the subject.
   yes no somewhat

3. The speakers were helpful in answering my questions.
   yes no somewhat

4. The most helpful thing I learned today was . . .

5. The least helpful part of this workshop was . . .

6. I still need . . .

Thank You!

Pretests and Posttests

Learning based on pretests and posttests is best evaluated when situations are used and the learner must apply the knowledge to scenarios that may occur in the clinical environment. Although a trainer cannot predict whether students will use their new concepts and skills in their daily worklives, using situations from the worker's environment, followed with discussion, will produce measurable data regarding learning. Whether the skills or knowledge becomes practice on the job will be best reflected by actual observation of clinical practice, interactions with other staff, assignments that have been made, charting, and problem resolution and follow-through.

RN Delegation Review

This tool will help evaluate the education nurses possess before a delegation/supervision workshop, and how much of the basic information they were able to absorb during a seminar. This will not, however, evaluate how well they are able to implement the leadership roles when involved in clinical practice. (First things first!)

Tool #60: RN Delegation Review

- How do you determine what tasks you will delegate to members of your team?

- Where would you find information about the safe practice of delegation of tasks to other personnel on your team that would help you determine if your "license is on the line"?

Circle the correct answer to each of the following questions:

- According to my state practice act, supervision means
  1. to watch over and inspect the persons with whom the RN is working
  2. to provide guidance and evaluation of the accomplishment of a nursing task or activity
  3. to have the authority to terminate an unlicensed person
  4. anyone who is providing care for the patient must be given an evaluation

- Delegation is defined by the nurse practice act as
  1. assigning tasks to other individuals
  2. retaining the responsibility for the other person's performance
  3. transferring the performance of selected nursing tasks to competent individuals in selected situations
  4. transferring the performance of any nursing task to another individual

- When delegating a task to a multiskilled worker, the registered nurse must
  1. only delegate the tasks that the delegate prefers to do
  2. ensure the competency of the delegate
  3. retain accountability for the performance of the delegate
  4. be on the unit at all times while the delegate is performing the task and observe the performance

- Do you know the roles and the skills of other members of your team? YES/NO

- If you have questions about team members' roles and skills, how would you get the information you need?

Tool #61: Scenarios

The following scenarios are designed for RNs and assistive personnel to determine whether they are able to apply the concepts learned during a seminar to situations that they may encounter during their daily worklives. You will note that many of these emphasize the employee's accountability for taking action and the need to be clear about the roles of others in the team. An educator or trainer can develop scenarios that are relevant to instructional objectives related to the experiences that have occurred that may indicate a need for training or team building. Review incident reports or anecdotal notes from managers or risk managers to develop the situational questions that will best serve your needs in your specific setting. Ask any staff member for a problematic situation that he or she has encountered, and a trainer will be afforded a wealth of ideas within minutes!

Visiting Nurse Scenario

Two of the newest admissions to your caseload may require the assistance of a home health aide. The first patient, Mrs. Frank, is a long-term diabetic patient with frequent readmissions to the hospital with diabetic crises (either hypo- or hyperglycemia). The hospital has made it very clear that it would appreciate some assistance in keeping Mrs. Frank in the community setting. She is also a suspected alcoholic and has difficulty seeing. Her level of education and ability regarding home administration of glucose testing and insulin injection (on a sliding scale) is in question. Her toes and feet are beginning to show the effects of poor glucose control.

The second patient, Ms. Oswald, is a new mother of twins. She has been an abusive parent previously, and despite all your attempts to have the new babies placed in foster care, the twins are at home. Previous siblings are placed in foster care and the eldest is in long-term care for mental disabilities. One of the conditions enabling her to take the children home was for her to go through a drug rehabilitation program, which was completed just before delivery.

1. Determine the outcomes you would like to achieve with the patients in these two homes.
2. A new home health aide was assigned to you last week. Consider what tasks you may ask her to do, and how you would determine her competency.
3. How will you make certain the home health aide understands the planned outcomes and when to report?

The "Bossy" RN

Estelle, CNA, came in to report, obviously upset. "Do they think we are superwomen or what? I can't take on any more work! It seems that the RNs are spending an awful lot of time at the desk talking on the phone while we do the real work here!"

Pamela, LPN, said, "Frankly, I do find this new care delivery system to be a challenge, but I'd like to try it for a bit to see how we can work together to make it the best for the patients. Maybe you should say something to the RNs if you have a question or problem with what they are doing."

Estelle rejoined, "Oh, sure, little Goodie Two Shoes! You are always the favorite of that old battle-ax Gertrude. She is very bossy, tells me what to do all the time, and never says thank you like a polite person. I don't feel very valued here!"

As Pamela, how would you respond to Estelle? Where is Estelle's accountability here? If Gertrude's behavior toward you were demeaning in any way, how would you handle it?

Role play how you would deal with this situation.

Who Is in Charge?

Pat, RN, began the shift by refusing to work with Jerri again. "Don't you know what it's like? Here I am, just out of school, and only 25 years old! Jerri, Patient Care Assistant, is older than my grandma, and she thinks she knows everything in the world there is to know about nursing and medicine to boot! I can't figure out how to supervise someone like that! Besides, she tells me what to do all the time."

Joe, the charge nurse, responds, "Well, Pat, you'll need to learn to deal with this some time. Get with the program, OK? We're too busy to deal with personality issues, you know."

Under her breath, Pat says, "Well, nurse practice act be hanged! I am keeping out of Jerri's way and I'll be dipped if I'll tell HER what to do!"

What advice would you give Pat, Jerri, and Joe? What's wrong with this picture? What is Pat's legal accountability? Using the skills you've learned today, discuss what you'd do to make certain patient care quality is maintained and teamwork is enhanced.

Missing in Action

When you worked with Pat (RN), you had developed a kind of routine about the shift. Often, Pat did the assessments while you did the vital signs and helped with baths. Now, you have started to work with another RN, Brad. Brad is new and hasn't been telling you about the outcomes you and he are trying to achieve this shift. And now, when you've found that there is a problem with a high fever in a patient, you don't know how to find Brad. He is nowhere to be found on the unit, and the unit secretary doesn't know where he is.

What will you do with the information about the fever?

How will you approach Brad with your concerns?

Boundaries

One of your colleagues, Ellen, is interested in going to nursing school next year. She is very excited about all that she is learning in her special care provider position. Today, as you walk by a room, you note that Ellen is discontinuing an IV line in a patient's hand, something that you know is beyond her job description and scope of practice. What will you do about this situation?

Workload "Equality"

Susan, another LPN, began to laugh as she saw your assignment. "Oh, you really get the rotten deal, don't you? Doesn't your RN think she is the Queen of the World! MY RN never makes me do all the I and Os (Intakes and Outputs) and the baths!"

"This assignment does seem like more than I had to do the last month, and it is more than what we were told in classes. I have never worked with Grace, RN, before, but I did hear that the unit doesn't have enough staff today."

"Well, don't be a chump! Refuse to do more than the rest of us.... If you don't make waves, you'll always get dumped on!"

What will you do in this situation? Use the skills you've learned today.

Diabetic Crisis

One of your patients is diabetic, on routine finger sticks and insulin control. You are working with a newly hired LPN who does the glucose testing before lunch. She obtained a blood glucose of 20 but does not report it to you. You are busy with another patient who is actively bleeding and you do not check the glucose right away. When lunch trays are delivered, the patient is found while having a seizure. The patient is treated with D50 and sent to the CCU.

What went wrong with the delegation process? Using the positive problem-solving process, solve this problem with attention to short-term and long-term outcomes. Practice giving feedback to the LPN. What conflict resolution choice seems best in this case? What is the LPN's accountability in this situation? What is the RN's accountability in this situation?

Staffing

Mary called the evening supervisor to discuss ill calls and the resulting low staffing. "It's not safe! Patients will be dying!" she sobbed over the phone. The evening supervisor, Lois, stated calmly, "Pull yourself together, you are out of control. You have plenty of staff for your needs."

How should the two resolve the problem, from an immediate and long-term perspective? How can Lois and Mary give each other feedback about their behavior? What choice of conflict resolution did you use?

The Unhappy Daughter

You have assigned tasks to your patient care assistant, Joel, for this night shift. As you are making rounds, one of the patients' daughters comes to you with a scowl on her face. "I told the day shift that you are to keep Mother comfortable! We left our Hawaiian vacation early because we weren't sure you knew what you were doing. She wants to die in comfort! Maybe you weren't aware that I am an attorney and will be glad to go to the Administration tomorrow morning! The nurse who just came into the room to take her vital signs said she couldn't have any more pain medication yet. Besides, I have noted that she wasn't turned from her left side all evening."

You know that Joel has just been in this patient's room. You realize that there is a problem (or several) that will require your attention.

What will you say to the daughter? How will you approach Joel regarding the alleged behavior? What went wrong with the delegation process? What can you do to avoid a similar problem in the future? What are short-term and long-term solutions to these problems?

Homework Assignment

The following tool (#62) has been developed for nurses who have attended the two-day Land in Sight workshop, as a continual reminder of the concepts presented and practiced. Reinforcement is necessary, particularly as nurses who have made a commitment to professional role growth meet with the resistance and scoffing of other colleagues who have not yet attended the workshop.

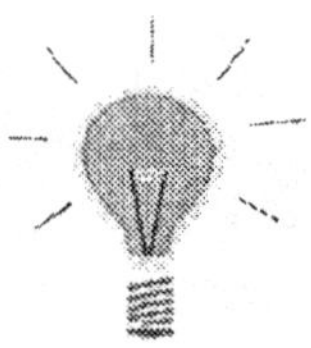

Tool #62: Homework Assignment

FOLLOW-UP SURVEY FOR RN WORKSHOP "NO LAND IN SIGHT"

Have You Done Your Homework?

About a month ago, you attended a two-day workshop focusing on the changes being made as a result of the redesign efforts at Memorial Medical Center. Throughout the two days, several actions were recommended as "homework," items for you to continue to work on that would help to ensure your continued professional growth, as well as the success of the unit redesign.

Please take a moment to answer the following questions and return the survey to your unit manager, or your resource educator, within a week. Thank you!

1. Obtain a copy of the nurse practice act—I have
   ____ called the Nursing Commission and requested a copy
   ____ asked the education department for a copy
   ____ read the one on the unit
   ____ forgotten, but I'm going to take action now

2. Attend a meeting of the Nursing Commission within the year
   ____ I have called the Commission and been placed on the mailing list for agendas
   ____ I have already attended one
   ____ I have reviewed the schedule printed in the newsletter and made plans to attend
   ____ I'm not sure I'll make the time

3. Plan patient care based on outcomes and communicate to the assistive personnel
   ____ I have started by planning outcomes for two patients and talking to the team members about them
   ____ I do this for my entire assignment and it works!
   ____ I have not had the time to start and am still doing report in the same way

4. Create your own "sound bite" for describing your practice as an RN
   ____ I have read some of the quotes in the workshop and developed my own response
   ____ I have shared my description with colleagues, friends, anyone who will listen
   ____ I have not taken the time to do this—but will soon!
   ____ I have introduced myself to the patients using my name and title

Role Development Reinforcement and Evaluation

Postworkshop rounding of managers, charge nurses, shift supervisors, and clinical specialists will allow evaluation of the real learning that has taken place. As you have read throughout this toolbook, many organizations find that new roles must be incorporated on a temporary basis to support implementation of the learning and to sustain the role redesign process. These individuals (sometimes named project consultants, professional development personnel, or implementation specialists) would focus on the assisting personnel in adapting to new roles and processes and, in doing so, would be positioned pivotally to recognize RN leadership performance as discussed in the following tool. This guide encourages those evaluating to focus on parts of the leadership process and those areas that will be beneficial in producing the positive clinical outcomes expected. We encourage those using the tool to jot down examples and to give as much positive feedback as possible when they observe staff efforts and successes.

Tool #63: RN Role Development Workshop Follow-Up

Memorial Medical Center

The following behaviors can be evaluated on rounds on the nursing units to judge whether staff who have attended the workshops are able to implement the concepts in practical situations. Reinforcement of workshop concepts and sharing of success stories will enhance positive outcomes in the redesign process.

1. Are registered nurses supervising assistive personnel by giving initial direction, periodic follow-up and evaluation, and feedback regarding problems?

2. Have RNs discussed patient outcomes for this shift, or long-term plans, with the oncoming shift or other members of their team?

3. Have RNs used the positive problem-solving approach, and are they actively involved in solving problems on the unit?

4. Is there evidence of outcomes-based communication, the feedback process, and/or conflict resolution skills being used?

5. Have roles or expectations for assistive personnel and colleagues been discussed?

Success Story: Evaluating Training

The following success story relates to evaluation of role training at Huntington Memorial Hospital in Pasadena, California. We thank Joyce Johnson and Elaine Goehner for contributing this story and advice. We previously discussed the comprehensive education efforts at this hospital in the Intervention section of this book.

Huntington Memorial Hospital, Pasadena, California

Training outcomes are currently being measured for each role with recommendations for changes and continuing education. Examples of the educational outcomes include:

Excerpt from RN Role Development Survey

The survey results indicate a high regard for teamwork among both the registered nurses and their managers. *Problem solving and critical thinking happen in the majority of cases, although in 18 percent of the nurses the managers saw no evidence of these behaviors*. Delegation of tasks to assistive personnel happen frequently, although some of the registered nurses added comments implying that they were not always comfortable delegating "nursing care" (even though the questions explicitly stated "tasks appropriate to the job descriptions"). Registered nurses are still performing tasks that could be done by an unlicensed caregiver, and according to both manager and self-report, this happens very frequently.

Excerpts from Job Satisfaction Survey (PCA, PSA, BSA)

The majority of people in the new positions think that *the job is important (96 percent) and the work is meaningful (95 percent). They are proud and would reapply for their jobs (78 percent). Seventy-four percent indicated they had enough training, but 40 percent would have liked more.* The PCAs reported a significantly lower mean regarding training for the job than did the PSAs. Based on PCA comments, this reflects the phlebotomy and patient care aspects of the job that have a greater learning curve and require practice and repetition to gain competency and confidence. More education in computer use, phlebotomy, and ECG was requested by PCAs.

We continue to evaluate the effectiveness of both the initial training and the orientation of new employees to these roles, changing our training programs as the need arises.

What Worked and What Did Not

The Redesign Committee (a multidisciplinary steering committee including physicians) chose to implement PFC one role at a time. Just-in-time training was used with the non-RN roles. However, because not all roles on a unit were implemented together at the same time, the ability to use education for team building was reduced. If roles are implemented one at a time, later team-building sessions are necessary. Our strategy to improve teamwork, especially RN leadership, includes

- on-unit consultation
- job description redesign
- distinguished scholar lectures
- on-site education (BSN program)
- precepted learning experiences

- **Lesson learned:** From an educational perspective, just-in-time training unit by unit as a team would have increased the effectiveness of our educational efforts.

As previously described, manager involvement affects the transfer of learning to the worksite. The clearer the vision and the more obvious the involvement and manager support, the better the transition for the staff.

- **Lesson learned:** Strategies to gain manager support should be developed before training implementation.

One PCA stated, *"Personally, I needed more on-the-job training from individuals who were knowledgeable, competent teachers. It would have helped me become a better PCA faster. Some nurses don't have good teaching skills. However, there were several nurses who were excellent teachers and I learned a great deal from them."* Since the skills must be refined in the clinical setting, the nursing staff must be able to assist them in the transfer process.

- **Lesson learned:** Adequate preparation of RNs for precepting other caregivers is critical.

To be cost-effective and time-efficient, the tendency is to structure the learning environment in classrooms with groups. Due to the nature of what is being taught, many of the skills would have been better taught in small groups in the clinical setting with the patients. We experienced an unexpected decline in opportunities for phlebotomy experiences during the training. This inhibited our ability to provide as much real patient opportunities as we would have liked. This lengthened the learning curve and reduced PCA confidence. Although we emphasized cognitive, affective, and psychomotor skills, the latter two are more difficult to attain in the classroom setting.

- **Lesson learned:** Structure the learning in the real care environment as much as possible with knowledgeable, committed, and excited preceptors.

Faculty was recruited from all parts of the organization. They taught the skills and concepts within their specialty area. All the faculty were receptive to assistance and coaching by the education staff in preparing materials, selecting teaching methodologies, and evaluating learning outcomes. One example of this expertise was the phlebotomy trainer who came to us from the clinical laboratory. She had extensive experience in training and supervision. Her excitement and support of the project enabled learners to overcome their fear and increase their confidence. Because this was such an important area for patient comfort, it was helpful to have such competent faculty.

- **Lesson learned:** Have the clinical experts do the training.

Financial accounting for our education program was structured through a separate cost center. We included not only the learners time but also the instructor time, supplies and materials, and other related costs. This allowed us to identify exact costs of our PFC education and to discriminate them from other educational efforts.

- **Lesson learned:** Develop an accounting method for tracking financial performance.

If we were asked to give our advice about educating for restructuring, we would say:

- plan carefully
- do not rush the process
- use a multidisciplinary team
- make sure managers are knowledgeable and supportive
- expect to adjust and revise along the way
- use clinical experts as faculty
- identify outcome measures early, within the process and post
- expect to reinforce learning many times and in varied ways
- celebrate your successes, even the little ones!

Courtesy of E. Goehner and J. Johnson, Huntington Memorial Hospital, Pasadena, California. Previously printed in R. Hansten and M. Washburn, *Successful Restructuring,* Vol. 1, No. 5, pp. 4–5, © 1996, Aspen Publishers, Inc.

KEEPING IT ALL GOING: ONGOING EVALUATION CRITERIA

A fellow consultant, Betty Noyes of Noyes & Associates, Ltd., Bainbridge Island, Washington, offers some measurement criteria that can be quantified throughout the reengineering processes in the tool below. This tool is based on the need for ongoing criteria for evaluation: in the beginning for assessment of the current state of affairs, for benchmarking, for course correction along the way, and for evaluation of the most current revision of your redesign plan. Betty bases her evaluation criteria on these truths about the illusive measurement of "quality": Quality is doing the right thing right. It is the most appropriate, effective, efficient, ongoing, customer-focused method of delivering services. Quality is definable, measurable, multifaceted, and multidimensional and must be meaningful to practitioners. It includes employee satisfaction measures, patient satisfaction, physician satisfaction, departmental service, and financial cost per day.

Betty encourages three or four people to be deployed on specific missions (perhaps in disguise!) to gather the following facts. It is possible to establish numerical scoring based on your assessment benchmarks.

Tool #64: Evaluation Criteria

1. Count the number of patients in the admitting area who are waiting for more than 30 minutes to be registered.
2. Count the number of patients waiting to be escorted from admitting to the inpatient unit for more than 10 minutes.
3. Go to an inpatient surgical unit. Ask a unit secretary for a patient record who had blood drawn (not a STAT order) and whose results have been reported. Find out when the blood was drawn and when it was reported on the record. Was it done before the attending physician's rounds? If not, was the laboratory called and by whom?
4. Look at a table of the organization and get a copy of position control by cost center. How many departments have two levels of supervision between the vice president and the supervisory employee with less than 15 employees?
5. Look at the number of administrative manager meetings per month.
6. Compare a copy of the inpatient and outpatient admitting "face sheets." Count the number of redundant data fields.
7. Review each of the Clinical Ancillary Services documentation records. Count the number of data fields that require duplicate information from that appearing on the nursing assessment sheet.
8. Go to an inpatient medical unit during morning or afternoon rounds. Ask the first three physicians whom you encounter whether (a) the nurses communicate with them about the patient's discharge needs when they are present on rounds and (b) when is the last time she or he was called for new orders due to missed medications or treatments.
9. In a patient room, have a patient or family member count how many different faces enter the room during a given 24-hour period.
10. Count how many simple respiratory treatments are ordered and not provided.
11. Wait for an elevator connecting physical therapy and a nursing unit. Count the minutes.
12. Count the number of trips for physical therapy treatments that did not require major equipment and could have been provided on the unit. Then multiply the number of minutes times the number of trips by the hourly salary of the transporter.
13. How many different consent forms are needed for an average surgical procedure?
14. Count how many people write in the medical record and what percentage of their time is taken in that activity. Multiply that times their hourly salary.
15. Go to a nursing unit on Sunday evening or night shift. Count the number of sheets, towels, and washcloths and towels that remain for patient use during the night.
16. Look at the physician's order sheet for medication or IV orders, then trace the time the medication was actually given. Subtract the two to determine the time for order completion.
17. What is your pet peeve? Put a cost on it!
18. How many calls were made to pharmacy for missing medications in the past 24 hours?
19. Interview the discharge planner, social worker, or utilization review personnel regarding the hours (or days!) patients wait to transfer from unit to unit, from the OR or ED to a unit, to an extended care facility or home.
20. Ask medical records to review charts for the number of admits or ED visits from patients who have been discharged from an inpatient setting within the past 14 days.

Courtesy of Betty Noyes, Noyes & Associates, Ltd., Bainbridge Island, Washington.

Are We There Yet?

We end where we began. Call it assessment or evaluation, the ongoing process and evolution of care delivery systems cannot cease if we expect to continue to create systems that will meet the ever-changing needs of individuals, families, and groups within our communities. This never-ending process could seem daunting if we had not taking the time along the way to measure, and celebrate, the positive successes we have achieved. We encourage you all to continuously evaluate your progress, make course corrections, and adapt to the fluid nature of health care delivery. Use the tools we have featured with vitality and creativity, confident that the assessment, planning, intervening, and evaluation that you have done will keep you on the route to your team's chosen vision. Best wishes!

He that will not apply new remedies, must expect new evils: for Time is the greatest innovator: and if Time, of course, alter things to the worse, and wisdom and counsel shall not alter them to the better, what shall be the end?

Francis Bacon, 1576

References for Section Four: Evaluation

Bacon, F. (1561–1626) (English philosopher, essayist, statesman). *Essays,* "Of Innovations" (1597–1625) (final quote in book).

Bushick, B. 1996. Performance indicators for achieving goals at Allina. *Quality Letter for Healthcare Leaders 8,* no. 5:10–15.

Hansten, R., and M. Washburn. 1996. *Successful Restructuring 1,* no. 1:3.

Hansten, R., and M. Washburn. 1996. *Successful Restructuring 1,* no. 5:4–5.

Krapohl, G., and E. Larson. 1996. The Impact of unlicensed assistive personnel on nursing care delivery. *Nursing Economic$ 14,* no. 2:99–122.

Mark, B., and D. L. Burleson. 1995. Measurement of patient outcomes: Data availability and consistency across hospitals. *JONA 25,* no. 4:52–59.

Phillips, D. T. 1992. *Lincoln on Leadership.* New York: Time Warner Books.

Pine, J., and J. C. Tingley. 1993. ROI on soft skills training. *Training 30* (February):55–60.

Stanley, S., and S. R. Foer. 1996. Preserving patient safety and quality nursing care. *Nursing Policy Forum 2,* no. 3:18–20.

Towers, J. 1996. What do you know about NCQA? *Nursing Policy Forum 2,* no. 3:30.

Wheatley, M. 1992. *Leadership and the New Science.* San Francisco: Berrett-Kohler Publications.

INDEX

9 780834 209077

Printed in Dunstable, United Kingdom

88190712R00179